LEIF ERIKSON DISCOVERS A NEW WORLD.

(From a drawing by Heller.)

THE discovery of America by Norsemen about the year 1000, is so well authenticated as to be no longer a matter of mere tradition, but to whom the honor is due is less easy to prove by the historical sagas. The claim set up in favor of Bjarne Herjulfson is well substantiated, but if the discovery be credited to Bjarne, to Leif Erikson belongs the fame of having founded the first settlement in the New World. This flourished for a time and was frequently visited by other voyagers, until all the settlers it is supposed perished from a plague known as the Black Death.

LEIF ERIKSON DISCOVERS A NEW WORLD.

(From a drawing by Heller.)

THE discovery of America by Norsemen about the year 1000, is so well authenticated as to be no longer a matter of mere tradition, but to whom the honor is due is less easy to prove by the historical sagas. The claim set up in favor of Bjarne Herjulfson is well substantiated, but if the discovery be credited to Bjarne, to Leif Erikson belongs the fame of having founded the first settlement in the New World. This flourished for a time and was frequently visited by other voyagers until all the settlers it is supposed perished from a plague known as the Black Death.

THE NORSE
DISCOVERY OF AMERICA

*A Compilation in Extenso of all the Sagas, Manuscripts,
and Inscriptive Memorials Relating to the Finding
and Settlement of the*

New World in the Eleventh Century.

*With Presentations of Freshly Discovered Proofs, in the form of
Church Records Supplied by the Vatican of Rome,
Never Before Published.*

TRANSLATIONS AND DEDUCTIONS BY

ARTHUR MIDDLETON REEVES,
NORTH LUDLOW BEAMISH,
HON. RASMUS B. ANDERSON.

HON. RASMUS B. ANDERSON, LL.D.,
EDITOR IN CHIEF.

J. W. BUEL, Ph.D.,
MANAGING EDITOR.

PUBLISHED BY THE
NORRŒNA SOCIETY,
LONDON STOCKHOLM COPENHAGEN BERLIN NEW YORK
1907

LIST OF PHOTOGRAVURES.

———

———

PLATES AND MAPS.

CONTENTS.

(NORSE DISCOVERY OF AMERICA.)

CONTENTS

Page

Freydis Murders two Men and five Women 96
Death of Gudrid, Father of Snorre (Snorri) 101

CHAPTER V.

Wineland in the Icelandic Annals 102
Bishop of Greenland goes to Wineland 103
The Church Fathers in the New World 105
Last Historic Reference to Wineland 107

CHAPTER VI.

Notices of Doubtful Value 108
The Wonderful Story of Biorn 109
Evidences of Irish Occupation of America 113
Difficulty in Locating "Newland" 115
Sagas that Puzzle Historians 117

CHAPTER VII.

Publication of the Wineland Discovery 119
Adam of Bremen Writes of Wineland....................121
First Printed Theory Concerning Wineland 123
Arni Magnusson's Collection of Manuscripts 124
Sagas of which their Accuracy is Confirmed 125
Prof. Storm's Treatise upon the Wineland Discovery 126
Notes Explanatory of Prof. Reeves' Text 128

BOOK II.

Arguments and Evidences Respecting the Wineland Dis-
  covery 148
Introduction to a Study of Icelandic Records..............149
Scalds and Sagamen in Icelandic Literature 150
Establishment of Law in Iceland 153
Origin of the Saga 155
Records of Great Deeds Preserved by Skalds.............157
Important Position Held by the Skalds 159
Preservation of Ancient Traditions 161
Second Period of Icelandic Literature 162
Purpose served by Skaldic Verse 163
Subjects Treated by the Sagamen 165
Passion for Travel among Icelanders 169
Arne Magnussen (Arni Magnusson) the Learned..........171
Third Period in Icelandic Literature 174
Effect of Christianity's Introduction 175
Importance of the Islendingabok 177
Link that Connects the Written and Oral Annals..........179
First of Icelandic Historians 181
Chronology of the Historical Sagas 183
Last Period of Icelandic Literature 184

CONTENTS

CONTENTS

NORUMBEGA IN AMERICA.

By HON. R. B. ANDERSON.

CHAPTER I.

CHAPTER II.

CHAPTER III.

CHAPTER IV.

PREFACE.

In this work is brought together for the first time the interpretation of the best authorities respecting the evidences, historical, archaeologic, inscriptive and deductive, of Norse discovery, occupation, and colonization of America five centuries before the time of Columbus. The subject, though it has engaged in a general way the attention of historians for a long time, has only within recent years been brought into great prominence by a serious study of the Saga writers of Iceland and Scandinavia. The beginning of this interest dates from 1837 in which year was published, by the Royal Danish Society of Northern Antiquaries, a large quarto volume of old Icelandic documents, in which the proofs were set forth that the discovery credited to Columbus was anticipated by sea-roving Norsemen five hundred years earlier. This great work was edited by Prof. C. C. Rafn, founder of the Royal Danish Society, and was the result of painstaking labor and expensive research by that very distinguished antiquarian.

Interest in the subject thus aroused by Prof. Rafn was further promoted by Dr. R. B. Anderson's "America not First Discovered by Columbus," published in 1874, which ran through several editions and was translated into French, German and probably other languages.

Inspired by Dr. Anderson's work, Prof. Reeves entered most earnestly into a study of the question, for which he prepared himself by becoming a master of the Danish tongue, with a view to investigating all the original documents in possession of the Antiquarian Society. Not being fully satisfied with what he was able to find in Copenhagen, Stockholm, Trondhjem, and other Scandinavian centers, in 1879 he set sail for Iceland and there continued his examination of records and his enquiries, results of which were published in London in 1895, which with a work by Prof. Beamish, are reproduced in this volume.

While Prof. Reeves does not in all matters pertaining thereto agree perfectly with Professor Rafn, there is sufficient concurrence in their arguments to establish corroboration of conclusions; this is most important because Professor Rafn's work was not freely translated into English, and thus escaped the notice of American historians, while Professor Reeves, a master of the Danish tongue, took up the work of investigating, in the original, the documents submitted by the Antiquarian Society in 1879.

It may truly be said that thirty years ago only a very cultured few professed even the least familiarity with the literature of the Gothic people, notwithstanding our descent from that sturdy race. The Vatican exhibit at the Louisiana Purchase Exposition, 1904, intensified the interest aroused by Professor Reeves' investigations among the libraries of Copenhagen, Christiana, Stockholm and Reykjavik, Iceland's capital. Some had theretofore conjectured that the Church of Rome had maintained a brief relation to Pre-Columbian America, but not until the records were produced and placed on exhibition at St. Louis, did many believe that the Holy Church had established itself so successfully in the New World as early as the year 1000, as to require the services of an archbishop, whose See extended from Greenland to Vineland (Massachusetts?) This almost coincident, and in a way co-operative, enlightenment of the educated, scarcely

PREFACE

less than of the popular mind on the subject of American
discovery, has led to the liveliest appreciation of the Norsemen, and particularly so since with an understanding of their
early visits to these shores we have learned that Americans,
through the English, are descended from these rugged, fearless, sea-roving, liberty-loving people. The interest that
has thus been aroused in the deeds of our Scandinavian
ancestors has led to a wide-spread desire for knowledge respecting their civilization, by which the masses are coming
to know that the Norsemen were not only the greatest of
seamen, but even in their remote isolation, on Iceland's frig-
idly inhospitable coast, they developed a literature, as well
also a popular form of government, the excellence of
which is scarcely to be equalled by that of any other ancient people.

That America was discovered and colonized by Norsemen
nine hundred years ago has been a disputed claim over which
historians have for a long while contended, like enemies
struggling in the dark, but in the light of recently exhumed
evidence, resurrected out of the age-invested tome reposito-
ries of the Vatican, and libraries of the North, the question
is fully resolved and the credit may now be properly placed.
The argument and evidences that establish this claim are set
forth in this volume by such distinguished authorities as
Arthur Reeves, Charles Christian Rafn, North Ludlow
Beamish and Rasmus B. Anderson. There is also printed,
in connection with the historical presentation of the subject,
confirmatory proofs, in the form of reproduced manuscripts,
ancient maps, and church records not heretofore accessible
to the general reader. In fact, some of these documents were
not known to exist until accidentally discovered by very
recent investigation and are now published as a whole for
the first time.

PREFACE

The allusions herein made to the tradition of Irish discovery of America will not wholly satisfy the critical enquirer, but it may lead to a more general study of this much
neglected chapter of Irish history. This much may be set
down as fact: Sixty-five years before the discovery of Iceland by Norsemen, Irish sea-rovers had not only visited but
erected habitations on that island. About the year 725 Irish
ecclesiastics are known to have sought seclusion on the
Faroe Islands. In the Tenth Century voyages between Ireland and Iceland were so frequent as to be ordinary occurrences. Finally, in the Eleventh Century, a county west of
Iceland and South of Vinland, known to the Norsemen as
White-Man's Land, or Great Ireland, was discovered, and
probably settled by Irish. All that history recounts, or that
known documents confirm, regarding the New World anterior to the time of Columbus, will be found gathered and
sifted in this volume, to which is added Professor Anderson's most interesting description of Norumbega, a supposed settlement of Norsemen established near Boston, about
A. D. 1008.

J. W. BUEL.

INTRODUCTION.

THE Icelandic discovery of America was first announced, in print, more than two centuries and a half ago. Within the past fifty years of this period, the discovery has attracted more general attention than during all of the interval preceding,—a fact, which is no doubt traceable to the publication, in 1837, of a comprehensive work upon the subject prepared by the Danish scholar, Carl Christian Rafn. Although it is now more than half a century since this book was published, Rafn is still very generally regarded as the standard authority upon the subject of which he treats. But his zeal in promulgating the discovery seriously prejudiced his judgment. His chief fault was the heedless confusing of all of the material bearing directly or indirectly upon his theme,—the failure to winnow the sound historical material from that which is unsubstantiated. Rafn offered numerous explanations of the texts which his work contained, and propounded many dubious theories and hazardous conjectures. With these the authors, who have founded their investigations upon his work, have more concerned themselves than with the texts of the original documents. If less effort had been applied to the dissemination and defence of fantastic speculations, and more to the determination of the exact nature of the facts which have been preserved in the Icelandic records, the discovery should not have failed to be accepted as clearly established by sound historical data. Upon any other hypothesis than this it is difficult to account for the disposition American historians have shown to treat the Icelandic discovery as possible, from conjectural causes, rather than as determined by the historical records preserved by the fellow-countrymen of the discoverers.

Bancroft, in his History of the United States, gave form to this tendency many years ago, when he stated, that:

"The story of the colonization of America by Norsemen rests on narratives mythological in form, and obscure in meaning, ancient yet not contemporary. The intrepid mariners who colonized Greenland could easily have extended their voyages to Labrador, and have explored the coasts to the south of it. No clear historic evidence establishes the natural probability that they accomplished the passage, and no vestige of their presence on our continent has been found."

The latest historian of America, traversing the same field, virtually iterates this conclusion, when he says:

"The extremely probable and almost necessary pre-Columbian knowledge of the northeastern parts of America follows from the venturesome spirit of the mariners of those seas for fish and traffic, and from the easy transition from coast to coast by which they would have been lured to meet more southerly climes. The chances from such natural causes are quite as strong an argument in favor of the early Northmen venturings as the somewhat questionable representations of the Sagas."

The same writer states, elsewhere, in this connection, that:

"Everywhere else where the Northmen went they left proofs of this occupation on the soil, but nowhere in America, except on an island on the east shore of Baffin's Bay, has any authentic runic inscription been found outside of Greenland."

If the authenticity of the Icelandic discovery of America is to be determined by runic inscriptions or other archælogical remains left by the discoverers, it is altogether probable that the discovery will never be confirmed. The application of this same test, however, would render the discovery of Iceland very problematical. The testimony is the same in both cases, the essential difference between the two discoveries being, after all, that the one led to practical results, while the other, apparently, did not (1). The absence of any Icelandic remains south of Baffin's Bay makes neither for nor against the credibility of the Icelandic discovery,—although it may be said, that it is hardly reasonable to expect that, in the brief period of their sojourn, the explorers would have left any buildings or implements behind them, which would be likely to survive the ravages of the nine centuries that have elapsed since the discovery.

The really important issue, which is raised by the paragraphs quoted, is the broader one of the credibility of the Icelandic records. These records, in so far as they relate to the discovery, disentangled from wild theories and vague assumptions, would seem to speak best for themselves. It is true that Icelandic historical sagas do differ from the historical works of other lands, but this difference is one of form. The Icelandic saga is peculiarly distinguished for the presentation of events in a simple, straightforward manner, without embellishment or commentary by the author. Fabulous sagas there are in Icelandic literature, but this literature is by no means unique in the possession of works both of history and romance, nor has it been customary to regard works of fiction as discrediting the historical narratives of a people which has created both. It is possible to discriminate these two varieties of literary creation in other languages, so is it no less possible in Icelandic. There is, indeed, no clear reason why the statements of an historical saga should be called in question, where these statements are logically consistent and collaterally confirmed.

The information contained in Icelandic literature relative to the discovery of America by the Icelanders, has been brought together here, and an attempt has been made to trace the history of each of the elder manuscripts containing this information. Inconsistencies have been noted, and discriminations made in the material, so far as the facts have seemed to warrant, and especially has an effort been made to avoid any possibility of confusion between expressions of opinion and the facts.

It is not altogether consistent with the plan of this book, to suggest what seems to be established by the documents which it presents, these documents being offered to bear witness for themselves, but a brief recapitulation of the conclusions to which a study of the documents has led may not be amiss, since these conclusions differ radically, in many respects, from the views advanced by Rafn and his followers, and are offered with a view to point further enquiry, rather than to supplant it.

The eldest surviving manuscript containing an account of the discovery of Wineland the Good, as the southernmost land reached by the Icelandic discoverers was called, was written not later than 1334. This, and a more recent manuscript containing virtually the same saga, present the most cogent and consistent account of the discovery which has been preserved. Many of the important incidents therein set forth are confirmed by other Icelandic records of contemporary events, and the information which this saga affords is simply, naturally and intelligibly detailed. This information is of such a character that it is natural to suppose it to have been derived from the statements of those who had themselves visited the lands described; it is not conceivable from what other source it could have been obtained, and, except its author was gifted with unparalleled prescience, it could not have been a fabrication. According to this history, for such it clearly is, Wineland was discovered by a son of Eric Thorvaldsson, called the Red, the first Icelandic explorer and colonist of Greenland. This son, whose name was Leif, returning from a voyage to Norway, probably not later than the year 1000, was driven out of the direct track to Greenland, and came upon a country of which he had previously had no knowledge. He returned thence to Greenland, and reported what he had found, and an ineffectual attempt was made soon after to reach this

strange land again. A few years later one Thorfinn Thor-
darson, called Karlsefni, an Icelander, who had recently
arrived in Greenland, determined to renew the effort to
find and explore the unknown country which Leif had
seen. He organized an expedition and sailed away from
Greenland toward the south-west. He first sighted a
barren land, which, because of the large flat stones that lay
strewn upon its surface, received the name of Helluland.
Continuing thence, with winds from the north, the explorers next found a wooded land, to which they gave the
name of Markland, from its trees, which, to these inhabitants of a treeless land, were a sufficiently distinguishing
characteristic. Proceeding thence, they next described a
coast-land, along which they sailed, having the land upon
their starboard side. The first portion of this land-fall
proved to be a long, sandy shore, but when they had followed it for some time, they found it indented with bays
and creeks, and in one of these they stopped, and sent two
of their company inland to explore the country. These
explorers, when they returned, brought with them, the one
a bunch of grapes, the other an ear of wild ["self-sown"]
grain. They hoisted anchor then, and sailed on until they
came to a bay, at the mouth of which was an island with
strong currents flowing about it. They laid their course
into the bay, and, being pleased with the country thereabouts, decided to remain there the first winter, which
proved to be a severe one. In the following year, Karlsefni, with the greater portion of his company, continued
the advance southward, halting finally at a river, which
flowed down from the land into a lake and thence into

the sea. About the mouth of this river was shoal water, and it could only be entered at flood-tide; they proceeded up the river with their ship, and established themselves not far from the sea, and remained here throughout the second winter. There were woods here, and in low-lands fields of wild "wheat," and on the ridges grapes growing wild. Here for the first time they encountered the inhabitants of the country, to whom they gave the name of Skrellings, a name which seems to bear evidence of their opprobrium. In the spring after their arrival at this spot, they were visited for the second time by the Skrellings, with whom they now engaged in barter; their visitors, however, becoming alarmed at the bellowing of a bull, which Karlsefni had brought with him, fled to their skin-canoes and rowed away. For three weeks after this, nothing was seen of the natives; but, at the end of this interval, they returned in great numbers and gave battle to Karlsefni and his companions. The Skrellings finally withdrew, having lost several of their number, while two of Karlsefni's men had fallen in the affray. The explorers, although they were well content with the country, decided, after this experience, that it would be unwise for them to attempt to remain in that region longer, and they accordingly returned to the neighbourhood in which they had passed the first winter, where they remained throughout the third winter, and in the following spring set sail for Greenland.

In a manuscript written probably between 1370 and 1390, but certainly before the close of the fourteenth century, are two detached narratives which, considered together, form another version of the history of the discovery and exploration of Wineland. In this account the discovery is ascribed to one Biarni Heriulfsson, and the date assigned to this event is fixed several years anterior to that of Leif Ericsson's voyage; indeed, according to this account, Leif's voyage to Wineland is not treated as accidental, but as the direct result of Biarni's description of the land which he had found. This version differs further, from that already described, in recounting three voyages besides that undertaken by Leif, making in all four voyages of exploration—the first headed by Leif, the second by Leif's brother, Thorvald, the third by Karlsefni, and the fourth and last led by Freydis, a natural daughter of Eric the Red. This account of the discovery is treated at length, and certain of its inconsistencies pointed out in another place, and it is, therefore, not necessary to examine it more particularly here. The statement concerning the discovery of Wineland by Biarni Heriulfsson is not confirmed by any existing collateral evidence, while that which would assign the honour to Leif Ericsson is; moreover, beyond the testimony of this, the Flatey Book, version, there is no reason to believe that more than a single voyage of exploration took place, namely, that of Thorfinn Karlsefni. So far as the statements of this second version coincide with that of the first, there seems to be no good reason for calling them in question; where they do not, they may well receive more particular scrutiny than has been directed to them, hitherto, since the Flatey Book narrative is that which has generally been treated as the more important, and

its details have, in consequence, received the greater pub-
licity.

Especially has one of the statements, which appears in
this second version, claimed the attention of writers, who
have sought to determine from it the site of Wineland.
Rafn, by the ingenious application of a subtile theory,
succeeded in computing from this statement the exact
latitude, to the second, of the southernmost winter-quar-
ters of the explorers, and for nearly fifty years after its
publication Rafn's method of interpretation remained
essentially unassailed. In 1883, however, Professor
Gustav Storm, of Christiana, propounded a novel, but
withal a simple and scientific interpretation of this passage, which can hardly fail to appeal to the discernment
of any reader who may not in advance have formed his
conclusions as to where Wineland ought to have been.
Professor Storm's method of interpretation does not seek
to determine from the passage the exact spot which the
explorers reached (for which, it may be remarked, the
passage does not afford sufficiently accurate data), but
he is enabled by his process of reasoning to determine a
limit, north of which Wineland could not have been, and
this limit is approximately 49°. A region not far removed
to the southward of this latitude conforms sufficiently
well to the description of the country, given in the narratives of the exploration, to serve to confirm Professor
Storm's result, and also the relative accuracy of the
mooted passage itself. It will be apparent from an examination of this author's treatise that it is not necessarily
proven that Wineland may not have been situated to the

southward of latitude 49°, but it would seem to be well-nigh certain that thus far south it must have been.

There is no suggestion in Icelandic writings of a permanent occupation of the country, and after the exploration at the beginning of the eleventh century, it is not known that Wineland was ever again visited by Icelanders, although it would appear that a voyage thither was attempted in the year 1121, but with what result is not known. That portion of the discovery known as Markland was revisited however, in 1347, by certain seamen from the Icelandic colony in Greenland.

It will be seen from this summary that the Wineland history is of the briefest, but brief as it is, it has been put in jeopardy no less by those who would prove too much, than by those who would deny all. It may not be unprofitable in the present aspect of the question to appeal to the records themselves.

ARTHUR M. REEVES.

ARGUMENTS AND PROOFS

THAT SUPPORT THE CLAIM OF NORSE DISCOVERY OF AMERICA
BY ARTHUR M. REEVES.

CHAPTER I.

EARLY FRAGMENTARY REFERENCES TO WINELAND.

WINELAND the Good is first mentioned in Icelandic literature by the Priest Ari Thorgilsson, in a passage contained in his so-called Islendingabok [Icelanders' Book]. Ari, commonly called the Learned, an agnomen which he received after his death, was born in Iceland in the year 1067, and lived to the ripe age of eighty-one, acquiring a positive claim to the appellation "hinn gamli" [the Old, the Elder], which is once given him; in this instance, however, to distinguish him from another of the same name. Of Ari, the father of Icelandic historiography, the author of Heimskringla, the most comprehensive of Icelandic histories, says in the prologue to his work:

"The priest Ari Thorgilsson the Learned, Gelli's grandson, was the first of men here in the land [Iceland] to write ancient and modern lore in the Northern tongue; he wrote chiefly in the beginning of his book concerning Iceland's colonization and legislation, then of the law-speakers (2), how long each was in office, down to the introduction of Christianity into Iceland, and then on to his own day. Therein he also treats of much other old lore, both of the lives of the kings of Norway and Denmark, as well as of those of England, as likewise of the

I

important events, which have befallen here in the land, and all of his narrations seem to me most trustworthy. . . . It is not strange that Ari should have been well-informed in the ancient lore, both here and abroad, since he had both acquired it from old men and wise, and was himself eager to learn and gifted with a good memory."

In the introduction to the Islendingabok, Ari says:

"I first composed an Islendingabok for our Bishops Thorlak [Thorlakr] and Ketil [Ketill], and showed it to them, as well as to Sæmund (Sæmundr) the Priest. And forasmuch as they were pleased [either] to have it thus, or augmented, I accordingly wrote this, similar in character, with the exception of the genealogy and lives of the kings, and have added that of which I have since acquired closer knowledge, and which is now more accurately set forth in this [the 'libellus'] than in that."

These words conjoined with the quoted statement concerning the character of the historian's work, and supplemented by references to Ari in other Icelandic writings, have given rise to a controversy as to the probable scope of Ari's literary activity. Whether the conclusion be reached that Ari was the author of several books, as has been claimed, or that the Islendingabok, which has perished, to which he refers in the words above quoted, was a much larger and more comprehensive work than the so-called Islendingabok which has been preserved to us, there seems to be abundant reason for the belief that all of Ari's historical material was by no means comprised in the only book of his now existing, about whose authorship there can be no room for dispute. Of this book, the so-called Islendingabok, the oldest manuscripts are two paper copies, of a lost parchment manuscript, belonging to the Arna-Magnæan Collection in the University Library of Copenhagen, which are known as 113*a* and 113*b* fol. At the end of 113*a*, the scribe has written as follows:

"These 'Schedæ' and narratives of the priest Ari the Learned are copied from a vellum in his own hand, as men believe, at Villingaholt, by the priest John Ellindsson [Jon Erlendsson], Anno domini 1651, the next Monday after the third Sunday after Easter."

This John Erlendsson is known to have made transcripts of many of the sagas for Bryniolf [Brynjolfr] Sveinsson, Bishop of Skalholt. To this worthy bishop's literary ardour, and zeal in collecting the neglected treasures of his language, we owe the preservation of many manuscripts, which would, but for him, doubtless, have perished before the coming of the indefatigable collector, Arni Magnusson.

Bishop Bryniolf, unfortunately, left no heir interested in the preservation of his library, and his books were soon scattered. When Arni Magnusson visited Iceland, thirty years after the Bishop's death and ransacked the island for surviving manuscripts, the vellum of the Islendingabok, doubtless one of the oldest of Icelandic manuscripts, had entirely disappeared. Concerning the two paper copies of this vellum, which he succeeded in obtaining, Arni has inserted the following memorandum in the manuscript described at 113*b* fol.:

"The various different readings noted here throughout in my hand, are taken from another copy [113*a*. fol.]

written by the Rev. John Erlendsson in 1651. This was formerly the property of the Rev. Torfi Jonsson [Jonsson] of Bær, who inherited it from Bishop Bryniolf Sveinsson; I obtained it, however, from Thorlak, son of Bishop Thord [Thorlakr Pordarson]; it formed originally a portion of a large book, which I took apart, separating the treatises. This copy I have called "Codex B," signifying either "Baiensis," or the second, from the order of the letters of the alphabet. Concerning 'Codex B,' it is my conjecture that the Rev. John copied it first from the vellum; that Bishop Bryniolf did not like the copy [for this Codex is less exact than Codex A, as may be seen by comparing them] . . . wherefore the Rev. John made a new copy of the parchment manuscript, taking greater care to follow the original literally, whence it is probable that this Codex A was both the later and the better copy."

Both of the paper manuscripts "A" and "B" were written, it is believed, within the same year, and in each of them the paragraphs containing the reference to Wineland are almost identical; the Icelandic name in "A" being spelt Winland, in "B" Vinland, a clerical variation, devoid of significance. This paragraph, which is the sixth in Ari's history, is as follows:

"That country which is called Greenland, was discovered and colonized from Iceland. Eric the Red [Eirekr enn Rauthi] was the name of the man, an inhabitant of Breidafirth, who went out thither from here, and settled at that place, which has since been called Ericsfirth [Eiriksfiorthr]. He gave a name to the country, and called it Greenland, and said that it must persuade men to go thither, if the land had a good name. They found there, both east and west in the country, the dwellings of men, and fragments of boats, and stone implements, such that it may be perceived from these that that manner of people had been there who have inhabited Wineland, and whom the Greenlanders call Skrellings. And this, when he set about the colonization of the country, was XIV or XV winters before the introduction of Christianity here in Iceland, according to that which a certain man [lit. he], who himself accompanied Eric the Red thither, informed Thorkel Gellisson."

This mention of Wineland, which in itself may appear to be of little importance, acquires its greatest value from that which it leaves unsaid; for had Ari not known that his reference to Wineland and its inhabitants would be entirely intelligible to his readers, he would hardly have employed it, as he does, to inform his Greenland chronicle. This passing notice, therefore, indicates a general diffusion of the knowledge of the Wineland discoveries among Ari's contemporaries at the time when the paragraph was composed. The "libellus" [Islendingabok] was probably written about the year 1134, and we are accordingly apprised that at that time the facts concerning the Wineland discovery, upon an acquaintance with which Ari seems to rely, were notorious. It is impossible, however, to determine whether Ari presumed upon a knowledge derived from particulars, which he had himself previously published, or upon a prevalent acquaintance with the accounts of the explorers themselves. It

5

is, at least, questionable whether Ari would have been content to presuppose such local historical knowledge if he had not already sealed it with his own authority elsewhere. Nor is the importance which he may have assigned to the Wineland discovery material to this view. He had set about writing a chronicle of his fatherland, and his passing allusion to Wineland, without a word of explanation, appears incompatible with the duty which he had assumed, unless, indeed, he had already dealt with the subject of the Wineland discovery in a previous work. Be this as it may, however, certain it is that Wineland has found further mention in two Icelandic works, which in their primitive form have been very generally accredited to Ari, namely the Landnamabok [Book of Sentiment] and the Kristni-Saga [the Narrative of the Introduction of Christianity into Iceland]. The first of these, in a passage already cited, expressly acknowledges Ari's share in the authorship. One manuscript of this work, from which the passage is taken [No. 371, 4to, in the Arna-Magnæan Collection], while it is the oldest extant manuscript containing the Landnamabok [now in an incomplete state] presents this in a later review of the original work, than that which is contained in the much more modern manuscript, AM. 107, fol. This latter manuscript, like the copy of Islendingabok, was written by the Rev. John Erlendsson for Bishop Bryniolf Sveinsson. Both of the references to Wineland in the Landnamabok occur incidentally in the course of the history, and are of the briefest. The first of these treats of the adventure of Ari Marsson [Mars-

6

son]; it is to be found in Chapter 22, of the second part of the book, and is as follows:

". . . their son was Ari. He was driven out of his course at sea to White-men's-land [Hvitramanna-land], which is called by some persons Ireland the Great (58); it lies westward in the sea near Wineland the Good; it is said to be six "dœgra" sail west of Ireland; Ari could not depart thence, and was baptized there." The first account of this was given by Rafn who sailed to Limerick (3) [Hlimreksfari], and who remained for a long time at Limerick in Ireland. So Thorkel Geitisson states that Icelanders report, who have heard Thorfinn, Earl of the Orkneys (4) say, that Ari had been recognized there, and was not permitted to leave [*lit.* could not leave], but was treated with great respect there.

The names of Ari Marsson's wife, and of his three sons are given in the same passage from which the quotation is made, and additional concurrent evidence is not wanting to serve to establish the existence of this man; any particulars, however, which might serve to enlighten this narrative, or aid in determining whence Rafn and Earl Thorfinn derived their intelligence, are lacking. Without free conjectural emendation to aid in its interpretation, this description of Ari Marsson's visit to Ireland the Great is of the same doubtful historical value as a later account of another visit to an unknown land, to be considered hereafter.

The second reference to Wineland in the Landnamabok is contained in a list of the descendants of Snorri Head-Thord's son.

"Their son was Thord Horse-head, father of Karl-sefni, who found Wineland the Good, Snorri's father," etc. A genealogy which entirely coincides with that of the histories of the discovery of Wineland, as well as with that of the episcopal genealogy appended to the Islend-ingabok. The Landnamabok contained no other mention of Wineland, but a more extended notice is contained in the work already named, which, in its present form, is supposed to retain evidence of the learned Ari's pen.

The Kristni-Saga, which is supplementary, historically, to the Landnamabok, is given in its entirety in AM. 105, fol. This is a paper copy of an earlier manuscript made by the same industrious cleric, John Erlendsson, for Bishop Bryniolf. A portion of the same history has also been preserved along with the detached leaves of the Landnamabok now deposited in the Arna-Magnæan Collection, No. 371, 4to. These fragments of the two histories originally belonged to one work, the so-called Hauk's Book, a vellum manuscript of the fourteenth century, hereafter to be more fully described. The history of the Wineland discovery is contained in the eleventh chapter of the printed edition of the Kristni-Saga, in the following words:

"That summer (5) King Olaf [Tryggvason] went from the country southward to Vindland [the land of the Wends]; then, moreover, he sent Leif Ericsson [Leifr Eiriksson] to Greenland, to proclaim the faith there. On this voyage [lit. then] Leif found Wineland the Good; he also found men on a wreck at sea, wherefore he was called Leif the Lucky."

8

Of the same tenor as this brief paragraph of the Kristni-Saga, is a chapter in the Codex Frisianus [Frissbok], number 45, fol., of the Arna-Magnæan manuscripts. This Codex Frisianus, or, as it has been more appropriately called, the Book of Kings, is a beautifully written and well-preserved parchment manuscript of 124 leaves; it obtains its name from a former owner, Otto Friis of Salling; it subsequently became the property of one Jens Rosenkranz, and next passed into the possession of Arni Magnusson. Friis' Book was, in all probabilities, written about the beginning of the fourteenth century; and if the conjectures as to its age are correct, it is, perhaps, the oldest extant Icelandic manuscript containing an account of the Wineland discovery. It is believed, from internal evidence, that the greater part of the Codex was written by an Icelander, in Norway, possibly for a Norwegian, and that the manuscript was never in Iceland. The early history of the Codex is not known. Certain marginal notes appear to have been inserted in the manuscript about the year 1550 by Lawman Laurents Hansson, and it is conjectured that the book was then owned in Bergen; fifty years later we find it in Denmark; for about the year 1600 a Dane, by the name of Slangerup, inserted his name upon a fly-leaf in the book, which leaf, Arni Magnusson tells us, was removed when he had the manuscript bound. This "Book of Kings," the saga of Olaf Tryggvason, in which the history of the discovery of Wineland occurs, follows closely the same saga as it was written in the two lost parchment manuscripts of the "Heimskringla," as we are enabled to determine from the copies of these lost vellums made by the Icelander, Asgeir Jonsson. It is not known whether the author of the "Heimskringla" had access to the history of the Wineland discovery in some such extended form as that contained in Hauk's Book; indeed it has been suggested that he may only have been acquainted with the brief narrative of the Kristni-Saga; but certain it is, that his account of the discovery was not influenced by the version presented in the Flatey Book, which narrative appears in the first printed edition of the "Heimskringla," where it was interpolated by the editor, Johann Peringskiold. Similarly, any trace of the Flatey Book version of the discovery is lacking from Friis' Book, although the author of the saga of Olaf Tryggvason, therein contained, appears to have been acquainted with a somewhat more detailed account of Leif Ericssons' life than that afforded by the Kristni-Saga, if we may judge from his own language, as we find it in column 136, page 34*b,* of the manuscript:

"WINELAND THE GOOD FOUND.

"Leif, a son of Eric the Red, passed this same winter, in good repute, with King Olaf, and accepted Christianity. And that summer, when Gizur went to Iceland, King Olaf sent Leif to Greenland to proclaim Christianity there. He sailed that summer to Greenland. He found men upon a wreck at sea and succoured them. Then, likewise, he discovered Wineland the Good, and arrived in Greenland in the autumn. He took with him thither a priest and other spiritual teachers, and went to Brattahlid to make his home with his father, Eric. People afterwards called him Leif the Lucky. But his father, Eric, said that one account should balance the other, that Leif had rescued the ship's crew, and that he had brought the trickster to Greenland. This was the priest."

Almost identical with the history of the discovery contained in Friis' Book is that of the so-called longer saga of Olaf Tryggvason. This saga, in its printed form, has been compiled from several manuscripts of the Arna-Magnæan collection, the most important of which is No. 61, fol., a codex dating from about the year 1400. This account is contained in the 231st chapter of the printed version as follows:

"King Olaf then sent Leif to Greenland to proclaim Christianity there. The king sent a priest and other holy men with him, to baptize the people there, and to instruct them in the true faith. Leif sailed to Greenland that summer, and rescued at sea the men of a ship's crew, who were in great peril and were clinging to [*lit.* lay upon] the shattered wreckage of a ship; and on this same voyage he found Wineland the Good, and at the end of the summer arrived in Greenland, and betook himself to Brattahlid, to make his home with his father, Eric. People afterwards called him Leif the Lucky, but his father, Eric, said that the one [deed] offset the other, in that Leif had on the one hand rescued and restored the men of the ship's crew to life, while on the other he had brought the trickster to Greenland, for thus he called the priest."

In composition, doubtless, much more recent than the

notices already cited, is a passage in the collectanea of Middle-age wisdom of the Arna-Magnæan Library. This manuscript contains fifty-two pages, part of which are in Icelandic and part in Latin, written between the years 1400-1450. From a slip in Arni Magnusson's hand, inserted in the collection, it appears that Arni obtained it from the Rev. Thorvald Stephensson in the year 1707. Whatever its condition may have been at that time, the parchment upon which it is written is now in a sad state of decay. In this respect page 10 of the vellum, upon the back of which the Wineland chirography is written, is Icelandic, is no exception; fortunately, however, the lacunae are so inconsiderable in this page that they may be readily supplied from that which survives, and the Wineland passage appears as follows:

"Southward from Greenland is Helluland, then comes [*lit.* is] Markland; thence it is not far to Wineland the Good, which some men believe extends from Africa, and, if this be so, then there is an open sea flowing in between Wineland and Markland. It is said, that Thorfinn Karlsefni hewed a "house-neat-timber" (6) and then went to seek Wineland the Good, and came to where they believed this land to be, but they did not succeed in exploring it, or in obtaining any of its products (7). Leif the Lucky first found Wineland, and he then found merchants in evil plight at sea, and restored them to life by God's mercy; and he introduced Christianity into Greenland, which waxed there so *that an episcopal seat was established there,* at the place called Gardar. England and Scotland are one island, although each of them is a kingdom. Ireland is a great island. Iceland is also a great island [to the north of] Ireland. These countries are all in that part of the world which is called Europe."

In a fascicle of detached vellum fragments, brought together in AM. No. 736, 4to, there are two leaves containing, besides certain astronomical material, a concise geographical compilation. In this Wineland is assigned a location identical with that in the codex from which the quotation has just been made, and the notice of Wineland is limited to this brief statement:

"From Greenland to the southward lies Helluland, then Markland; thence it is not far to Wineland, which some men believe extends from Africa. England and Scotland are one island," etc.

While the reference to Wineland omits the account of Thorfin's visit and Leif's discovery, the language in which the location of the land is given, as well as the language of the context, has so great a likeness to that of 194, 8vo, that, although it was perhaps written a few years earlier, there seems to be a strong probability that each of the scribes of these manuscripts derived his material from a common source.

Somewhat similar in character to the above notices is the brief reference written in the vellum fragment contained in AM. 764, 4to. This fragment comprises a so-called "totius orbis brevis descriptio," written probably about the year 1400. Upon the second page of this "brief description" is the passage:

"From Biarmaland uninhabited regions extend from the north, until Greenland joins them. South from

13

Greenland lies Helluland, then Markland. Thence it is not so far to Wineland. Iceland is a great island," etc.

Differing in nature from these geographical notices [but of even greater interest and historical value by reason of the corroborative evidence which it affords of certain particulars set forth in the leading narrative of the Wineland discovery] is the mention of Wineland contained in a chapter of the Eyrbyggja Saga [Saga of the People of Eyrr]. No complete vellum manuscript of this saga has been preserved. The eldest manuscript remnant of the saga consists of two leaves written about 1300; these leaves do not, however, contain that portion of the saga, with which we are concerned. Of another vellum codex containing this saga, which has entirely perished, we have certain knowledge. This was the so-called Vatnshyrna or Vatnshorn's Book, a manuscript which at one time belonged to the eminent Danish scholar, Peder Hans Resen, from whom it received the name by which it is sometimes cited, Codex Resenianus. It was bequeathed by Resen to the University Library of Copenhagen, where it was deposited after his death in 1688. It perished in the great fire of October, 1728, but fortunately paper copies, which had been made from it, survived the conflagration. The Vatnshorn Codex, it has been conjectured, was prepared for the same John Haconsson, to whom we are indebted for the great Flatey Book, and was, apparently, written about the year 1400, or, possibly, toward the close of the fourteenth century. The most complete vellum manuscript of the Eyrbyggja Saga now extant forms a part of the Ducal Library of Wolfenbuttel, purchased in the seventeenth century at a public sale in Holstein. This manuscript was probably written about the middle of the fourteenth century, and although the first third of the Eyrbyggja Saga has been lost from the codex, that portion of the history which contains the chapter referring to Wineland has been preserved, and is as follows:

"After the reconciliation between Steinthor and the people of Alpta-firth, Thorbrand's sons, Snorri and Thorleif Kimbi, went to Greenland. From him Kimba-firth (in Greenland), gets its name. Thorleif Kimbi lived in Greenland to old age. But Snorri went to Wineland the Good with Karlsefni; and when they were fighting with the Skrellings there in Wineland, Thorbrand Snorrason, a most valiant man, was killed."

The foregoing brief notices of Wineland, scattered through so many Icelandic writings, yield no very great amount of information concerning that country. They do afford, however, a clear insight into the wide diffusion of the intelligence of the discovery in the earlier saga period, and in every instance confirm the Wineland history as unfolded in the leading narrative of the discovery, now to be considered.

CHAPTER II.

THE SAGA OF ERIC THE RED.

THE clearest and most complete narrative of the discovery of Wineland, preserved in the ancient Icelandic literature, is that presented in the Saga of Eric the Red. Of this narrative two complete vellum texts have survived. The eldest of these texts is contained in the Arna-Magnæan Codex, No. 544, 4to, which is commonly known as Hauk's Book [Hauksbok]. This manuscript has derived its name from its first owner, for whom the work was doubtless written, and who himself participated in the labour of its preparation. This man, to whom the manuscript traces its origin, has, happily, left, not only in the manuscript itself, but in the history of his time, a record which enables us to determine, with exceptional accuracy, many dates in his life, and from these it is possible to assign approximate dates to that portion of the vellum which contains the narrative of the discovery. This fact possesses the greater interest since of no one of those who participated in the conservation of the elder sagas, have we data so precise as those which have been preserved to us of Hauk Erlendsson, to whose care, actual and potential, this manuscript owes its existence.

We know that Jorunn, the mother of this man, was the direct descendant of a famous Icelander. His paternal ancestry is not so clearly established. It has been conjectured that his father, Erlend Olafsson, surnamed the

Stout [Erlendr sterki Olafsson], was the son of a man of humble parentage, and by birth a Norwegian. This view has been discredited, however, and the fact pretty clearly established that Erlend's father, Olaf, was no other than a certain Icelander called Olaf Tot. Hauk's father, Erlend, was probably the "Ellindr bondi" of a letter addressed by certain Icelanders to the Norwegian king, Magnus Law-Amender, in the year 1275. In the year 1283 we find indubitable mention of him in Icelandic annals as "legifer," he having in that year "come out" to Iceland from Norway vested with the dignity of "law-man." It is as the incumbent of a similar office, to which he appears to have been appointed in 1294, that we first find Hauk Erlendsson mentioned. It is not unlikely that Hauk had visited Norway prior to 1301; there can be no doubt that he was in that country in the latter part of that year, for he was a "lawman" in Oslo [the modern Christiania] upon the 28th of January, 1302, since upon that date he published an autographic letter, which is still in existence. Whether the rank of knighthood, which carried with it the title of "herra" (Earl), had already been conferred upon him at this time is not certain. He is first mentioned with this title, in Icelandic annals, in 1306, elsewhere in 1305, although it has been claimed that he had probably then enjoyed this distinction for some years, but upon what authority is not clear. While Hauk revisited Iceland upon more than one occasion after the year 1302, much of the remainder of his life appears to have been spent in Norway, where he died in the year 1334.

On the back of page 21 of Hauk's Book Arni Magnusson has written, probably with a view to preserve a fading entry upon the same page, the words: "This book belongs to Teit Paulsson [Teitr Palsson], if he be not robbed." It is not known who this Teit Paulsson was, but it is recorded that a man of this name sailed from Iceland to Norway in the year 1344. He may have been the one-time owner of the book, and, if the manuscript was then in Norway, may have carried it back to Iceland with him. Apart from this conjecture, the fact remains that the early history of Hauk's Book is shrouded in obscurity. It is first mentioned in the beginning of the seventeenth century by John the Learned, possibly about 1600, and a few years later by Arngrim Jonsson; it was subsequently loaned to Bishop Bryniolf Sveinsson, who caused the transcripts of the Landnamabok and the Kristni Saga to be made from it, as has already been related. This part of the codex the Bishop may have returned to the owner, himself retaining the remainder, for, with the exception of the two sagas named, Arni Magnusson obtained the codex from Gualveriabœr in the south of Iceland, and subsequently the remaining leaves of the missing sagas from the Rev. Olaf Jonsson, who was the clergyman at Stad in Grunnavik, in north-western Iceland, between the years 1703 and 1707.

Hauk's Book originally contained about 200 leaves, with widely varied contents. Certain leaves of the original manuscript have been detached from the main body of the book, and are now to be found in the Arna-Magnæan Collection; a portion has been lost, but 107 leaves of the original codex are preserved. With the exception of those portions just referred to, that part of the manuscript which treats of the Wineland discovery is to be found in this last mentioned volume, from leaves 93 to 101 [*back*] inclusive. The saga therein contained has no title contemporary with the text, but Arni Magnusson has inserted, in the space left vacant for the title, the words: "Here begins the Saga of Thorfinn Karlsefni and Snorri Thorbrandsson," although it is not apparent whether he himself invented this title, or derived it from some now unknown source.

The Saga of Thorfinn Karlsefni was written by three different persons; the first portion is in a hand commonly ascribed to Hauk's so-called "first Icelandic secretary." On p. 99, l. 14, the ink and the hand change, and beginning with the words *Eirikr svarar vel,* the chirography is Hauk's own, as is readily apparent from a comparison with the autographic letter of 1302, already referred to. Hauk's own work continues throughout this and the following page, ceasing at the end of the second line on p. 100, with the words *kolludu i Hopi,* where he gives place to a new scribe, his so-called "second Icelandic secretary." Hauk, however, again resumes the pen on the back of p. 101, and himself concludes the saga. Two of the leaves upon which the saga is written are of an irregular shape, and there are holes in two other leaves; these defects were, however, present in the vellum from the beginning, so that they in no wise affect the integrity of the text; on the other hand the lower right-hand corner of p. 99 has become badly blackened, and is, in conse-

quence, partially illegible, as is also the left-hand corner
of p. 101; similarly pp. 100 and 101 [*back*] are somewhat indistinct, but, in the original, still not undecipher-
able. Initial letters are inserted in red and blue, and the
subtitles in red ink, which has sadly faded. There are
three paginations, of which the latest, in red, is the one
here adopted.

The genealogy appended to the saga has been brought
down to Hauk's own time, and Hauk therein traces his
ancestry to Karlsefni's Wineland-born son. By means
of this genealogical list, we are enabled to determine, approximately, the date of this transcript of the original
saga, for we read in this list of Hallbera, "Abbess of Reyniness," and since we know that Hallbera was not consecrated abbess until the year 1299, it becomes at once
apparent that the saga could not have been completed before that year. This conclusion is corroborated by additional evidence furnished by this ancestral list, for in this
list Hauk has given himself his title "herra," (earl).
As has been stated, Hauk is first accorded this title in
1305, he is last mentioned without the title in 1304;
which fact not only confirms the conclusion already
reached, but enables us to advance the date, prior to which
the transcript of the saga could not have been concluded,
to 1304. It is not so easy to determine positively when
the saga was finished. As Hauk's own hand brings the
saga to a conclusion, it is evident that it must have been
completed before, or not later than, the year 1334, the
year of his death. If we accept the words of the genealogical list literally, it would appear that Hauk wrote this

list not many years before his death, for it is there stated
that Fru Ingigerd's daughter *"was"* Fru Hallbera, the
Abbess. But Hallbera lived until 1330, and the strict
construction of Hauk's language might point to the conclusion that the reference to Hallbera was made after her
death, and therefore after 1330. Hauk was in Iceland
in the years 1330 and 1331, doubtless for the last time.
One of the scribes who aided him in writing the codex
was probably an Icelander, as may be gleaned from his
orthography, and as it is highly probable that the contents of the codex were for the most part copied from
originals owned in Iceland; it may be that the transcript
of this saga, as well as the book itself, was completed during this last visit. It has been claimed that a portion of
Hauk's book, preceding the Saga of Thorfinn, was written prior to Hauk's acquirement of his title, a view
founded upon the fact that his name is there cited without the addition of his title, and this view is supported by
the corresponding usage of the Annals. If this be true,
then, upon the above hypothesis, a period of more than
twenty-five years must have elapsed between the incep-
tion of the work and the completion of the "Thorfinn's
Saga." Doubtless a considerable time was consumed in
the compilation and transcription of the contents of this
manuscript; but it seems scarcely probable that so long a
time should have intervened between the preparation of
the different portions of the work. Wherefore, if the
reference to the Abbess Hallbera be accepted literally, the
conjecture that the earlier portion of the codex was
written prior to 1299 would appear to be doubtful, and it

may be necessary either to advance the date of this portion of the manuscript or place the date of the Saga of Thorfinn anterior to that suggested. However this may be, two facts seem to be clearly established, first, that this saga was not written before 1299, and second, that this eldest surviving detailed narrative of the discovery of Wineland was written not later than the year 1334.

In the vellum codex, known as Number 557, 4to, of the Arna-Magnæan Collection, is an account of the Wineland discovery, so strikingly similar to that of Hauk's Book that there can be no doubt that both histories were derived from the same source. The history of the discovery contained in the above codex is called the "Saga of Eric the Red." This may well have been the primitive title of the saga of Hauk's Book, which, as has been noted, obtains its modern name, "Thorfinns Saga Karlsefnis," from the entry made by Arni Magnusson, early in the eighteenth century. That both sagas were copied from the same vellum is by no means certain; if both transcripts be judged strictly by their contents it becomes at once apparent that this could not have been the fact, and such a conjecture is only tenable upon the theory that the scribes of Hauk's Book edited the saga which they copied. This, while it is very doubtful in the case of the body of the text of the Hauk's Book Saga of Thorfinn, may not even be conjectured of the Saga of Eric the Red. The latter saga was undoubtedly a literal copy from the original, for there are certain minor confusions of the text, which indicate, unmistakably, either the heedlessness of the copyist, or that the scribe was working from a somewhat illegible original whose defects he was not at pains to supply. If both sagas were copied from different early vellums, the simpler language of the Saga of Eric the Red would seem to indicate that it was a transcript of a somewhat earlier form of the saga than that from which the saga of Hauk's Book was derived. This, however, is entirely conjectural, for the codex containing the Saga of Eric the Red was not written for many years after Hauk's Book, and probably not until the following century. So much the orthography and hand of 557, 4to, indicate, and, from the application of this test, the codex has been determined to date from the fifteenth century, and has been ascribed by very eminent authority to *ca.* 1400.

The Saga of Eric the Red begins with the thirteenth line of page 27 of the codex [the title appears at the top of this page], and concludes in the fifth line on the back of page 35, the hand being the same throughout. Spaces were left for initial letters, but these were not inserted, except in one case by a different and indifferent penman. With the exception of a very few words, or portions of words, upon page 30 [*back*] and page 31, the manuscript of the saga is clearly legible throughout. Certain slight defects in the vellum have existed from the beginning, and there is, therefore, no material hiatus in the entire text, for the sense of the few indistinct words is either clearly apparent from the context, or may be supplied from the sister text of Hauk's Book.

In his catalogue of parchment manuscripts, Arni Magnusson states that he obtained this manuscript from

23

Bishop John Vidalin and adds the conjecture, that it had either belonged to the Skaholt Church, or came thither from among Bishop Bryniolf's books. This conjecture, that the book belonged to the Church of Skaholt, has, however, been disputed, and the place of its compilation, at the same time, assigned to the north of Iceland.

The Saga of Eric the Red [and both texts are included under this title] presents a clear and graphic account of the discovery and exploration of Wineland the Good. In this narrative the discovery is ascribed to Leif, the son of Eric the Red, who hit upon the land, by chance, during a voyage from Norway to Greenland. This voyage, as has already been stated, probably took place in the year 1000.

After his return to Greenland, Leif's account of the land which he had discovered seems to have persuaded his brother, Thorstein, and possibly his father, to undertake an expedition to the strange country. This voyage, which was not destined to meet with a successful issue, may well have fallen in the year following Leif's return, and therefore, it may be conjectured, in the year 1001. About this time there had arrived in Greenland an Icelander of considerable prominence, an old friend of Eric's, named Thorbiorn Vifilsson, who had brought with him his daughter, Gudrid, or, as she is also called, Thurid. He must have arrived before Thorstein Ericsson's voyage, for we are told that it was in Thorbiorn's ship that this voyage was undertaken. It seems probable that Thorbiorn arrived at Brattahlid [Eric's home] during Leif's absence from Greenland, and if this be true it fol-

lows that Thorbiorn and Gudrid must have been converted to Christianity before its acceptance in Iceland
as the legalized religion of the land; for very soon after
their arrival in Greenland Gudrid alludes to the fact
of her being a Christian, and, from the language of the
saga, there can be no question that her father had likewise embraced the new faith. The presence of these
companions in the faith may have materially aided Leif
in the work of proselytism, in which he engaged upon
his return to Greenland. We are told that Thorbiorn
did not arrive at Brattahlid until the second year after
his departure from Iceland, wherefore, if the assumption
that he arrived during Leif's absence be sound, it becomes apparent that he must have left Iceland in the
summer of the year 998 or 999.

Eric's son, Thorstein, wooed and married Gudrid, and
the wedding was celebrated at Brattahlid in the autumn.
It is recorded in the saga that Gudrid was regarded as
a most desirable match. Thorstein may have promptly
recognized her worth, and his marriage may have occurred in the autumn of the same year in which he returned from his unlucky voyage. It could not well have
been celebrated in the previous year, for Thorstein's allusions on his death-bed to the religion of Greenland, indicate that Christianity must have been for a longer time
the accepted faith of the land than it could have been at
the close of the year 1000.

In the winter after his marriage, Thorstein died, and
in the spring, Gudrid returned to Brattahlid. Thorfinn
Karlsefni arrived at Brattahlid about this time, possibly

the next autumn after Thorstein's death, and in his company came Snorri Thorbrandsson. Karlsefni was married to Gudrid shortly after the Yule-tide following his arrival. If he arrived in Greenland in the autumn of the year 1002, this wedding may, accordingly, have taken place about the beginning of the year 1003. In the summer following his marriage, Thorfinn appears to have undertaken his voyage of exploration to Wienland, that is to say in the summer of the year 1003. A longer time may well have elapsed after Gudrid's arrival before her marriage with Thorstein, and similarly it is even more probable that a longer interval elapsed between Thorstein's death and Gudrid's second marriage. The purpose of this conjectural chronology is to determine, if possible, a date prior to which Thorfinn Karlsefni's voyage to Wineland could not have been undertaken. While therefore it is altogether probable that this voyage was made after the year 1003, it does not appear to be possible, for the reasons presented, that it could have taken place before that year.

Problems suggested by the text of another version of the history of the discovery and exploration, namely, that contained in the Flatey Book, are considered elsewhere, as are also points of difference between that narrative and the history as set forth in the Saga of Eric the Red. It remains to be said, that the text of this saga does not present such difficulties as those which are suggested by a critical examination of the narrative of the Flatey Book. This version of the history of the discovery does contain, however, one statement which is not altogether intelligible and which is not susceptible of very satisfactory explanation, namely, that "there came no snow" in the land which the Wineland explorers had found. This assertion does not agree with our present knowledge of the winter climate of the eastern coast of that portion of North America situated within the latitude which was probably reached by the explorers. The observation may, perhaps, be best explained upon the theory that the original verbal statement of the explorers was, that there was no snow in Wineland, such as that to which they were accustomed in the countries with which they were more familiar. With this single exception there appears to be no statement in the Saga of Eric the Red which is not lucid, and which is not reasonably consistent with our present knowledge of the probable regions visited. The incident of the adventure with the Uniped may be passed without especial mention in this connection; it gives evidence of the prevalent superstition of the time, it is true, but it in no way reflects upon the keenness of observation or relative credibility of the explorers. It follows, therefore, that the accounts of the discovery contained in Hauk's Book and AM. 557, 4to, whether they present the eldest form of the narrative of the Wineland explorers or not, do afford the most graphic and succinct exposition of the discovery, and, supported as they are throughout by contemporaneous history, appear in every respect most worthy of credence.

THE SAGA OF ERIC THE RED, ALSO CALLED THE SAGA OF
THORFINN KARLSEFNI AND SNORRI THORBRANDSSON.

Olaf was the name of a warrior-king, who was called
Olaf the White. He was the son of King Ingiald,
Helgi's son, the son of Olaf, Gudraud's son, son of Halfdan Whiteleg, king of the Uplands-men (8). Olaf engaged in a Western freebooting expedition and captured
Dublin in Ireland and the Shire of Dublin, over which
he became king (9). He married Aud the Wealthy,
daughter of Ketil Flatnose, son of Biorn Buna, a famous
man of Norway. Their son was called Thorstein the
Red. Olaf was killed in battle in Ireland, and Aud (10)
and Thorstein went then to the Hebrides (11); there
Thorstein married Thurid, daughter of Eyvind Easterling, sister of Helgi the Lean; they had many children.
Thorstein became a warrior-king, and entered into fel-
lowship with Earl Sigurd the Mighty, son of Eystein
the Rattler. They conquered Caithness and Sutherland,
Ross and Moray, and more than the half of Scotland.
Over these Thorstein became king, ere he was betrayed
by the Scots, and was slain there in battle. Aud was at
Caithness when she heard of Thorstein's death; she thereupon caused a ship (12) to be secretly built in the forest, and when she was ready, she sailed out to the Orkneys. There she bestowed Groa, Thorstein the Red's
daughter, in marriage; she was the mother of Grelad,
whom Earl Thorfinn, Skull-cleaver, married. After this
Aud set out to seek Iceland, and had on board her ship
twenty freemen (13). Aud arrived in Iceland, and

passed the first winter at Biarnarhofn with her brother, Biorn. Aud afterwards took possession of all the Dale country (14) between Dogurdar river and Skraumuhlaups river. She lived at Hvamm, and held her orisons at Krossholar, where she caused crosses to be erected, for she had been baptized and was a devout believer. With her there came out [to Iceland] many distinguished men, who had been captured in the Western freebooting expedition, and were called slaves. Vifil was the name of one of these; he was a highborn man, who had been taken captive in the Western sea, and was called a slave before Aud freed him; now when Aud gave homesteads to the members of her crew, Vifil asked wherefore she gave him no homestead, as to the other men. Aud replied, that this should make no difference to him, saying that he would be regarded as a distinguished man wherever he was. She gave him Vifilsdal (15) and there he dwelt. He married a woman whose name was . . . their sons were Thorbiorn and Thorgeir. They were men of promise, and grew up with their father.

ERIC THE RED FINDS GREENLAND.

There was a man named Thorvald; he was a son of Asvald, Ulf's son, Eyxna-Thori's son. His son's name was Eric. He and his father went from Jaederen (16) to Iceland, on account of manslaughter, and settled on Hornstrandir, and dwelt at Drangar (17). There Thorvald died, and Eric then married Thorhild, a daughter of Jorund, Atli's son, and Thorbiorg the Ship-chested who had been married before to Thorbiorn of the Hauk-

adal family. Eric then removed from the North, and
cleared land in Haukadal, and dwelt at Ericsstadir by
Vatnshorn. Then Eric's thralls caused a land-slide on
Valthiof's farm, Valthiofsstadir. Eyiolf the Foul, Valthiof's kinsman, slew the thralls near Skeidsbrekkur above
Vatnshorn. For this Eric killed Eyiolf the Foul, and he
also killed Duelling-Hrafn, at Leikskalar. Geirstein and
Odd of Jorva, Eyiolf's kinsmen, conducted the prosecu-
tion for the slaying of their kinsmen, and Eric was, in
consequence, banished from Haukadal. He then took
possession of Brokey and Eyxney, and dwelt at Tradir on
Sudrey, the first winter (18). It was at this time that
he loaned Thorgest his outer dais-boards (19); Eric afterwards went to Eyxney, and dwelt at Ericsstad. He
then demanded his outer dais-boards, but did not obtain
them. Eric then carried the outer dais-boards away
from Breidabolstad, and Thorgest gave chase. They
came to blows a short distance from the farm of Drangar
(20). There two of Thorgest's sons were killed and
certain other men besides. After this each of them retained a considerable body of men with him at his home.
Styr gave Eric his support, as did also Eyiolf of Sviney,
Thorbiorn, Vifil's son, and the sons of Thorbrand of
Alptafirth; while Thorgest was backed by the sons of
Thord the Yeller, and Thorgeir of Hitardal, Aslak of
Langadal and his son, Illugi. Eric and his people were
condemned to outlawry at Thorsness-thing (21). He
equipped his ship for a voyage, in Ericsvag; while Eyiolf
concealed him in Dimunarvag (22), when Thorgest and
his people were searching for him among the islands.

He said to them, that it was his intention to go in search of that land which Gunnbiorn (23), son of Ulf the Crow, saw when he was driven out of his course, westward across the main, and discovered Gunnbiorns-skerries. He told them that he would return again to his friends, if he should succeed in finding that country. Thorbiorn, and Eyiolf, and Styr accompanied Eric out beyond the islands, and they parted with the greatest friendliness; Eric said to them that he would render them similar aid, so far as it might lie within his power, if they should ever stand in need of his help. Eric sailed out to sea from Snaefells-iokul, and arrived at that ice-mountain (24) which is called Blacksark. Thence he sailed to the southward, that h? might ascertain whether there was habitable country in that direction. He passed the first winter at Ericsey, near the middle of the West-ern-settlement. In the following spring he proceeded to Ericsfirth, and selected a site there for his homestead. That summer he explored the western uninhabited re-gion, remaining there for a long time, and assigning many local names there. The second winter he spent at Ericsholms beyond Hvarfsgnipa. But the third summer he sailed northward to Snaefell, and into Hrafnsfirth. He believed then that he had reached the head of Erics-firth; he turned back then, and remained the third win-ter at Ericsey at the mouth of Ericsfirth (25). The following summer he sailed to Iceland, and landed in Breidafirth. He remained that winter with Ingolf (26) at Holmlatr. In the spring he and Thorgest fought to-gether, and Eric was defeated; after this a reconciliation was effected between them. That summer Eric set out to colonize the land which he had discovered, and which he called Greenland, because, he said, men would be the more readily persuaded thither if the land had a good name.

CONCERNING THORBIORN.

Thorgeir, Vifil's son, married, and took to wife Arnora, daughter of Einar of Laugarbrekka, Sigmund's son, son of Ketil Thistil, who settled Thistilsfirth. Einar had another daughter named Hallveig; she was married to Thorbiorn, Vifil's son (27), who got with her Laugarbrekka-land on Hellisvellir. Thorbiorn moved thither, and became a very distinguished man. He was an excellent husbandman, and had a great estate. Gudrid was the name of Thorbiorn's daughter. She was the most beautiful of her sex, and in every respect a very superior woman. There dwelt at Arnarstapi a man named Orm, whose wife's name was Halldis. Orm was a good husbandman, and a great friend of Thorbiorn, and Gudrid lived with him for a long time as a foster-daughter. There was a man named Thorgeir, who lived at Thorgeirsfell (28); he was very wealthy and had been manumitted; he had a son named Einar, who was a handsome, well-bred man, and very showy in his dress. Einar was engaged in trading-voyages from one country to the other, and had prospered in this. He always spent his winter alternately either in Iceland or in Norway.

Now it is to be told that one autumn, when Einar was in Iceland, he went with his wares out along Snaefellsness, with the intention of selling them. He came to Arnarstapi, and Orm invited him to remain with him, and Einar accepted this invitation, for there was a strong friendship [between Orm and himself]. Einar's wares were carried into a store-house, where he unpacked them, and displayed them to Orm and the men of his household, and asked Orm to take such of them as he liked. Orm accepted this offer, and said that Einar was a good merchant, and was greatly favoured by fortune. Now, while they were busied about the wares, a woman passed before the door of the store-house. Einar enquired of Orm: "Who was that handsome woman who passed before the door? I have never seen her here before." Orm replies: "That is Gudrid, my foster-child, the daughter of Thorbiorn of Laugarbrekka." "She must be a good match," said Einar; "has she had any suitors?" Orm replies: "In good sooth she has been courted, friend, nor is she easily to be won, for it is believed that both she and her father will be very particular in their choice of a husband." "Be that as it may," quoth Einar, "she is the woman to whom I mean to pay my addresses, and I would have thee present this matter to her father in my behalf, and use every exertion to bring it to a favourable issue, and I shall reward thee to the full of my friendship, if I am successful. It may be that Thorbiorn will regard the connection as being to our mutual advantage, for [while] he is a most honourable man and has a goodly home, his personal effects, I am told, are somewhat on the wane; but neither I nor my father are lacking in lands or chattels, and Thorbiorn would be greatly aided thereby, if this match should be brought about." "Surely I believe myself to be thy friend," replies Orm, "and yet I am by no means disposed to act in this matter, for Thorbiorn hath a very haughty spirit, and is moreover a most ambitious man." Einar replied that he wished for nought else than that his suit should be broached; Orm replied that he should have his will. Einar fared again to the South until he reached his home. Sometime after this, Thorbiorn had an autumn feast, as was his custom, for he was a man of high position. Hither came Orm of Arnarstapi, and many other of Thorbiorn's friends. Orm came to speech with Thorbiorn, and said that Einar of Thorgeirsfell had visited him not long before, and that he was become a very promising man. Orm now makes known the proposal of marriage in Einar's behalf, and added that for some persons and for some reasons it might be regarded as a very appropriate match: "thou mayest greatly strengthen thyself thereby, master, by reason of the property." Thorbiorn answers: "Little did I expect to hear such words from thee, that I should marry my daughter to the son of a thrall (29); and that, because it seems to thee that my means are diminishing, wherefore she shall not remain longer with thee since thou deemest so mean a match as this suitable for her." Orm afterward returned to his home, and all of the invited guests to their respective households, while Gudrid remained behind with her father, and tarried at home that winter. But in the spring Thorbiorn gave an entertainment to his friends, to which many came, and it was a noble feast, and at the banquet Thorbiorn called for si-

34

lence, and spoke: "Here have I passed a goodly life-time, and have experienced the good-will of men toward me, and their affection; and, methinks, our relations together have been pleasant; but now I begin to find myself in straitened circumstances, although my estate has hitherto been accounted a respectable one. Now will I rather abandon my farming than lose my honour, and rather leave the country than bring disgrace upon my family; wherefore I have now concluded to put that promise to the test, which my friend Eric the Red made, when we parted company in Breidafirth. It is my present design to go to Greenland this summer, if matters fare as I wish." The folk were greatly astonished at this plan of Thorbiorn's, for he was blessed with many friends, but they were convinced that he was so firmly fixed in his purpose that it would not avail to endeavour to dissuade him from it. Thorbiorn bestowed gifts upon his guests, after which the feast came to an end, and the folk returned to their homes. Thorbiorn sells his lands and buys a ship, which was laid up at the mouth of Hraunhofn (30). Thirty persons joined him in the voyage; among these were Orm of Arnarstapi, and his wife, and other of Thorbiorn's friends, who would not part from him. Then they put to sea. When they sailed the weather was favourable, but after they came out upon the high seas the fair wind failed, and there came great gales, and they lost their way, and had a very tedious voyage that summer. Then illness appeared among their people, and Orm and his wife Halldis died, and the half of their company. The sea began to run high, and

35

they had a very wearisome and wretched voyage in many
ways, but arrived, nevertheless, at Heriolfsness in Greenland, on the very eve of winter.   At Heriolfsness lived
a man named Thorkel.   He was a man of ability and an
excellent husbandman.   He received Thorbiorn and all of
his ship's company, and entertained them well during the
winter.   At that time there was a season of great dearth
in Greenland; those who had been at the fisheries had had
poor hauls, and some had not returned.   There was a
certain woman there in the settlement, whose name was
Thorbiorg.   She was a prophetess, and was called Little
Sibyl (31).   She had had nine sisters, all of whom were
prophetesses, but she was the only one left alive.   It was
Thorbiorg's custom in the winters to go to entertainments, and she was especially sought after at the homes
of those who were curious to know their fate, or what
manner of season might be in store for them; and inasmuch as Thorkel was the chief yeoman in the neighbourhood it was thought to devolve upon him to find out
when the evil time, which was upon them, would cease.
Thorkel invited the prophetess to his home, and careful
preparations were made for her reception, according to
the custom which prevailed, when women of her kind
were to be entertained.   A high seat was prepared for
her, in which a cushion filled with poultry feathers was
placed.   When she came in the evening, with the man
who had been sent to meet her, she was clad in a dark-
blue cloak, fastened with a strap, and set with stones
quite down to the hem.   She wore glass beads around
her neck, and upon her head a black lamb-skin hood,

lined with white cat-skin. In her hands she carried a staff, upon which there was a knob, which was ornamented with brass, and set with stones up about the knob. Circling her waist she wore a girdle of touch-wood, and attached to it a great skin pouch, in which she kept the charms which she used when she was practising her sorcery. She wore upon her feet shaggy calf-skin shoes, with long, tough latchets, upon the ends of which there were large brass buttons. She had cat-skin gloves upon her hands, which were white inside and lined with fur. When she entered, all of the folk felt it to be their duty to offer her becoming greetings. She received the salutations of each individual according as he pleased her. Yeoman Thorkel took the sibyl by the hand, and led her to the seat which had been made ready for her. Thorkel bade her run her eyes over man and beast and home. She had little to say concerning all these. The tables were brought forth in the evening, and it remains to be told what manner of food was prepared for the prophetess. A porridge of goat's beestings was made for her, and for meat there were dressed the hearts of every kind of beast, which could be obtained there. She had a brass spoon, and a knife with a handle of walrus tusk, with a double hasp of brass around the haft, and from this the point was broken. And when the tables were removed Yeoman Thorkel approached Thorbiorg, and asked how she was pleased with the home, and the character of the folk, and how speedily she would be likely to become aware of that concerning which he had questioned her, and which the people were anxious to know. She replied that she could not give an opinion in this matter before the morrow, after that she had slept there through the night. And on the morrow, when the day was far spent, such preparations were made as were necessary to enable her to accomplish her soothsaying. She bade them bring her those women, who knew the incantation, which she required to work her spells, and which she called War-locks; but such women were not to be found. Thereupon a search was made throughout the house, to see whether any one knew this [incantation]. Then said Gudrid: "Although I am neither skilled in the black art nor a sibyl, yet my foster-mother, Halldis, taught me in Ice-land that spell-song, which she called Warlocks." Thor-biorg answered: "Then are thou wise in season!" Gudrid replied: "This is an incantation and ceremony of such a kind, that I do not mean to lend it any aid, for that I am a Christian woman." Thorbiorg answered: "It might so be that thou couldst give thy help to the company here, and still be no worse woman than before; however I leave it with Thorkel to provide for my needs." Thorkel now so urged Gudrid, that she said she must needs comply with his wishes. The women then made a ring round about, while Thorbiorg sat up on the spell-dais. Gudrid then sang the song, so sweet and well that no one remembered ever before to have heard the melody sung with so fair a voice as this. The sorceress thanked her for the song, and said: "She has indeed lured many spirits hither, who think it pleasant to hear this song, those who were wont to forsake us hitherto and refuse to submit themselves to us. Many things are now revealed to me which

38

hitherto have been hidden, both from me and from others. And I am able to announce that this period of famine will not endure longer, but the season will mend as spring approaches. The visitation of disease, which has been so long upon you, will disappear sooner than expected. And thee, Gudrid, I shall reward out of hand for the assistance which thou hast vouchsafed us, since the fate in store for thee is now all made manifest to me. Thou shalt make a most worthy match here in Greenland, but it shall not be of long duration for thee, for thy future path leads out to Iceland, and a lineage both great and goodly shall spring from thee, and above thy line brighter rays of light shall shine than I have power clearly to unfold. And now fare well and health to thee, my daughter!" After this the folk advanced to the sibyl, and each besought information concerning that about which he was most serious. She was very ready in her responses, and little of that which she foretold failed of fulfillment. After this they came for her from a neighbouring farmstead, and she thereupon set out thither. Thorbiorn was then sent for, since he had not been willing to remain at home while such heathen rites were practising. The weather improved speedily when the spring opened, even as Thorbiorg had prophesied. Thorbiorn equipped his ship and sailed away, until he arrived at Brattahlid. Eric received him with open arms, and said that it was well that he had come thither. Thorbiorn and his household remained with him during the winter, while quarters were provided for the crew among the farmers. And the following spring Eric gave Thor-

39

biorn land on Stokkaness, where a goodly farmstead was founded, and there he lived thenceforward.

CONCERNING LEIF THE LUCKY AND THE INTRODUCTION OF CHRISTIANITY INTO GREENLAND.

Eric was married to a woman named Thorhild, and had two sons; one of these was named Thorstein, and the other Leif. They were both promising men. Thorstein lived at home with his father, and there was not at that time a man in Greenland who was accounted of so great promise as he. Leif had sailed (32) to Norway, where he was at the court of King Olaf Tryggvason. When Leif sailed from Greenland, in the summer, they were driven out of their course to the Hebrides. It was late before they got fair winds thence, and they remained there far into the summer. Leif became enamored of a certain woman, whose name was Thorgunna. She was a woman of fine family, and Leif observed that she was possessed of rare intelligence (33): When Leif was preparing for his departure Thorgunna (34) asked to be permitted to accompany him. Leif enquired whether she had in this the approval of her kinsmen. She replied that she did not care for it. Leif responded that he did not deem it the part of wisdom to abduct so high-born a woman in a strange country, "and we so few in number." "It is by no means certain that thou shalt find this to be the better decision," said Thorgunna. "I shall put it to the proof, notwithstanding," said Leif. "Then I tell thee," said Thorgunna, "that I am no longer a lone woman, for I am pregnant, and upon thee I charge it. I foresee that I shall give birth to a male child. And though thou give this no heed, yet will I rear the boy, and send him to thee in Greenland, when he shall be fit to take his place with other men. And I foresee that thou wilt get as much profit of this son as is thy due from this our parting; moreover, I mean to come to Greenland myself before the end comes." Leif gave her a gold finger-ring, a Greenland wadmal mantle, and a belt of walrus-tusk. This boy came to Greenland, and was called Thorgils. Leif acknowledged his paternity, and some men will have it that this Thorgils came to Iceland in the summer before the Froda-wonder (35). However, this Thorgils was afterwards in Greenland, and there seemed to be something not altogether natural about him before the end came. Leif and his companions sailed away from the Hebrides, and arrived in Norway in the autumn. Leif went to the court of King Olaf Tryggvason. He was well received by the king, who felt that he could see that Leif was a man of great accomplishments. Upon one occasion the king came to speech with Leif, and asked him, "Is it thy purpose to sail to Greenland in the summer?" "It is my purpose," said Leif, "if it be your will." "I believe it will be well," answers the king, "and thither thou shalt go upon my errand, to proclaim Christianity there." Leif replied that the king should decide, but gave it as his belief that it would be difficult to carry this mission to a successful issue in Greenland. The king replied that he knew of no man who would be better fitted for this undertaking, "and in thy hands the cause will surely prosper." "This can only be," said Leif, "if I enjoy the grace of your protection." Leif put to sea when his ship was ready for the voyage. For a long time he was tossed about upon the ocean, and came upon lands of which he had previously had no knowledge. There were self-sown wheat fields and vines growing there. There were also those trees there which are called "mausur" (36), and of all these they took specimens. Some of the timbers were so large that they were used in building. Leif found men upon a wreck, and took them home with him, and procured quarters for them all during the winter. In this wise he showed his nobleness and goodness, since he introduced Christianity into the country, and saved the men from the wreck; and he was called Leif the Lucky ever after. Leif landed in Ericsfirth, and then went home to Brattahlid; he was well received by every one. He soon proclaimed Christianity throughout the land, and the Catholic faith, and announced King Olaf Tryggvason's messages to the people, telling them how much excellence and how great glory accompanied this faith. Eric was slow in forming the determination to forsake his old belief, but Thiodhild (37) embraced the faith promptly, and caused a church to be built at some distance from the house. This building was called Thiodhild's Church, and there she and those persons who had accepted Christianity, and they were many, were wont to offer their prayers. Thiodhild would not have intercourse with Eric after that she had received the faith, whereat he was sorely vexed.

At this time there began to be much talk about a voyage of exploration to that country which Leif had discovered. The leader of this expedition was Thorstein Ericsson, who was a good man and an intelligent, and blessed with many friends. Eric was likewise invited to join them, for the men believed that his luck and foresight would be of great furtherance. He was slow in deciding, but did not say nay, when his friends besought him to go. They thereupon equipped that ship in which Thorbiorn had come out, and twenty men were selected for the expedition. They took little cargo with them, nought else save their weapons and provisions. On that morning when Eric set out from his home he took with him a little chest containing gold and silver; he hid this treasure, and then went his way. He had proceeded but a short distance, however, when he fell from his horse and broke his ribs and dislocated his shoulder, whereat he cried, "Ai, ai!" By reason of this accident he sent his wife word that she should procure the treasure which he had concealed, for to the hiding of the treasure he attributed his misfortune (38). Thereafter they sailed cheerily out of Ericsfirth in high spirits over their plan. They were long tossed about upon the ocean, and could not lay the course they wished. They came in sight of Iceland, and likewise saw birds from the Irish coast. Their ship was, in sooth, driven hither and thither over the sea. In the autumn they turned back, worn out by toil, and exposure to the elements, and exhausted by their labours, and arrived at Ericsfirth at the very beginning of winter. Then said Eric, "More cheerful were we in the summer, when we put out of the firth, but we still live, and it might have been much worse." Thorstein answers, "It will be a princely deed to endeavour to look well after the wants of all these men who are now in need, and to make provision for them during the winter." Eric answers, "It is ever true, as it is said, that 'it is never clear ere the answer comes,' and so it must be here. We will act now upon thy counsel in this manner." All of the men, who were not otherwise provided for, accompanied the father and son. They landed thereupon, and went home to Brattahlid, where they remained throughout the winter.

THORSTEIN ERICSSON WEDS GUDRID; APPARITIONS.

Now it is to be told that Thorstein Ericsson sought Gudrid, Thorbiorn's daughter, in wedlock. His suit was favourably received both by herself and by her father, and it was decided that Thorstein should marry Gudrid, and the wedding was held at Brattahlid in the autumn. The entertainment sped well, and was very numerously attended. Thorstein had a home in the Western-settlement at a certain farmstead, which is called Lysufirth. A half interest in this property belonged to a man named Thorstein, whose wife's name was Sigrid. Thorstein went to Lysufirth, in the autumn, to his namesake, and Gudrid bore him company. They were well received, and remained there during the winter. It came to pass that sickness appeared in their home early in the winter. Gard was the name of the overseer there; he had few friends; he took sick first and died. It was not long before one after another took sick and died. Then Thorstein, Eric's son, fell sick, and Sigrid, the wife of Thorstein, his name-

44

sake; and one evening Sigrid wished to go to the house, which stood over against the outer-door, and Gudrid accompanied her; they were facing the outer-door when Sigrid uttered a loud cry. "We have acted thoughtlessly," exclaimed Gudrid, "yet thou needest not cry, though the cold strikes thee; let us go in again as speedily as possible." Sigrid answered, "This may not be in this present plight. All of the dead folk are drawn up here before the door now; among them I see thy husband, Thorstein, and I can see myself there, and it is distressful to look upon." But directly this had passed she exclaimed, "Let us go now, Gudrid; I no longer see the band!" The overseer had vanished from her sight, whereas it had seemed to her before that he stood with a whip in his hand and made as if he would scourge the flock. So they went in, and ere the morning came she was dead, and a coffin was made ready for the corpse; and that same day the men planned to row out to fish, and Thorstein accompanied them to the landing-place, and in the twilight he went down to see their catch. Thorstein, Eric's son, then sent word to his namesake that he should come to him, saying that all was not as it should be there, for the housewife was endeavouring to rise to her feet, and wished to get in under the clothes beside him, and when he entered the room she was come up on the edge of the bed. He thereupon seized her hands and held a pole-axe (39) before her breast. Thorstein, Eric's son, died before night-fall. Thorstein, the master of the house, bade Gudrid lie down and sleep, saying that he would keep watch over the bodies during the night; thus she did, and

45

early in the night Thorstein, Eric's son, sat up and spoke, saying that he desired Gudrid to be called thither, for that it was his wish to speak with her: "It is God's will that this hour be given me for my own and for the betterment of my condition." Thornstein, the master, went in search of Gudrid, and waked her, and bade her cross herself, and pray God to help her; "Thorstein, Eric's son, has said to me that he wishes to see thee; thou must take counsel with thyself now, what thou wilt do, for I have no advice to give thee." She replied, "It may be that this is intended to be one of those incidents which shall afterward be held in remembrance, this strange event, and it is my trust that God will keep watch over me; wherefore, under God's mercy, I shall venture to go to him, and learn what it is that he would say, for I may not escape this if it be designed to bring me harm. I will do this, lest he go further, for it is my belief that the matter is a grave one." So Gudrid went and drew near to Thorstein, and he seemed to her to be weeping. He spoke a few words in her ear, in a low tone, so that she alone could hear them; but this he said so that all could hear, that those persons would be blessed who kept well the faith, and that it carried with it all help and consolation, and yet many there were, said he, who kept it but ill. "This is no proper usage, which has obtained here in Greenland since Christianity was introduced here, to inter men in unconsecrated earth, with nought but a brief funeral service. It is my wish that I be conveyed to the church, together with the others who have died here; Gard, however, I would have you burn upon a pyre, as speedily as possible,

46

since he has been the cause of all of the apparitions which have been seen here during the winter." He spoke to her also of her own destiny, and said that she had a notable future in store for her, but he bade her beware of marrying any Greenlander; he directed her also to give their property to the church and to the poor, and then sank down again a second time. It had been the custom in Greenland, after Christianity was introduced there, to bury persons on the farmsteads where they died, in unconsecrated earth; a pole was erected in the ground, touching the breast of the dead, and subsequently, when the priests came thither, the pole was withdrawn and holy water poured in [the orifice], and the funeral service held there, although it might be long thereafter. The bodies of the dead were conveyed to the church at Ericsfirth, and the funeral services held there by the clergy. Thorbiorn died soon after this, and all of his property then passed into Gudrid's possession. Eric took her to his home and carefully looked after her affairs.

CONCERNING THORD OF HOFDI.

There was a man named Thord, who lived at Hofdi on Hofdi-strands. He married Fridgerd, daughter of Thori the Loiterer and Fridgerd, daughter of Kiarval the King of the Irish. Thord was a son of Biorn Chestbutter, son of Thorvald Spine, Asleik's son, the son of Biorn Iron-side, the son of Ragnar Shaggy-breeks. They had a son named Snorri. He married Thorhild Ptarmigan, daughter of Thord the Yeller. Their son was Thord Horse head. Thorfinn Karlsefni* was the name of

---

Karlsefni, one who gives promise of becoming a man.

47

Thord's son (40). Thorfinn's mother's name was
Thorunn. Thorfinn was engaged in trading voyages,
and was reputed to be a successful merchant. One summer Karlsefni equipped his ship, with the intention of
sailing to Greenland. Snorri, Thorbrand's son, of Alptafirth (41) accompanied him, and there were forty men on
board the ship with them. There was a man named
Biarni, Grimolf's son, a man from Briedafirth, and another named Thorhall, Gamli's son (42), an East-firth
man. They equipped their ship, the same summer as
Karlsefni, with the intention of making a voyage to
Greenland; they had also forty men in their ship. When
they were ready to sail, the two ships put to sea together.
It has not been recorded how long a voyage they had;
but it is to be told that both of the ships arrived at Ericsfirth in the autumn. Eric and other of the inhabitants of
the country rode to the ships, and a goodly trade was
soon established between them. Gudrid was requested
by the skippers to take such of their wares as she wished,
while Eric, on his part, showed great munificence in return, in that he extended an invitation to both crews to
accompany him home for winter quarters at Brattahlid.
The merchants accepted this invitation, and went with
Eric. Their wares were then conveyed to Brattahlid; nor
was there lack there of good and commodious store-
houses, in which to keep them; nor was there wanting
much of that which they needed, and the merchants
were well pleased with their entertainment at Eric's
home during that winter. Now as it drew toward Yule
Eric became very taciturn, and less cheerful than had

48

been his wont. On one occasion Karlsefni entered into conversation with Eric, and said: "Hast thou aught weighing upon thee, Eric? The folk have remarked, that thou are somewhat more silent than thou hast been hitherto. Thou hast entertained us with great liberality, and it behooves us to make such return as may lie within our power. Do thou now but make known the cause of thy melancholy." Eric answers: "Ye accept hospitality gracefully, and in manly wise, and I am not pleased that ye should be the sufferers by reason of our intercourse; rather am I troubled at the thought, that it should be given out elsewhere, that ye have never passed a worse Yule than this, now drawing nigh, when Eric the Red was your host at Brattahlid in Greenland." "There shall be no cause for that," replied Karlsefni, "we have malt, and meal, and corn in our ships, and you are welcome to take of these whatsoever you wish, and to provide as liberal an entertainment as seems fitting to you." Eric accepted this offer, and preparations were made for the Yule feast (43), and it was so sumptuous, that it seemed to the people they had scarcely ever seen so grand an entertainment before. And after Yule Karlsefni broached the subject of a marriage with Gudrid to Eric, for he assumed that with him rested the right to bestow her hand in marriage. Eric answered favourably, and said that she would accomplish the fate in store for her, adding that he had heard only good reports of him. And not to prolong this the result was that *Thorfinn* was betrothed to *Thurid,* and the banquet was augmented, and their wedding was celebrated; and this befell at Brattahlid during the winter.

49

BEGINNING OF THE WINELAND VOYAGES.

About this time there began to be much talk at Bratt-ahlid, to the effect that Wineland the Good should be explored, for, it was said, that country must be possessed of many goodly qualities. And so it came to pass, that Karlsefni and Snorri fitted out their ship, for the purpose of going in search of that country in the spring. Biarni and Thorhall joined the expedition with their ship, and the men who had borne them company. There was a man named Thorvard; he was wedded to Freydis (44) a natural daughter of Eric the Red. He also accompanied them, together with Thorvald, Eric's son, and Thorhall, who was called the Huntsman. He had been for a long time with Eric as his hunter and fisherman during the summer, and as his steward during the winter. Thorhall was stout and swarthy, and of giant stature; he was a man of few words, though given to abusive language when he did speak, and he ever incited Eric to evil. He was a poor Christian; he had a wide knowledge of the unsettled regions. He was on the same ship with Thorvard and Thorvald. They had that ship which Thorbiorn had brought out. They had in all one hundred and sixty men, when they sailed to the Western settlement (45), and thence to Bear Island. Thence they bore away to the southward two "dœgr" (46). Then they saw land, and launched a boat, and explored the land, and found there large flat stones [*hellur*], and many of these were twelve ells wide; there were many Arctic foxes there. They gave a name to the country, and called it Helluland [the land of flat stones]. Then they sailed with northerly winds two "dœgr," and land then lay before them, and upon it was a great wood and many wild beasts; an island lay off the land to the southeast, and there they found a bear, and they called this Biarney [Bear Island], while the land where the wood was they called Markland [Forest-land]. Thence they sailed southward along the land for a long time, and came to a cape; the land lay upon the starboard; there were long strands and sandy banks there. They rowed to the land and found upon the cape there the keel of a ship (47) and they called it there Kialarnes [Keelness]; they also called the strands Furdustrandir [Wonder-strands], because they were so long to sail by. Then the country became indented with bays, and they steered their ships into a bay. It was when Leif was with King Olaf Tryggvason, and he bade him proclaim Christianity to Greenland, that the king gave him two Gaels (48); the man's name was Haki, and the woman's Haekia. The king advised Leif to have recourse to these people, if he should stand in need of fleetness, for they were swifter than deer. Eric and Leif had tendered Karlsefni the services of this couple. Now when they had sailed past Wonder-strands they put the Gaels ashore, and directed them to run to the southward, and investigate the nature of the country, and return again before the end of the third half-day. They were each clad in a garment which they called "kiafal," which was so fashioned that it had a hood at the top, was open at the sides, was sleeveless, and was fastened between the legs with buttons and loops, while elsewhere they were naked. Karlsefni and his companions cast anchor, and lay there during their absence; and when they came again, one of them carried a bunch of grapes and the other an ear of new-sown wheat. They went on board the ship, whereupon Karlsefni and his followers held on their way, until they came to where the coast was indented with bays. They stood into a bay with their ships. There was an island out at the mouth of the bay, about which there were strong currents, wherefore they called it Straumey [Stream Isle]. There were so many birds there that it was scarcely possible to step between the eggs. They sailed through the firth, and called it Straumfiord [Streamfirth], and carried their cargoes ashore from the ships, and established themselves there. *They had brought with them all kinds of live-stock.* It was a fine country there. There were mountains thereabouts. They occupied themselves exclusively with the exploration of the country. They remained there during the winter, and they had taken no thought for this during the summer. The fishing began to fail, and they began to fall short of food. Then Thorhall the Huntsman disappeared. They had already prayed to God for food, but it did not come as promptly as their necessities seemed to demand. They searched for Thorhall for three half-days, and found him on a projecting crag. He was lying there and looking up at the sky, with mouth and nostrils agape, and mumbling something. They asked him why he had gone thither; he replied that this did not concern anyone. They asked him then to go home with them, and he did so. Soon after this a whale appeared there, and they captured it, and flensed it, and no one could tell what manner of whale it was; and when the cooks had prepared it they ate of it, and were all made ill by it. Then Thorhall, approaching them, said: "Did not the Red-beard (49) prove more helpful than your Christ? This is my reward for the verses which I composed to Thor, the Trustworthy; seldom has he failed me." When the people heard this they cast the whale down into the sea, and made their appeals to God. The weather then improved, and they could now row out to fish, and thenceforward they had no lack of provisions, for they could hunt game on the land, gather eggs on the island, and catch fish from the sea.

CONCERNING KARLSEFNI AND THORHALL.

It is said that Thorhall wished to sail to the northward beyond Wonder-strands, in search of Wineland, while Karlsefni desired to proceed to the southward, off the coast. Thorhall prepared for his voyage out below the island, having only nine men in his party, for all the remainder of the company went with Karlsefni. And one day when Thorhall was carrying water aboard his ship, and was drinking, he recited this ditty:

> When I came, these brave men told me,
>   Here the best of drink I'd get,
> Now with water-pail behold me,—
>   Wine and I are strangers yet.
> Stooping at the spring, I've tested
>   All the wine this land affords;
> Of its vaunted charms divested,
>   Poor indeed are its rewards.

And when they were ready, they hoisted sail; whereupon Thorhall recited this ditty:

> Comrades, let us now be faring
>   Homeward to our own again!
> Let us try the sea-steed's daring,
>   Give the chafing courser rein.
> Those who will may bide in quiet,
>   Let them praise their chosen land,
> Feasting on a whale-steak diet,
>   In their home by Wonder-strand.*

Then they sailed away to the northward past Wonder-strands and Keelness, intending to cruise to the westward around the cape. They encountered westerly gales, were driven ashore in Ireland, where they were grievously maltreated and thrown into slavery. There Thorhall lost his life, according to that which traders have related.

It is now to be told of Karlsefni, that he cruised southward off the coast, with Snorri and Biarni, and their people. They sailed for a long time, and until they came at last to a river which flowed down from the land into a lake, and so into the sea. There were great bars at the mouth of the river, so that it could only be entered at the height of the flood-tide. Karlsefni and his men sailed into the mouth of the river, and called it there Hop [a small land-locked bay]. They found self-sown wheat-fields on the land there; wherever there were hollows, and wherever there was hilly ground, there were vines (50). Every brook there was full of fish. They dug

---

*The prose sense of the verse is: Let us return to our countrymen, leaving those, who like the country here, to cook their whale on Wonder-strands.

pits on the shore where the tide rose highest, and when the tide fell there were halibut (51) in the pits. There were great numbers of wild animals of all kinds in the woods. They remained there half a month, and enjoyed themselves, and kept no watch. They had their live-stock with them. Now one morning early when they looked about them they saw a great number of skin-ca-noes, and staves (52) were brandished from the boats, with a noise like flails, and they were revolved in the same direction in which the sun moves. Then said Karlsefni: "What may this betoken?" Snorri, Thorbrand's son, an-swered him: "It may be that this is a signal of peace, wherefore let us take a white shield (53) and display it." And thus they did. Thereupon the strangers rowed to-ward them, and went upon the land, marvelling at those whom they saw before them. They were swarthy men and ill-looking, and the hair of their heads was ugly. They had great eyes, and were broad of cheek (54). They tarried there for a time looking curiously at the people they saw before them, and then rowed away, and to the southward around the point.

Karlsefni and his followers had built their huts above the lake, some of their dwellings being near the lake, and others farther away. Now they remained there that win-ter. No snow came there, and all of their live-stock lived by grazing (55). And when spring opened they dis-covered, early one morning, a great number of skin-ca-noes rowing from the south past the cape, so numerous that it looked as if coals had been scattered broadcast out before the bay; and on every boat staves were waved.

Thereupon Karlsefni and his people displayed their shields and when they came together they began to barter with each other. Especially did the strangers wish to buy red cloth, for which they offered in exchange peltries and quite grey skins. They also desired to buy swords and spears, but Karlsefni and Snorri forbade this. In exchange for perfect unsullied skins, the Skrellings would take red stuff a span in length, which they would bind around their heads. So their trade went on for a time, until Karlsefni and his people began to grow short of cloth, when they divided it into such narrow pieces that it was not more than a finger's breadth wide, but the Skrellings still continued to give just as much for this as before, or more.

It so happened that a bull, belonging to Karlsefni and his people, ran out from the woods, bellowing loudly. This so terrified the Skrellings, that they sped out to their canoes, and then rowed away to the southward along the coast. For three entire weeks nothing more was seen of them. At the end of this time, however, a great multitude of Skrelling boats was discovered approaching from the south, as if a stream were pouring down, and all of their staves were waved in a direction contrary to the course of the sun, and the Skrellings were all uttering loud cries. Thereupon Karlsefni and his men took red shields (53) and displayed them. The Skrellings sprang from their boats, and they met then, and fought together. There was a fierce shower of missiles, for the Skrellings had war-slings. Karlsefni and Snorri observed that the Skrellings raised up on a pole a great ball-shaped body, almost the size of a sheep's belly, and nearly black in colour, and this they hurled from the pole upon the land above Karlsefni's followers, and it made a frightful noise where it fell. Whereat a great fear seized upon Karlsefni and all his men, so that they could think of nought but flight, and of making their escape up along the river bank, for it seemed to them that the troop of the Skrellings was rushing towards them from every side, and they did not pause until they came to certain jutting crags, where they offered a stout resistance. Freydis came out, and seeing that Karlsefni and his men were fleeing, she cried: "Why do ye flee from these wretches, such worthy men as ye, when, meseems, ye might slaughter them like cattle. Had I but a weapon, methinks, I would fight better than any one of you!" They gave no heed to her words. Freydis sought to join them, but lagged behind, for she was not hale; she followed them, however, into the forest, while the Skrellings pursued her; she found a dead man in front of her; this was Thorbrand, Snorri's son, his skull cleft by a flat stone; his naked sword lay beside him; she took it up, and prepared to defend herself with it. The Skrellings then approached her, whereupon she stripped down her shift, and slapped her breast with the naked sword. At this the Skrellings were terrified and ran down to their boats, and rowed away. Karlsefni and his companions, however, joined her and praised her valour. Two of Karlsefni's men had fallen and a great number of the Skrellings. Karlsefni's party had been overpowered by dint of superior numbers. They now returned to their

57

dwellings, and bound up their wounds, and weighed carefully what throng of men that could have been, which had seemed to descend upon them from the land; it now seemed to them that there could have been but the one party, that which came from the boats, and that the other troop must have been an ocular delusion. The Skrellings, however, found a dead man, and an axe lay beside him. One of their number picked up the axe, and struck at a tree with it, and one after another [they tested it], and it seemed to them to be a treasure, and to cut well; then one of their number seized it, and hewed at a stone with it, so that the axe broke, whereat they concluded that it could be of no use, since it would not withstand stone, and they cast it away.

It now seemed clear to Karlsefni and his people that although the country thereabouts was attractive, their life would be one of constant dread and turmoil by reason of the [hostility of the] inhabitants of the country, so they forthwith prepared to leave, and determined to return to their own country. They sailed to the northward off the coast, and found five Skrellings, clad in skin-doublets, lying asleep near the sea. There were vessels beside them containing animal marrow, mixed with blood. Karlsefni and his company concluded that they must have been banished from their own land. They put them to death. They afterwards found a cape, upon which there was a great number of animals, and this cape looked as if it were one cake of dung, by reason of the animals which lay there at night. They now arrived again at Streamfirth, where they found great abundance of all those things

58

DEATH OF THORVALD ERIKSON.

(From a drawing by Kendrick.)

THORVALD, a son of Eric the Red, was a man cast in a mould as heroic as that from which issued his historically better known brother, Leif Erikson. To him the credit is due of having been with Karlsefni, the first white man to explore the American coast south of what is now Massachusetts. His death from an arrow wound, received at the hands of the Skrellings (Indians), was the first tragedy enacted in the settlement of the New World, and his dying words were prophetic of the greatness which the country would some day attain because of its fruitfulness.

DEATH OF THORVALD ERIKSON.

(*From a drawing by Kendrick.*)

THORVALD, a son of Eric the Red, was a man cast in a mould as heroic as that from which issued his historically better known brother, Leif Erikson. To him the credit is due of having been with Karlsefni, the first white man to explore the American coast south of what is now Massachusetts. His death from an arrow wound, received at the hands of the Skrellings (Indians), was the first tragedy enacted in the settlement of the New World, and his dying words were prophetic of the greatness which the country would some day attain because of its fruitfulness.

of which they stood in need. Some men say that Biarni and Freydis remained behind here with a hundred men, and went no further; while Karlsefni and Snorri proceeded to the southward with forty men, tarrying at Hop barely two months, and returning again the same summer. Karlsefni then set out with one ship in search of Thorhall the Huntsman, but the greater part of the company remained behind. They sailed to the northward around Keelness, and then bore to the westward, having land to the larboard. The country there was a wooded wilderness, as far as they could see, with scarcely an open space; and when they had journeyed a considerable distance, a river flowed down from the east toward the west. They sailed into the mouth of the river, and lay to by the southern bank.

THE SLAYING OF THORVALD, ERIC'S SON.

It happened one morning that Karlsefni and his companions discovered in an open space in the woods above them, a speck, which seemed to shine toward them, and they shouted at it; it stirred and it was a Uniped (56), who skipped down to the bank of the river by which they were lying. Thorvald, a son of Eric the Red, was sitting at the helm, and the Uniped shot an arrow into his inwards. Thorvald drew out the arrow, and exclaimed: "There is fat around my paunch; we have hit upon a fruitful country, and yet we are not like to get much profit of it." Thorvald died soon after from this wound. Then the Uniped ran away back toward the north. Karlsefni and his men pursued him, and saw him from time

6   59

to time. The last they saw of him, he ran down into a creek. Then they turned back; whereupon one of the men recited this ditty:

> Eager, our men, up hill, down dell,
>   Hunted a Uniped;
> Hearken, Karlsefni, while they tell
>   How swift the quarry fled!

Then they sailed away back toward the north, and believed they had got sight of the land of the Unipeds; nor were they disposed to risk the lives of their men any longer. They concluded that the mountains of Hop, and those which they had now found, formed one chain, and this appeared to be so because they were about an equal distance removed from Streamfirth, in either direction. They sailed back, and passed the third winter at Stream-firth. Then the men began to divide into factions, of which the women were the cause; and those who were without wives endeavoured to sieze upon the wives of those who were married, whence the greatest trouble arose. Snorri, Karlsefni's son, was born the first autumn, and he was three winters' old when they took their departure. When they sailed away from Wineland, they had a southerly wind, and so came upon Markland, where they found five Skrellings, of whom one was bearded, two were women, and two were children. Karlsefni and his people took the boys, but the others escaped, and these Skrellings sank down into the earth. They bore the lads away with them, and taught them to speak, and they were baptized. They said that their mother's name was Vætilldi, and their father's Uvægi. They said that kings governed the Skrellings, one of whom was called Avalldamon, and the other Valldidida (57). They stated, that there were no houses there, and that the people lived in caves or holes. They said that there was a land on the other side over against their country, which was inhabited by people who wore white garments, and yelled loudly, and carried poles before them, to which rags were attached; and people believe that this must have been Hvitramanna-land [White-men's-land], or Ireland the Great (58). Now they arrived in Greenland, and remained during the winter with Eric the Red.

Biarni, Grimolf's son, and his companions were driven out into the Atlantic, and came into a sea, which was filled with worms,* and their ship began to sink beneath them. They had a boat which had been coated with seal-tar; this the sea-worm does not penetrate. They took their places in this boat, and then discovered that it would not hold them all. Then said Biarni: "Since the boat will not hold more than half of our men, it is my advice, that the men who are to go in the boat be chosen by lot, for this selection must not be made according to rank." This seemed to them all such a manly offer that no one opposed it. So they adopted this plan, the men casting lots; and it fell to Biarni to go in the boat, and half of the men with him, for it would not hold more. But when the men were come into the boat an Icelander, who was in the ship, and who had accompanied Biarni

---

*This reference is to the toredo, or ship worm, that bores into wood and is often a source of danger to unsheathed vessels.

from Iceland, said: "Dost thou intend, Biarni, to forsake me here?" "It must be even so," answers Biarni. "Not such was the promise thou gavest my father," he answers, "when I left Iceland with thee, that thou wouldst thus part with me, when thou saidst that we should both share the same fate." "So be it, it shall not rest thus," answered Biarni; "do thou come hither, and I will go to the ship, for I see that thou art eager for life." Biarni thereupon boarded the ship, and this man entered the boat, and they went their way, until they came to Dublin in Ireland, and there they told this tale; now it is the belief of most people that Biarni and his companions perished in the maggot-sea, for they were never heard of afterward.

The following summer Karlsefni sailed to Iceland and Gudrid with him, and he went home to Reyniness (59). His mother believed that he had made a poor match, and she was not at home the first winter. However, when she became convinced that Gudrid was a very superior woman, she returned to her home, and they lived happily together. Hallfrid was a daughter of Snorri, Karlsefni's son, she was the mother of Bishop Thorlak, Runolf's son (60). They had a son named Thorbiorn, whose daughter's name was Thorunn [she was] Bishop Biorn's mother. Thorgeir was the name of a son of Snorri, Karlsefni's son, [he was] the father of Ingveld, mother of Bishop Brand the Elder. Steinunn was a daughter of Snorri, Karlsefni's son, who married Einar, a son of

Grundar-Ketil, a son of Thorvald Crook, a son of Thori of Espihol. Their son was Thorstein the Unjust, he was the father of Gudrun, who married Jorund of Keldur. Their daughter was Halla, the mother of Flosi, the father of Valgerd, the mother of Herra Erlend, the Stout, the father of Herra Hauk the Lawman. Another daughter of Flosi was Thordis, the mother of Fru Ingigerd the Mighty. Her daughter was Fru Hallbera, Abbess of Reyniness at Stad (59). Many other great people in Iceland are descended from Karlsefni and Thurid, who are not mentioned here. God be with us, Amen!

CHAPTER III.

THE WINELAND HISTORY OF THE FLATEY BOOK.

THE Flatey Book [Flateyjarbok] is the most extensive and most perfect of Icelandic manuscripts. It is in itself a comprehensive historical library of the era with which it deals, and so considerable are its contents that they fill upwards of 1700 large octavo pages of printed text. On the title-page of the manuscript we are informed, that it belonged originally to John Haconsson for whom it was written by the priests John Thordsson and Magnus Thorhallsson. We have no information concerning the date when the book was commenced by John Thordsson; but the most important portion of the work appears to have been completed in the year 1387, although additions were made to the body of the work by one of the original scribes, and the annals appended to the books, brought them down to the year 1394. Toward the close of the fifteenth century, the then owner of the book, whose name is unknown, inserted three quaternions of additional historical matter in the manuscript, to fill a hiatus in the historical sequence of the work, not, however, in that part of the manuscript which treats of Wineland.

It has been conjectured that the manuscript was written in the north of Iceland, but according to the editors of the printed text the facts are that the manuscript was owned in the west of Iceland as far back as we possess any knowledge of it, and there is no positive evidence where it was written. We have, indeed, no further particulars concerning the manuscript before the seventeenth century, when we find that it was in the possession of John Finsson, who dwelt in Flatey in Breidafirth as had his father, and his father's father before him. That the book had been a family heirloom is evident from an entry made in the manuscript by this same John Finsson:

"This book I, John Finsson, own; the gift of my deceased father's father, John Biarnsson," etc.

From John Finsson the book descended to his nephew, John Torfason, from whom that worthy bibliophile, Bishop Bryniolf of Skalholt, sought in vain to purchase it, as is related in an anecdote in the bishop's biography:

"Farmer John of Flatey, son of the Rev. Torfi Finsson, owned a large and massive parchment-book in ancient monachal writing, containing sagas of the Kings of Norway, and many others; and it is, therefore, commonly called Flatey Book. This Bishop Bryniolf endeavored to purchase, first for money, and then for five hundreds of land. But he nevertheless failed to obtain it; however, when John bore him company, as he was leaving the island, he presented him the book; and it is said that the Bishop rewarded him liberally for it."

The Flatey Book was among a collection of vellum manuscripts intrusted to the care of Thormod Torfæus, in 1662, as a present from Bishop Bryniolf to King Frederick the Third of Denmark, and thus luckily escaped the fate of others of the bishop's literary treasures. In the Royal Library of Copenhagen it has ever since remained, where it is known as No. 1005, fol. of the Old Royal Collection.

Interpolated in the Saga of Olaf Tryggvason in the Flatey Book are two minor historical narratives. The first of these, in the order in which they appear in the manuscript, is called, a Short Story of Eric the Red, the second, a Short Story of the Greenlanders. Although these short histories are not connected in any way in the manuscript, being indeed separated by over fifty columns of extraneous historical matter, they form, if brought together, what may be called, the Flatey Book version of history of the Wineland discovery,—a version which varies materially from the accounts of the discovery, as they have been preserved elsewhere. Before considering these points of difference, it may be stated that, as we have no certain knowledge where the Flatey Book was written, neither have we any definite information concerning the original material from which the transcripts of these two narratives were made. The original manuscripts of these narratives would appear to have shared a common fate with the other original forms from which the scribes of the Flatey Book compiled their work;—all of this vast congeries of early manuscripts has entirely disappeared. This is the conclusion reached by that eminent authority, the late Dr. Vigfusson, whose profound knowledge of the written literature of the North was supplemented in the present instance by that close acquaintance which he had gained with the Flatey Book, by reason of his having transcribed the entire manuscript for publication.

This total disappearance of all trace of the archetypes of the Flatey Book, although it is by no means the only case of the kind in the history of Icelandic paleography, is especially to be deplored in connection with the Wineland narrative, since it leaves us without a clue, which might aid us in arriving at a solution of certain enigmas which this narrative presents.

In the Flatey Book version of the discovery it is stated that Biarni Heriulfsson, during a voyage from Iceland to Greenland, having been driven to the southward out of his course, came upon unknown lands; that, following upon this, and as the direct result of Biarni's reports of his discoveries, Leif Ericsson was moved to go in search of the strange lands which Biarni had seen but not explored; that he found these in due course, "first that land which Biarni had seen last," and finally the southernmost land, to which, "after its products," he gave the name of Wineland. This account differs entirely from the history contained in the other manuscripts which deal with this subject, all of which agree in ascribing the discovery to

66

Leif Ericsson, and unite in the statement that he found Wineland *accidentally,* during a voyage from Norway to Greenland, which he had undertaken at the instance of King Olaf Tryggvasson, for the purpose of introducing Christianity to his fellow-countrymen in Greenland. Not only is Biarni's discovery unknown to any other Icelandic writing now existing, but the man himself, as well as his daring voyage, have failed to find a chronicler elsewhere, although his father was "a most distinguished man," the grandson of a "settler," and a kinsman of the first Icelandic colonist.

The first portion of the Flatey Book version, the "Short Story of Eric the Red," concludes with the words, "Biarni now went to his father, gave up his voyaging, and remained with his father during Heriulf's lifetime, and continued to dwell there after his father." The second portion of this version of the Wineland history, the "Short Story of the Greenlanders," begins with the words "It is now next to this, that Biarni Heriulfsson came out from Greenland on a visit to Earl Eric," etc. As has already been stated, the two portions of the history of the Wineland discovery, as they appear in the Flatey Book, are not in any way connected with each other. The first narrative occupies its appropriate place in the account of the life of King Olaf Tryggvason, as do the other narratives, similar in character, which are introduced into this as into the other sagas in the manuscript, and there appears to be no reason why the second narrative, "A Short Story of the Greenlanders," should be regarded as having received treatment different, in this respect, from other interpolated narratives of the same class. If, therefore, we interpret the opening words of this story of the Greenlanders, "It is now next to this," to mean that the incident which follows is related next in chronological order after that part of the saga which has immediately preceded it, it becomes apparent that Biarni's visit must have taken place after the battle of Svoldr in which King Olaf Tryggvason fell, and Earl Eric was victorious. This battle took place on the 9th of September, in the year 1000. As it is not probable that Biarni would have undertaken his voyage to Norway before the summer following, the earliest date which could reasonably be assigned for Biarni's sojourn at the Earl's court would appear to be the winter of the years 1001-1002. We are told in the same place that Biarni returned to Greenland the following summer, and that subsequent to his return Leif purchased his ship, and went in search of the land which Biarni had seen, but had failed to explore, in the year 985, according to the chronology of the "Short Story."

Leif's voyage of exploration, as described in the Flatey Book, could, therefore, scarcely have taken place before the year 1002. But, according to the other historical data already cited, Leif discovered Wineland during a voyage to Greenland, undertaken at the request, and during the lifetime, of King Olaf Tryggvason, hence obviously not later than the year 1000. The Flatey Book refers to this voyage in the following words: "That same summer he [King Olaf Tryggvason] sent Gizur and Hialti to Iceland, as has already been written. At that time King Olaf sent Leif to Greenland to preach

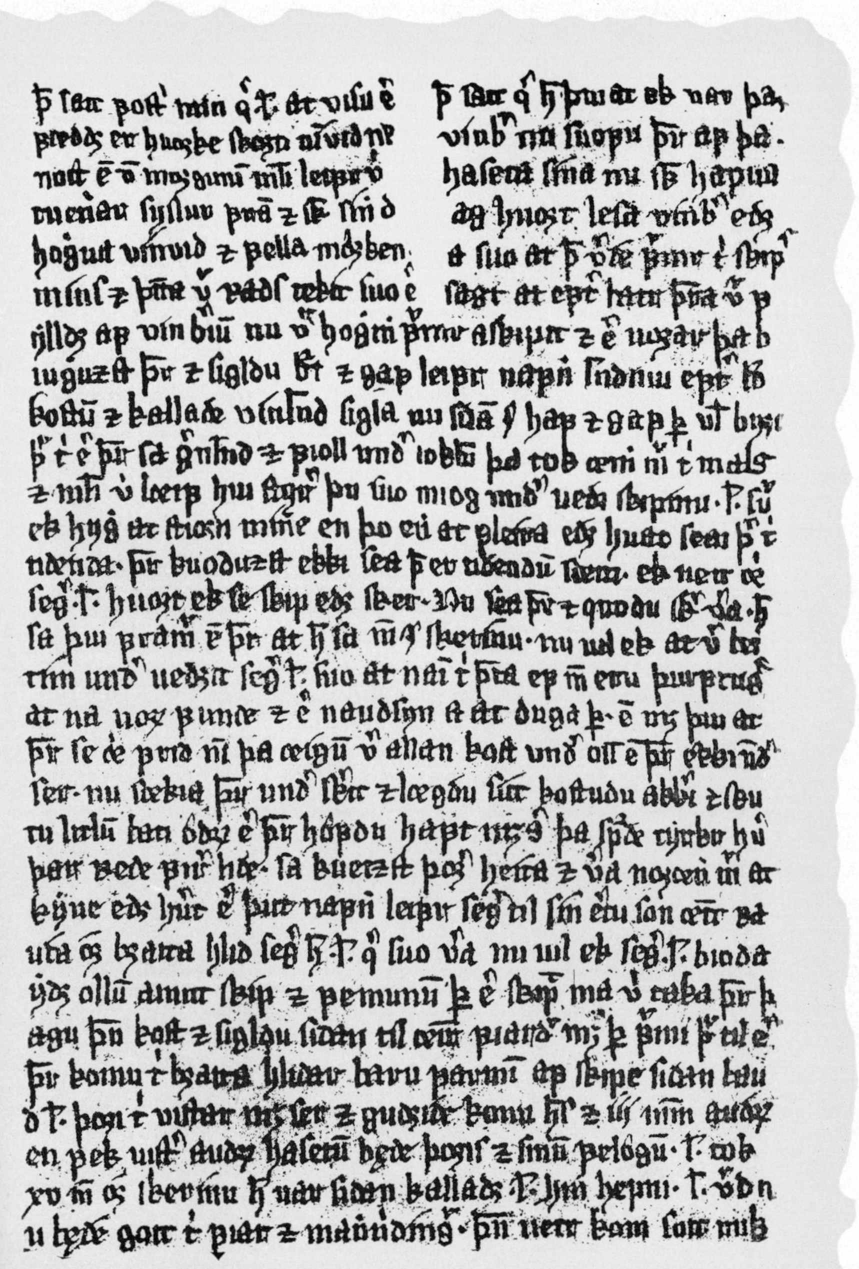

Christianity there. The King sent with him a priest and certain other holy men to baptize the folk, and teach them the true faith. Leif went to Greenland that summer and took [on board his vessel] a ship's crew of men, who were at the time in great peril upon a rock. He arrived in Greenland late in the summer, and went home to his father, Eric, at Brattahlid. The people afterwards called him Leif the Lucky, but his father, Eric, said that Leif's having rescued the crew and restored the men to life, might be balanced against the fact that he had brought the impostor to Greenland, so he called the priest. Nevertheless, through Leif's advice and persuasion, Eric was baptized, and all of the people of Greenland.

It will be observed, that in this record of Leif's missionary voyage no allusion is made to the discovery of Wineland, as in the other accounts of the same voyage, with which, in other respects, this passage agrees. By this variation a conflict with Biarni's claim to the priority of discovery, previously promulgated in the "Short Story of Eric the Red," is avoided. A portion of this passage may not, however, be so happily reconciled. It is said that, through Leif's advice and persuasion, Eric the Red was baptized, while we find in the "Short Story of the Greenlanders," the statement that "Eric the Red died before Christianity." Moreover, we have, in the "Short Story of the Greenlanders," in addition to this direct conflict of statement, an apparent repetition of the incident of the rescue of the shipwrecked mariners, when we are told that Leif effected a rescue of castaways on his return from a voyage of exploration to Wineland, and was therefore called Leif the Lucky. If this be not a repetition of the same incident, then we must conclude that Leif upon two different voyages saved the lives of a crew of shipwrecked mariners, for which he twice received the same title from the same people! In the description of the rescue, contained in the "Short Story of the Greenlanders," we read that the leader of the castaways was one Thori Easterling, whose wife, Gudrid, Thorbiorn's daughter, seems to have been among the rescued. This Thori is mentioned nowhere save in the Flatey Book. His wife was so famous a personage in Icelandic annals that it seems passing strange this spouse should have been so completely ignored by other Icelandic chronicles, which have not failed to record Gudrid's marriage to Thorstein Ericsson, and subsequently to Thorfinn Karlsefni. Indeed, according to the biography of this "most noble lady," as written in the Saga of Eric the Red, there is no place for Thori, for Gudrid is said to have come to Greenland in much less romantic fashion, namely, as an unmarried woman, in the same ship with, and under the protection of her father Thorbiorn.

Another chronological error occurs in that paragraph of the "Short Story of Eric the Red," wherein it is stated that, "after sixteen winters had lapsed from the time when Eric the Red went to colonize Greenland, Leif, Eric's son, sailed out from Greenland to Norway. He arrived in Drontheim in the autumn when King Olaf Tryggvason was come down from the North out of Halogaland." It has previously been stated in this same chronicle that Eric set out to colonize Greenland fifteen years before Christianity was legally adopted in Iceland, that is to say in the year 985. Whence it follows, from this chronology, that Leif's voyage must have been undertaken in the year 1001, but since Olaf Tryggvason was killed in the autumn of the year 1000, this is, from the context, manifestly impossible. If we may suppose that the scribe of the Flatey Book, by a careless verbal substitution wrote "for at byggja" [went to colonize], instead of "for at leita" [went in search of], the chronology of the narrative becomes reconcilable.

In the "Short Story of the Greenlanders" inaccuracies of lesser import occur, one of which, at least, appears to owe its origin to a clerical blunder. In the narrative of Freydis' voyage, we are told that she waited upon the brothers Helgi and Finnbogi, and persuaded them to join her in an expedition to Wineland; according to the text, however, she enters into an agreement governing the manning of their ships, not with them, but with Karlsefni. Yet it is obvious, from the context, that Karlsefni did not participate in the enterprise, nor does it appear that he had any interest whatsoever in the undertaking. The substitution of Karlsefni's name for that of Helgi or Finnbogi, by a careless scribe, may have given rise to this lack of sequence. A blunder, which has crept into the genealogical list, at the conclusion of the history, may, perhaps, owe its origin to a somewhat similar cause. In this list, it will be noted, Bishop Thorlak is called the grandson of Hallfrid, Snorri's daughter; in the words of the manuscript, "Hallfrid was the name of the daughter of Snorri, Karlsefni's son; she was the mother of Runolf, the father of Bishop Thorlak." Now Runolf was, indeed, the father of Bishop Thorlak, but he was the husband and not the son of Hallfrid. If we may suppose the heedless insertion of the word "mother" in the place of "wife," the palpable error, as the text now stands, would be removed.

It has been conjectured that the Wineland History of the Flatey Book has been drawn from a more primitive source than the narrative of the discovery which has been preserved in the two manuscripts, Hauk's Book and AM. 557, 4to. Two passages in the Flatey Book narrative lend a certain measure of plausibility to this conjecture. In the "Short Story of Eric the Red" it is stated, that Eric called his land-fall in Greenland Midiokul, in the words of the history; "this is now called Blacksark." In Hauk's Book this mountain is also called Blacksark; in AM. 557, 4to, it is called Whitesark; neither of these manuscripts, however, recalls the earlier name. Again, in the list of the descendants of Snorri, Karlsefni's Wineland-born son, appended to the "Short Story of the Greenlanders," Bishop Brand is so called without qualification, while in both texts of the Saga of Eric the Red he is referred to as Bishop Brand the Elder [hin fyrri]. The second Bishop Brand was ordained in 1263. This fact, while it would, without the other evidence which we possess, establish a date prior to which neither Hauk's Book nor AM. 557, 4to, could have been written, seems at the same time to afford negative evidence in support of the claim for the riper antiquity of the source from which the Flatey Book narrative was drawn. However this may be the lapses already noted, together with the introduction of such incidents as that of the apparition of the big-eyed Gudrid to her namesake, Karlsefni's spouse; the narrative of Freydis' unpalliated treachery; the account of Wineland grapes which produced intoxication, and which apparently ripened at all seasons of the year, of honey-dew grass, and the like, all seem to point either to a deliberate or careless corruption of the primitive history. Nevertheless, despite the discrepancies existing between the account of the Wineland discovery, as it has been preserved in the Flatey Book and as it is given elsewhere, so striking a parallelism is apparent in these different versions of this history, in the chief points of historical interest, as to point conclusively to their common origin.

The two disjoined "accounts" of the Flatey Book, which relate to the Wineland discovery, are brought together in the translation which follows.

CHAPTER IV.

A BRIEF HISTORY OF ERIC THE RED.

There was a man named Thorvald, a son of Osvald, Ulf's son, Eyxna-Thori's son. Thorvald and Eric the Red, his son, left Jaederen [in Norway], on account of manslaughter, and went to Iceland. At that time Iceland was extensively colonized. They first lived at Drangar on Horn-strands, and there Thorvald died. Eric then married Thorhild, the daughter of Jorund and Thorbiorg the Ship-chested, who was then married to Thorbiorn of the Haukadal family. Eric then removed from the north, and made his home at Ericsstadir by Vatnshorn. Eric and Thorhild's son was called Leif.

After the killing of Eyiulf the Foul, and Duelling-Hrafn, Eric was banished from Haukadal, and betook himself westward to Breidafirth, settling in Eyxney at Ericsstadir. He loaned his outer dais-boards to Thorgest, and could not get these again when he demanded them. This gave rise to broils and battles between himself and Thorgest, as Eric's Saga relates. Eric was backed in the dispute by Styr Thorgrimsson, Eyiulf of Sviney, the sons of Brand of Alptafirth and Thorbiorn Vifilsson, while the Thorgesters were upheld by the sons of Thord the Yeller, and Thorgeir of Hitardal. Eric was declared an outlaw at Thorsnessthing. He thereupon equipped his ship for a voyage, in Ericsvag, and when he was ready to sail Styr and the others accom-

panied him out beyond the islands. Eric told them that
it was his purpose to go in search of that country which
Gunnbiorn, son of Ulf the Crow, had seen, when he was
driven westward across the main, at the time when he discovered Gunnbiorns-skerries; he added, that he would
return to his friends, if he should succeed in finding this
country. Eric sailed out from Snaefellsiokul, and found
the land. He gave the name of Midiokul to his landfall;
this is now called Blacksark. From thence he proceeded
southward along the coast, in search of habitable land.
He passed the first winter at Ericsey, near the middle of
the Eastern-settlement, and the following spring he went
to Ericsfirth, where he selected a dwelling-place. In the
summer he visited the western uninhabited country, and
assigned names to many of the localities. The second
winter he remained at Holmar by Hrafnsgnipa, and the
third summer he sailed northward to Snæfell, and all the
way into Hrafnsfirth; then he said he had reached the
head of Ericsfirth. He then returned and passed the third
winter in Ericsey at the mouth of Ericsfirth. The next
summer he sailed to Iceland, landing in Breidafirth. He
called the country, which he had discovered, Greenland,
because, he said, people would be attracted thither if the
country had a good name. Eric spent the winter in Iceland, and the following summer set out to colonize the
country. He settled at Brattahlid in Ericsfirth, and
learned men say that in this same summer, in which
Eric set out to settle Greenland, thirty-five ships sailed
out of Breidafirth and Gorgarfirth; fourteen of these
arrived safely, some were driven back and some were

7   75

lost. This was fifteen years before Christianity was legally adopted in Iceland. During the same summer Bishop Frederick and Thorvald Kodransson (61) went abroad [from Iceland] Of those men, who accompanied Eric to Greenland, the following took possession of land there: Heriulf, Heriulfsfirth, he dwelt at Heriulfsness; Ketil, Ketilsfirth, Hrafn, Hrafnsfirth, Solvi, Solvadal; Helgi Thorbrandsson, Alptafirth; Thorbiorn Gleamer, Siglufirth; Einar, Einarsfirth; Hafgrim, Hafgrimsfirth and Vatnahverfi; Arnlaugsfirth; while some went to the Western settlement.

LEIF THE LUCKY BAPTIZED.

After that sixteen winters had lapsed, from the time when Eric the Red went to colonize Greenland, Leif, Eric's son, sailed out from Greenland to Norway. He arrived in Drontheim in the autumn, when King Olaf Tryggvasson was come down from the north, out of Halagoland. Leif put in to Nidaros with his ship, and set out at once to visit the king. King Olaf expounded the faith to him, as he did to other heathen men who came to visit him. It proved easy for the king to persuade Leif, and he was accordingly baptized, together with all of his shipmates. Leif remained throughout the winter with the king, by whom he was well entertained.

BIARNI GOES IN QUEST OF GREENLAND.

Heriulf (62) was a son of Bard Heriulfsson. He was a kinsman of Ingolf, the first colonist. Ingolf allotted land to Heriulf between Vag and Reykianess, and he

76

dwelt at first at Drepstok. Heriulf's wife's name was Thorgerd, and their son, whose name was Biarni, was a most promising man. He formed an inclination for voyaging while he was still young, and he prospered both in property and public esteem. It was his custom to pass his winters alternately abroad and with his father. Biarni soon became the owner of a trading-ship, and during the last winter that he spent in Norway, [his father] Heriulf determined to accompany Eric on his voyage to Greenland, and made his preparation to give up his farm. Upon the ship with Heriulf was a Christian man from the Hebrides, he it was who composed the Sea-Rollers' Song (63). Heriulf settled at Heriulfsness, and was a most distinguished man. Eric the Red dwelt at Bratahlid, where he was held in the highest esteem, and all men paid him homage. These were Eric's children: Leif, Thorvald, and Thorstein, and a daughter whose name was Freydis; she was wedded to a man named Thorvard, and they dwelt at Gardar, where the episcopal seat now is. She was a very haughty woman, while Thorvard was a man of little force of character, and Freydis had been wedded to him chiefly because of his wealth. At that time the people of Greenland were heathen.

Biarni arrived with his ship at Eyrar [in Iceland] in the summer of the same year, in the spring of which his father had sailed away. Biarni was much surprised when he heard this news, and would not discharge his cargo. His shipmates enquired of him what he intended to do, and he replied that it was his purpose to keep to his custom, and make his home for the winter with his father; "and I will take the ship to Greenland, if you will bear me company." They all replied that they would abide by his decision. Then said Biarni, "Our voyage must be regarded as foolhardy, seeing that no one of us has ever been in the Greenland Sea." Nevertheless they put out to sea when they were equipped for the voyage, and sailed for three days, until the land was hidden by the water, and then the fair wind died out, and north winds arose, and fogs, and they knew not whither they were drifting and thus it lasted for many "dœgr." Then they saw the sun again, and were able to determine the quarters of the heavens; they hoisted sail, and sailed that "dœgr" through before they saw land. They discussed among themselves what land it could be, and Biarni said that he did not believe that it could be Greenland. They asked whether he wished to sail to this land or not. "It is my counsel" [said he], "to sail close to the land." They did so, and soon saw that the land was level, and covered with woods, and that there were small hillocks upon it. They left the land on their larboard, and let the sheet turn toward the land. They sailed for two "dœgr" before they saw another land. They asked whether Biarni thought this was Greenland yet. He replied that he did not think this any more like Greenland than the former, "because in Greenland there are said to be many great ice-mountains." They soon approached this land, and saw that it was a flat and wooded country. The fair wind failed them then, and the crew took counsel together, and concluded that it would be wise to land there, but Biarni would not consent to this. They alleged that they were in need of both wood and water. "Ye have no lack of either of these,' says Biarni—a course, forsooth, which won him blame among his shipmates. He bade them hoist sail, which they did, and turning the prow from the land they sailed out upon the high seas, with southwesterly gales, for three "dœgr," when they saw the third land; this land was high and mountainous, with ice-mountains upon it (64). They asked Biarni then whether he would land there, and he replied that he was not disposed to do so, "because this land does not appear to me to offer any attractions." Nor did they lower their sail, but held their course off the land, and saw that it was an island. They left this land astern, and held out to sea with the same fair wind. The wind waxed amain, and Biarni directed them to reef, and not to sail at a speed unbefitting their ship and rigging. They sailed now for four "dœgr," when they saw the fourth land. Again they asked Biarni whether he thought this could be Greenland or not. Biarni answers, "This is likest Greenland, according to that which has been reported to me concerning it, and here we will steer to the land." They directed their course thither, and landed in the evening, below a cape upon which there was a boat, and there, upon this cape, dwelt Heriulf (65), Biarni's father, whence the cape took its name, and was afterwards called Heriulfsness. Biarni now went to his father, gave up his voyaging, and remained with his father while Heriulf lived, and continued to live there after his father.

HERE BEGINS THE BRIEF HISTORY OF THE GREENLANDERS.

Next to this is now to be told how Biarni Heriulfsson came out from Greenland on a visit to Earl Eric, by whom he was well received. Biarni gave an account of his travels [upon the occasion] when he saw the lands, and the people thought that he had been lacking in enterprise, since he had no report to give concerning these countries, and the fact brought him reproach. Biarni was appointed one of the Earl's men, and went out to Greenland the following summer. There was now much talk about voyages of discovery. Leif, the son of Eric the Red, of Brattahlid, visited Biarni Heriulfsson and bought a ship of him, and collected a crew, until they formed altogether a company of thirty-five men. Leif invited his father, Eric, to become the leader of the expedition, but Eric declined, saying that he was then stricken in years, and adding that he was less able to endure the exposure of sea-life than he had been. Leif replied that he would nevertheless be the one who would be most apt to bring good luck, and Eric yielded to Leif's solicitations, and rode from home when they were ready to sail. When he was but a short distance from the ship, the horse which Eric was riding stumbled, and he was thrown from his back and wounded his foot, whereupon he exclaimed, "It is not designed for me to discover more lands than the one in which we are now living, nor can we now continue longer together." Eric returned home to Brattahlid, and Leif pursued his way to the ship with his companions, thirty-five men; one of the company was a German named

Tyrker. They put the ship in order, and when they were ready, they sailed out to sea, and found first that land which Biarni and his ship-mates found last. They sailed up to the land and cast anchor, and launched a boat and went ashore, and saw no grass there; great ice mountains lay inland back from the sea, and it was as a [table-land of] flat rock all the way from the sea to the ice mountains, and the country seemed to them to be entirely devoid of good qualities. Then said Leif, "It has not come to pass with us in regard to this land as with Biarni, that we have not gone upon it. To this country I will now give a name, and call it Helluland." They returned to the ship, put out to sea, and found a second land. They sailed again to the land, and came to anchor, and launched the boat, and went ashore. This was a level wooded land, and there were broad stretches of white sand, where they went, and the land was level by the sea. Then said Leif, "This land shall have a name after its nature, and we will call it Markland." They returned to the ship forthwith, and sailed away upon the main with north-east winds, and were out two "dœgr" before they sighted land. They sailed toward this land, and came to an island which lay to the northward off the land. There they went ashore and looked about them, the weather being fine, and they observed that there was dew upon the grass, and it so happened that they touched the dew with their hands, and touched their hands to their mouths, and it seemed to them that they had never before tasted anything so sweet as this. They went aboard their ship again and sailed into a certain sound, which lay between the island and a cape, which jutted out from the land on the north, and they stood in westering past the cape. At ebb-tide there were broad reaches of shallow water there, and they ran their ship around there, and it was a long distance from the ship to the ocean; yet were they so anxious to go ashore that they could not wait until the tide should rise under their ship, but hastened to the land, where a certain river flows out from a lake. As soon as the tide rose beneath their ship, however, they took the boat and rowed to the ship, which they conveyed up the river, and so into the lake, where they cast anchor and carried their hammocks ashore from the ship, and built themselves booths there. They afterwards determined to establish themselves there for the winter, and they accordingly built a large house. There was no lack of salmon there either in the river or in the lake, and larger salmon than they had ever seen before. The country thereabouts seemed to be possessed of such good qualities that cattle would need no fodder there during the winters. There was no frost there in the winters, and the grass withered but little. The days and nights there were of more nearly equal length than in Greenland or Iceland. On the shortest day of winter the sun was up between "eyktarstad" and "dagmalastad (66)." When they had completed their house Leif said to his companions, "I propose now to divide our company into two groups, and to set about an exploration of the country; one half of our party shall remain at home at the house, while the other half shall investigate the land, and they must not go beyond a point from which they can return home the same evening, and are not to separate [from each other]." Thus they did for a time; Leif himself, by turns, joined the exploring party or remained behind at the house. Leif was a large and powerful man, and of a most imposing bearing, a man of sagacity, and a very just man in all things.

LEIF THE LUCKY FINDS MEN UPON A SKERRY AT SEA.

It was discovered one evening that one of their company was missing, and this proved to be Tyrker, the German. Leif was sorely troubled by this, for Tyrker had lived with Leif and his father for a long time, and had been very devoted to Leif, when he was a child. Leif severely reprimanded his companions, and prepared to go in search of him, taking twelve men with him. They had proceeded but a short distance from the house when they were met by Tyrker, whom they received most cordially. Leif observed at once that his foster-father was in lively spirits. Tyrker had a prominent forehead, restless eyes, small features, was diminutive in stature, and rather a sorry-looking individual withal, but was, nevertheless, a most capable handicraftsman. Leif addressed him, and asked: "Wherefore art thou so belated, foster-father mine, and astray from the others?" In the beginning Tyrker spoke for some time in German, rolling his eyes, and grinning, and they could not understand him; but after a time he addressed them in the Northern tongue: "I did not go much further [*than you*] and yet I have something of novelty to relate. I have found vines and grapes." "Is this indeed true, foster-father?" said Leif. "Of a certainty it is true," quoth he, "for I was born where there is no lack of either grapes or vines." They slept the night through, and on the morrow Leif said to his shipmates: "We will now divide our labours, and each day will either gather grapes or cut vines and fell trees, so as to obtain a cargo of these for my ship." They acted upon this advice, and it is said that their after-boat was filled with grapes. A cargo sufficient for the ship was cut, and when the spring came they made their ship ready, and sailed away; and from its products Leif gave the land a name, and called it Wineland. They sailed out to sea, and had fair winds until they sighted Greenland, and the fells below the glaciers; then one of the men spoke up, and said, "Why do you steer the ship so much into the wind?" Leif answers: "I have my mind upon my steering, but on other matters as well. Do ye not see anything out of the common?" They replied that they saw nothing strange. "I do not know," says Leif, "whether it is a ship or a skerry that I see." Now they saw it, and said that it must be a skerry; but he was so much keener of sight then they that he was able to discern men upon the skerry. "I think it best to tack," says Leif, "so that we may draw near to them, that we may be able to render them assistance, if they should stand in need of it; and if they should not be peaceably disposed, we shall still have better command of the situation than they." They approached the skerry, and lowered their sail cast anchor and launched a second small boat, which they had brought with them. Tyrker inquired who was the elder of the party? He

84

replied that his name was Thori, and that he was a Norseman; "but what is thy name?" Leif gave his name. "Art thou a son of Eric the Red of Brattahlid?" says he. Leif responded that he was. "It is now my wish," says Leif, "to take you all into my ship, and likewise so much of your possessions as the ship will hold." This offer was accepted, and [with their ship] thus laden, they held away to Ericsfirth, and sailed until they arrived at Brattahlid. Having discharged the cargo, Leif invited Thori, with his wife, Gudrid, and three others, to make their home with him, and procured quarters for the other members of the crew, both for his own and Thori's men. Leif rescued fifteen persons from the skerry. He was afterward called Leif the Lucky. Leif had now goodly store both of property and honour. There was serious illness that winter in Thori's party, and Thori and a great number of his people died. Eric the Red also died that winter. There was now much talk about Leif's Wineland journey, and his brother, Thorvald, held that the country had not been sufficiently explored. Thereupon Leif said to Thorvald: "If it be thy will, brother, thou mayest go to Wineland with my ship, but I wish the ship first to fetch the wood, which Thori had upon the skerry." And so it was done.

THORVALD GOES TO WINELAND.

Now Thorvald, with the advice of his brother, Leif, prepared to make this voyage with thirty men. They put their ship in order, and sailed out to sea; and there is no account of their voyage before their arrival at Leif's booths in Wineland. They laid up their ship there, and remained there quietly during the winter, supplying themselves with food by fishing. In the spring, however, Thorvald said that they should put their ship in order, and that a few men should take the after-boat and proceed along the western coast, and explore [the region] thereabouts during the summer. They found it a fair, well-wooded country; it was but a short distance from the woods to the sea, and [there were] white sands, as well as great numbers of islands and shallows. They found neither dwelling of man nor lair of beast; but in one of the westerly islands they found a wooden building for the shelter of grain (67). They found no other trace of human handiwork, and they turned back, and arrived at Leif's-booth in the autumn. The following summer Thorvald set out toward the east with the ship, and along the northern coast. They were met by a high wind off a certain promontory, and were driven ashore there, and damaged the keel of their ship, and were compelled to remain there for a long time and repair the injury to their vessel. Then said Thorvald to his companions: "I propose that we raise the keel upon this cape, and call it Keelness," and so they did. Then they sailed away, to the eastward off the land, and into the mouth of the adjoining firth, and to a headland, which projected into the sea there, and which was entirely covered with woods. They found an anchorage for their ship and put out the gangway to the land, and Thorvald and all of his companions went ashore. "It is a fair region here," said he, "and here I should like to make my home." They then

86

returned to the ship and discovered on the sands, in beyond the headland, three mounds; they went up to these, and saw that they were three skin-canoes, with three men under each. They thereupon divided their party, and succeeded in seizing all of the men but one, who escaped with his canoe. They killed the eight men, and then ascended the headland again and looked about them and discovered with the firth certain hillocks, which they concluded must be habitations. They were then so overpowered with sleep that they could not keep awake, and all fell into a [heavy] slumber, from which they were awakened by the sound of a cry uttered above them; and the words of the cry were these: "Awake, Thorvald, thou and all thy company, if thou wouldst save thy life; and board thy ship with all thy men, and sail with all speed from the land!" A countless number of skin-canoes then advanced toward them from the inner part of the firth, whereupon Thorvald exclaimed: "We must put out the war-boards (68), on both sides of the ship, and defend ourselves to the best of our ability, but offer little attack." This they did, and the Skrellings, after they had shot at them for a time, fled precipitately, each as best he could. Thorvald then inquired of his men whether any of them had been wounded, and they informed him that no one of them had received a wound. "I have been wounded in my arm-pit," says he; "an arrow flew in between the gunwale and the shield, below my arm. Here is the shaft, and it will bring me to my end! I counsel you now to retrace your way with the utmost speed. But me ye shall convey to that headland which seemed to me to offer so pleasant a dwelling-place; thus it may be fulfilled, that the truth sprang to my lips, when I expressed the wish to abide there for a time. Ye shall bury me there, and place a cross at my head, and another at my feet, and call it Crossness for ever after." At that time Christianity had obtained in Greenland; Eric the Red died, however, before [the introduction of] Christianity.

Thorvald died, and when they had carried out his injunctions, they took their departure, and rejoined their companions, and they told each other of the experiences which had befallen them. They remained there during the winter, and gathered grapes and wood with which to freight the ship. In the following spring they returned to Greenland, and arrived with their ship in Ericsfirth, where they were able to recount great tidings to Leif.

THORSTEIN ERICSSON DIES IN THE WESTERN SETTLEMENT.

In the meantime it had come to pass in Greenland that Thorstein of Ericsfirth had married, and taken to wife Gudrid, Thorbiorn's daughter, [she] who had been the spouse of Thori Eastman (69), as has been already related. Now Thorstein Ericsson, being minded to make the voyage to Wineland after the body of his brother, Thorvald, equipped the same ship, and selected a crew of twenty-five men of good size and strength, and taking with him his wife, Gudrid, when all was in readiness, they sailed out into the open ocean, and out of sight of land. They were driven hither and thither over the sea all that summer, and lost all reckoning, and at the end of the first week of winter they made the land at Lysufirth in Greenland, in the Western settlement. Thorstein set out in search of quarters for his crew, and succeeded in procuring homes for all of his shipmates; but he and his wife were unprovided for, and remained together upon the ship for two or more days. At this time Christianity was still in its infancy in Greenland. It befell, early one morning, that men came to their tent, and the leader inquired who the people were within the tent. Thorstein replies: "We are twain," says he; "but who is it who asks?" "My name is Thorstein, and I am known as Thorstein the Swarthy, and my errand hither is to offer you two, husband and wife, a home with me." Thorstein replied that he would consult with his wife, and she bidding him decide, he accepted the invitation. "I will come after you on the morrow with a sumpter-horse; for I am not lacking in means wherewith to provide for you both, although it will be lonely living with me, since there are but two of us, my wife and myself, for I, forsooth, am a very hard man to get on with; moreover, my faith is not the same as yours, albeit methinks that is the better to which you hold." He returned for them on the morrow, with the beast, and they took up their home with Thorstein the Swarthy, and were well treated by him. Gudrid was a woman of fine presence, and a clever woman and very happy in adapting herself to strangers.

Early in the winter Thorstein Ericsson's party was visited by sickness, and many of his companions died. He caused coffins to be made for the bodies of the dead, and had them conveyed to the ship, and bestowed there; "for it is my purpose to have all the bodies taken to Ericsfirth in the summer." It was not long before illness appeared in Thorstein's home, and his wife, whose name was Grimhild, was first taken sick. She was a very vigorous woman, and as strong as a man, but the sickness mastered her; and soon thereafter Thorstein Ericsson was seized with the illness, and they both lay ill at the same time; and Grimhild, Thorstein the Swarthy's wife, died, and when she was dead Thorstein went out of the room to procure a deal, upon which to lay the corpse. Thereupon Gudrid spoke. "Do not be absent long, Thorstein mine!" says she. He replied that so it should be. Thorstein Ericsson then exclaimed: "Our housewife is acting now in a marvellous fashion, for she is raising herself up on her elbow, and stretching out her feet from the side of the bed, and groping after her shoes." At that moment Thorstein, the master of the house, entered, and Grimhild laid herself down, wherewithal every timber in the room creaked. Thorstein now fashioned a coffin for Grimhild's body, and bore it away, and cared for it. He was a big man, and strong, but it called for all [his strength], to enable him to remove the corpse from the house. The illness grew upon Thorstein Ericsson and he died, whereat his wife, Gudrid, was sorely grieved. They were all in the room at the time, and Gudrid was seated upon a chair before the bench, upon which her husband, Thorstein was lying. Thorstein, the master of the house, then taking Gudrid in his arms, [carried her] from the chair, and seated himself, with her, upon another bench, over against her husband's body, and exerted himself in divers ways to console her, and endeavoured to reassure her, and promised her that he would accompany her to Ericsfirth with the body of her husband, Thorstein, and those of his companions. "I will likewise summon other persons hither," says he "to attend upon thee and entertain thee." She thanked him. Then Thorstein Ericsson sat up, and exclaimed: "Where is Gudrid?" Thrice he repeated the question, but Gudrid made no response. She then asked Thorstein, the master, "Shall I give answer to his question or not?" Thorstein, the master, bade her make no reply, and he then crossed the floor, and seated himself upon the chair, with Gudrid in his lap, and spoke, saying: "What dost thou wish, namesake?" After a little while, Thorstein replies: "I desire to tell Gudrid of the fate which is in store for her, to the end that she may be better reconciled to my death, for I am indeed come to a goodly resting place. This I have to tell thee, Gudrid, that thou art to marry an Icelander, and that ye are to have a long wedded life together, and a numerous and noble progeny, illustrious, and famous, of good odour and sweet virtues. Ye shall go from Greenland to Norway, and thence to Iceland, where ye shall build your home. There ye shall dwell together for a long time, but thou shalt outlive him, and shalt then go abroad and to the South, and shalt return to Iceland again, to thy home, and there a church shall then be raised, and thou shalt abide there and take the veil, and there thou shalt die." When he had thus spoken, Thorstein sank back again, and his body was laid out for burial, and borne to the ship. Thorstein, the master, faithfully performed all his promises to Gudrid. He sold his lands and live-stock in the spring, and accompanied Gudrid to the ship, with all his possessions. He put the ship in order, procured a crew, and then sailed to Ericsfirth. The bodies of the dead were now buried at the church, and Gudrid then went home to Leif at Brattahlid, while Thorstein the Swarthy made a home for himself on Ericsfirth, and remained there as long as he lived, and was looked upon as a very superior man.

OF THE WINELAND VOYAGES OF THORFINN AND HIS COMPANIONS.

That same summer a ship came from Norway to Greenland. The skipper's name was Thorfinn Karlsefni; he was a son of Thord Horsehead, and a grandson of Snorri, the son of Thord of Hofdi. Thorfin Karlsefni, who was a very wealthy man, passed the winter at Brattahlid with Leif Ericsson. He very soon set his heart upon Gudrid, and sought her hand in marriage; she referred him to Leif for her answer, and was subsequently betrothed to him, and their marriage was celebrated that same winter. A renewed discussion arose concerning a Wineland voyage, and the folk urged Karselfni to make the venture, Gudrid joining with the others. He determined to undertake the voyage, and assembled a company of sixty men and five women, and entered into an agreement with his shipmates that they should each share equally in all the spoils of the enterprise. They took with them all kinds of cattle, as it was their intention to settle the country, if they could. Karlsefni asked Leif for the

KARLSEFNI'S EXPEDITION ASCENDING CHARLES RIVER

IT appears most probable from the text that when Karlsefni sailed from Iceland to visit the *New World*, in about the year 1003, his expedition comprised more than two ships. The saga mentions two ships, and also relates that on one ship were forty men. Considering that there was a total of 160 men in the company, while the character of the vessels used scarcely allowed for provisions and accommodations for more than fifty men each, it is almost certain that three or more ships were included in the expedition. That these vessels were small or of very light draft is proved by their ability to navigate in rivers, as related in the saga. From the nature of the country described it is believed that the stream ascended was the Charles River, that issues near Boston.

KARLSEFNI'S EXPEDITION ASCENDING CHARLES RIVER.

IT appears most probable from the text that when Karlsefni sailed from Iceland to visit the New World, in about the year 1003, his expedition comprised more than two ships. The saga mentions two ships, and also relates that on one ship were forty men. Considering that there was a total of 160 men in the company, while the character of the vessels used scarcely allowed for provisions and accommodations for more than fifty men each, it is almost certain that three or more ships were included in the expedition. That these vessels were small or of very light draft is proved by their ability to navigate in rivers, as related in the saga. From the nature of the country described it is believed that the stream ascended was the Charles River, that issues near Boston.

house in Wineland, and he replied, that he would lend it but not give it. They sailed out to sea with the ship, and arrived safe and sound at Leifs-booths, and carried their hammocks ashore there. They were soon provided with an abundant and goodly supply of food, for a whale of good size and quality was driven ashore there, and they secured it, and flensed it, and had then no lack of provisions. The cattle were turned out upon the land, and the males soon became very restless and vicious; they had brought a bull with them. Karlsefni caused trees to be felled, and to be hewed into timbers, wherewith to load his ship, and the wood was placed upon a cliff to dry. They gathered somewhat of all of the valuable products of the land, grapes, and all kinds of game and fish, and other good things. In the summer succeeding the first winter, Skrellings were discovered. A great troop of men came forth from out the woods. The cattle were hard by, and the bull began to bellow and roar with a great noise, whereat the Skrellings were frightened, and ran away, with their packs wherein were grey furs, sables and all kinds of peltries. They fled towards Karlsefni's dwelling, and sought to effect an entrance into the house, but Karselfni caused the doors to be defended [against them]. Neither [people] could understand the other's language. The Skrellings put down their bundles then, and loosed them, and offered their wares [for barter], and were especially anxious to exchange these for weapons, but Karlsefni forbade his men to sell their weapons, and taking counsel with himself, he bade the women carry out milk to the Skrellings, which they no sooner saw than they wanted to buy it, and nothing else. Now the outcome of the Skrelling's trading was, that they carried their wares away in their stomachs, while they left their packs and peltries behind with Karlsefni and his companions, and having accomplished this [exchange] they went away. Now it is to be told that Karlsefni caused a strong wooden palisade to be constructed and set up around the house. It was at this time that Gudrid, Karlsefni's wife, gave birth to a male child, and the boy was called Snorri. In the early part of the second winter the Skrellings came to them again, and these were now much more numerous than before, and brought with them the same wares as at first. Then said Karlsefni to the women: "Do ye carry out now the same food, which proved so profitable before, and nought else." When they saw this they cast their packs in over the palisade. Gudrid was sitting within, in the doorway, beside the cradle of her infant son, Snorri, when a shadow fell upon the door, and a woman in a black namkirtle (70) entered. She was short in stature, and wore a fillet about her head; her hair was of a light chestnut colour, and she was pale of hue, and so big-eyed that never before had eyes so large been seen in a human skull. She went up to where Gudrid was seated, and said: "What is thy name?" "My name is Gudrid; but what is thy name?" "My name is Gudrid," says she. The housewife, Gudrid, motioned her with her hand to a seat beside her; but it so happened, that at that very instant Gudrid heard a great crash, whereupon the woman vanished, and at that same moment one of the Skrell-

94

ings, who had tried to seize their weapons, was killed by one of Karlsefni's followers. At this the Skrellings fled precipitately, leaving their garments and wares behind them; and not a soul, save Gudrid alone, beheld this woman. "Now we must needs take counsel together," says Karlsefni, "for that I believe they will visit us a third time, in great numbers, and attack us. Let us now adopt this plan: ten of our number shall go out upon the cape, and show themselves there, while the remainder of our company shall go into the woods and hew a clearing for our cattle, when the troop approaches from the forest. We will also take our bull, and let him go in advance of us." The lay of the land was such that the proposed meeting-place had the lake upon the one side and the forest upon the other. Karlsefni's advice was now carried into execution. The Skrellings advanced to the spot which Karlsefni had selected for the encounter, and a battle was fought there, in which great numbers of the band of the Skrellings were slain. There was one man among the Skrellings, of large size and fine bearing, whom Karlsefni concluded must be their chief. One of the Skrellings picked up an axe, and having looked at it for a time, he brandished it about one of his companions, and hewed at him, and on the instant the man fell dead. Thereupon the big man seized the axe and after examining it for a moment he hurled it as far as he could, out into the sea; then they fled helter-skelter into the woods, and thus their intercourse came to an end. Karlsefni and his party remained there throughout the winter, but in the spring Karlsefni announced that he was not minded

95

to remain there longer, but would return to Greenland.
They now made ready for the voyage, and carried away
with them much booty in vines and grapes and peltries.
They sailed out upon the high seas, and brought their
ship safely to Ericsfirth, where they remained during the
winter.

FREYDIS CAUSES THE BROTHERS TO BE PUT TO DEATH.

There was now much talk anew, about a Wineland-
voyage, for this was reckoned both a profitable and an
honourable enterprise. The same summer that Karlsefni arrived from Wineland, a ship from Norway arrived
in Greenland. This ship was commanded by two brothers, Helgi and Finnbogi, who passed the winter in
Greenland. They were descended from an Icelandic
family of the East-firths. It is now to be added that
Freydis, Eric's daughter, set out from her home at Gardar, and waited upon the brothers, Helgi and Finnbogi,
and invited them to sail with their vessel to Wineland,
and to share with her equally all of the good things which
they might succeed in obtaining there. To this they
agreed, and she departed thence to visit her brother, Leif,
and ask him to give her the house which he had caused
to be erected in Wineland, but he made her the same answer [as that which he had given Karlsefni], saying that
he would lend the house, but not give it. It was stipula-
ted between Karlsefni and Freydis, that each should have
on ship-board thirty able-bodied men, besides the women;
but Freydis immediately violated this compact, by con-
cealing five men more [than this number], and this the

brothers did not discover before they arrived in Wine-land. They now put out to sea, having agreed before-hand that they would sail in company, if possible, and although they were not far apart from each other, the brothers arrived somewhat in advance, and carried their belongings up to Leif's house. Now when Freydis arrived, her ship was discharged, and the baggage carried up to the house, whereupon Freydis exclaimed: "Why did you carry your baggage in here?" "Since we believed," said they, "that all promises made to us would be kept." "It was to me that Leif loaned the house," says she, "and not to you." Whereupon Helgi exclaimed: "We brothers cannot hope to rival thee in wrong-dealing." They thereupon carried their baggage forth, and built a hut, above the sea, on the bank of the lake, and put all in order about it; while Freydis caused wood to be felled, with which to load her ship. The winter now set in, and the brothers suggested that they should amuse themselves by playing games. This they did for a time, until the folk began to disagree, when dissensions arose between them, and the games came to an end, and the visits between the houses ceased; and thus it continued far into the winter. One morning early, Freydis arose from her bed, and dressed herself, but did not put on her shoes and stockings. A heavy dew had fallen, and she took her husband's cloak, and wrapped it about her, and then walked to the brothers' house, and up to the door, which had been only partly closed by one of the men, who had gone out a short time before. She pushed the door open, and stood silently in the doorway for a time. Finnbogi, who was lying on the innermost side of the room, was awake, and said: "What dost thou wish here, Freydis?" She answers: "I wish thee to rise, and go out with me, for I would speak with thee." He did so, and they walked to a tree, which lay close by the wall of the house, and seated themselves upon it. "How art thou pleased here?" says she. He answered: "I am well pleased with the fruitfulness of the land, but I am ill-content with the breach which has come between us, for, methinks, there has been no cause for it." "It is even as thou sayest," said she, "and so it seems to me; but my errand to thee is, that I wish to exchange ships with you brothers, for that ye have a larger ship than I, and I wish to depart from here." "To this I must accede," said he, "if it is thy pleasure." Therewith they parted, and she returned home, and Finnbogi to his bed. She climbed up into bed, and awakened Thorvard with her cold feet, and he asked her why she was so cold and wet. She answered, with great passion: "I have been to the brothers," said she, "to try to buy their ship, for I wish to have a larger vessel, but they received my overtures so ill, that they struck me, and handled me very roughly; what time thou, poor wretch, will neither avenge my shame nor thy own, and I find, perforce, that I am no longer in Greenland; moreover I shall part from thee unless thou wreakest vengeance for this." And now he could stand her taunts no longer, and ordered the men to rise at once, and take their weapons, and this they did, and they then proceeded directly to the house of the brothers, and entered it while the folk were asleep, and seized and bound them, and led each one out when he was bound; and as they came out, Freydis caused each one to be slain. In this wise all of the men were put to death, and only the women were left, and these no one would kill. At this Freydis exclaimed: "Hand me an axe!" This was done, and she fell upon the five women, and left them dead. They returned home, after this dreadful deed, and it was very evident that Freydis was well content with her work. She addressed her companions, saying: "If it be ordained for us to come again to Greenland, I shall contrive the death of any man who shall speak of these events. We must give it out that we left them living here when we came away." Early in the spring they equipped the ship, which had belonged to the brothers and freighted it with all of the products of the land, which they could obtain, and which the ship would carry. Then they put out to sea, and after a prosperous voyage arrived with their ship in Ericsfirth early in the summer. Karlsefni was there, with his ship all ready to sail, and was awaiting a fair wind; and people say that a ship richer laden than that which he commanded never left Greenland.

CONCERNING FREYDIS.

Freydis now went to her home, since it had remained unharmed during her absence. She bestowed liberal gifts upon all of her companions, for she was anxious to screen her guilt. She now established herself at her home; but her companions were not all so close-mouthed, concerning their misdeeds and wickedness, that rumours did not get abroad at last. These finally reached her brother, Leif, and he thought it a most shameful story. He thereupon took three of the men, who had been of Freydis' party, and forced them all at the same time to a confession of the affair, and their stories entirely agreed. "I have no heart," says Leif, "to punish my sister, Freydis, as she deserves, but this I predict of them, that there is little prosperity in store for their offspring." Hence it came to pass that no one from that time forward thought them worthy of aught but evil. It now remains to take up the story from the time when Karlsefni made his ship ready, and sailed out to sea. He had a successful voyage, and arrived in Norway safe and sound. He remained there during the winter, and sold his wares, and both he and his wife were received with great favour by the most distinguished men of Norway. The following spring he put his ship in order for the voyage to Iceland; and when all his preparations had been made, and his ship was lying at the wharf, awaiting favourable winds, there came to him a Southerner, a native of Bremen in the Saxonland, who wished to buy his "house-neat." "I do not wish to sell it," said he. "I will give the half a 'mork' in gold for it" (71), says the Southerner. This Karlsefni thought a good offer, and accordingly closed the bargain. The Southerner went his way, with the "house-neat," and Karlsefni knew not what it was, but it was "mosur," come from Wineland.

Karlsefni sailed away, and arrived with his ship in the north of Iceland, in Skagafirth. His vessel was beached there during the winter, and in the spring he bought

Glaumbœiar-land (59), and made his home there, and dwelt there as long as he lived, and was a man of the greatest prominence. From him and his wife, Gudrid, a numerous and goodly lineage is descended. After Karlsefni's death, Gudrid, together with her son, Snorri, who was born in Wineland, took charge of the farmstead; and when Snorri was married Gudrid went abroad and made a pilgrimage to the South, after which she returned again to the home of her son, Snorri, who had caused a church to be built at Glaumbœr. Gudrid then took the veil and became an anchorite, and lived there the rest of her days. Snorri had a son, named Thorgeir, who was the father of Ingveld, the mother of Bishop Brand. Hallfrid was the name of the daughter of Snorri, Karlsefni's son; she was the mother of Runolf, Bishop Thorlak's father. Biorn was the name of [another] son of Karlsefni and Gudrid; he was the father of Thorunn, the mother of Bishop Biorn. Many men are descended from Karlsefni, and he has been blessed with a numerous and famous posterity; and of all men Karlsefni has given the most exact accounts of all these voyages, of which something has now been recounted.

CHAPTER V.

WINELAND IN THE ICELANDIC ANNALS.

In addition to the longer sagas of the discovery of
Wineland, and the scattered references in other Icelandic
historical literature, already adduced, the country finds
mention in still another class of Icelandic records. These
records are the chronological lists of notable events, in
and out of Iceland, which are known as the Icelandic
Annals. It has been conjectured that the archetype of
these Annals was compiled either by the learned Ari, the
father of Icelandic historiography, or in the century in
which he lived. Although there is the best of reasons
for the belief, that the first writer of Icelandic Annals
was greatly indebted to Ari the Learned for the knowledge of many of the events which he records, such written
evidence as we have from the century in which Ari lived
would seem to indicate that this kind of literature had
not then sprung into being.

A recent writer in an able disquisition upon this subject arrives at the conclusion, that the first book of Annals
was written in the south of Iceland about the year 1280.
While this theory is apparently well grounded, it is, nevertheless, true that the first writer of Icelandic Annals of
whom we have definite knowledge, was an Icelandic
priest named Einar Haflidason, who was born in 1307,
and died in 1393. The fact that Einar was the compiler
of such a book is gleaned from his own work, through an

LETTER OF POPE INNOCENT III TO NORWAY BISHOPS

PERHAPS the greatest literary discovery of a century are encyclical letters addressed to the bishops of Norway by Popes Innocent III, IV, V, John XXI, Martin IV, Nicholas III, Clement III, Innocent VIII, and Martin V, in which reference are made to interests of the church in Greenland. The earliest of these documents thus far found is one from Innocent III, bearing date of February 13, 1206, and the mention therein of Greenland sets at rest, finally and absolutely, the long disputed question of the discovery of America by Norsemen several centuries before the time of Columbus. These manuscript letters were resurrected from their ancient repository in the Vatican in the year 1907, and by special authorization of Cardinal Merry del Val, Papal Secretary of State, they are reproduced, with English translations, and appear in print for the first time in the Flatey book volume of this Norroena series. A part of Pope Innocent III's letter is shown on the accompanying page.

LETTER OF POPE INNOCENT III TO NORWAY BISHOPS.

PERHAPS the greatest literary discovery of a century are encyclical letters addressed to the bishops of Norway by Popes Innocent III, IV, V, John XXI, Martin IV, Nicholas III, Clement IV, Innocent VIII, and Martin V, in which reference are made to interests of the church in Greenland. The earliest of these documents thus far found is one from Innocent III, bearing date of February 13, 1206, and the mention therein of Greenland sets at rest, finally and absolutely, the long disputed question of the discovery of America by Norsemen several centuries before the time of Columbus. These manuscript letters were resurrected from their ancient repository in the Vatican in the year 1903, and by special authorization of Cardinal Merry del Val, Papal Secretary of State, they are reproduced, with English translations, and appear in print for the first time in the Flatey book volume of this Norroena series. A part of Pope Innocent III's letter is shown on the accompanying page.

tuierut studio adimplé. 7 p̄ uniuersum orbem nīe p̄ se nīe p̄ legatos suos corrigēda corrigē
7 statuenda statuere sūmope studuerut/ Quoy̅ q̅ uestigia sublecut́ te. me. Eugeni̅ p̄p̄. ante
cessorum. de cōrigendis hijs que in regno Norwere correctōne uidebāt expostē z ūbo
ibi fidei semīnando iuxta sui officij debitū sollicat́ extitit. 7 q̄d̄ per se ip̄m uniūlalit́
ecclē cura obsistente nō potuit. p̄ legatū suū inch. tuit. f̄. Albanen̄ ep̄m qui postea in
Romanū pōtifice est assūpt́ executōri mādauit. Qui ad ptes illas accedēs sic a suo pa
tre familias accepat in mādatis. talentu tibi creditū langui est ad ulntā. 7 taq̅ fidel̄ ser
uus 7 prudēs multiplicatū inde fructū studuit reportare. Sic ema̅ uis q̄ ad laude illē
nois dei 7 mīsterij sui cōmendatōem impleuit. iuxta q̄d̄ p̄dc̄s ancessor n̄r eu p̄oparat. palleu
Joh̄i ancessori tuo indulsit. 7 ne decete puicie Norwere metropolitan̄ cura possit deesse. cō
missa gubnatōi. sue urbem Nidrosien̄ eide puicie p̄petuā metropolim ordinauit. 7 ei As
loen̄. A matripien̄. Bargen̄. Stauangrien̄. Insulas Orcades. Insulas Farue. Surthar̄. 7 Sladen̄
7 Grenelandie ep̄atus taq̅ua sue metropoli p̄petuis teporib̄ cōstituit sublīce. 7 eoy̅ ep̄os sub
metropolitans suis tam sibi q̄ suis successorib̄ obedire. Ne igit́ ad uiolentiā cōstitutiōi ipi̅
uilli unq̅ liceat aspirare. nos fe. me. p̄dc̄a Eugenij 7 Alex̄. atq̅ Clemētis p̄p̄. ny̅ roman̄ po
tifice uestigijs insteentes. ea.ns̄ cōstitom auc. a. d̄. 7 p̄ſ p̄ſ. pri̅. cō. Statuētes ut Nidrosien̄ ci
uitas sup̄dc̄m urbiu p̄petuis tprib̄ metropolis h̄atur. 7 eay̅ epi tā tibi q̄ tuis successorib̄
siut suo metropolitan̄ obediat́. 7 de manu tuā cōsecratōis grā̄ suscipiat. Successores aut́
tui ad Roman̄ pōtifice tui p̄ceptui domū cōsecratōis accedāt. 7 ei solūmodo 7 roman̄ ecclē
subiecti semp̄ existat. porro cōcesso tibi palleo. pōtifical̄ f̄. officij plenitudine. infra ecclā
tui ad sacra missay̅ sollēpnia p̄ uniusa p̄uicia tuā. hijs solūmodo diebus. uti sinifias
tua debebit. qui inferi̅ leguntur inscripti. Natiuitate dn̄i. Epiphā. Cena dn̄i. Resur
rectōe. Ascensōne. p̄decuste. In sollēpnitatib̄ be dei genitris sep̄q̅ uirg̅. marie. Nata
licio boru petri 7 pauli. Inuentōe. 7 exaltatōe sc̄e crucis. Natiuitate b̄i Joh̄is bapt̄e. festo
b̄i Joh̄is euāg̅liste. Cōmemoratōe oīum scō̄y̅. In cō̄ sectatiōib̄ ecclay̅. ul epōy̅. Benedicōib̄
altariu̅. ordinatiōib̄ p̄bōy̅. In die cōsecratōis ecclē tue. ac festis sc̄e trinitatis. 7 sc̄i Olaui
7 anniuersario tue cōsecratōis die. Studeat g̅ tua f̄. plenitudine̅ ātte dignitatis tue de
pta ita strenue cuctā page. quatn̄ mox tuoy̅ ornameta eide̅ ualeat̄ couenire. Sic ui
ta tua subditis exēplu̅. ut p̄ ea cognoscat́ quid debeat appete. quid cogan̄ uitare. Altud d̄t
exitie p̄cipuis. cogitatōe ītus. actōe puit́ discret́ in silēto. utile in ūbo. cura ubi sit́
magis.p̄dee h̄oib̄. q̅ p̄ee. Nō in te potestate ordinis. sed equitate op̄et p̄statē cōuisit́.
Stude ne iusta doctrinā destituar̄. nec rursus iuste doctrina cōtradicat. Mentio q̄d̄ earl
artium regum aliaru̅. Sup orā studiū tibi sit aplice se̅. decreta firmit́ obseruare. z ita
q̅ matri 7 dn̄e tuo ei hulte obedire. Ecce f̄r̄ in xp̄o k̄me. inr̄ multa alia h̄ siit palleu
h̄ sacerdotij. q̅ omnia facile. xp̄o adiuuate adimple potis. si uirtutu̅ omnīu̅ magnā
caritatē h̄ueris. z hulitatē. 7 q̄d̄ foris h̄re ostendis. intus h̄ebis. Decinu̅ g̅ z c̄ usq̅ in
sine. Dat́ rom̄ ap̄ſ.c̄.p̄. p̄ man̄ Jo. s̄c̄e. mar̄e. in Cosmidi. diac. card̄. s̄c̄e Roman̄ ecclē Cancella
rij. Jo̅ febr. Indict. vi. Incarn. dn̄ice anno. M. cc. v. Pontificat́ uo domini Innocētij. p̄p̄.
.iiij. anno Octauo. Eidem.

entry under the year 1304, in which his birth is recorded in such wise as to point unmistakably to his authorship. This collection of Annals is contained in the parchment manuscript AM. 420 *b*, 4to, which has received the name, "Lewman's Annals" probably from the office held by some one of its former owners. Under the year 1121, we find in these Annals the entry: "Bishop Eric Uppsi sought Wineland."

The next considerable collection of Annals, the date of which we are enabled to determine with tolerable accuracy, is that appended to the Flatey Book, the manuscript of which has already been described. These Annals were written by the priest Magnus Thorhallsson, and doubtless completed before the year 1395, for all entries cease in the previous year. Among the recorded events of the year 1121 it is stated that "Eric, the Bishop of Greenland, went in search of Wineland."

Of a riper antiquity than either of the foregoing works are, in all likelihood, the so-called Annales Reseniani, the original vellum manuscript of which was destroyed by the fire of 1728. A paper copy from this original, written by Arni Magnusson, is preserved in AM. 424, 4to. The dates included in these Annals extend from the year 228 to 1295 inclusive, and it has been conjectured that these records were compiled before the year 1319. Here, under the year 1121, occurs the statement: "Bishop Eric sought Wineland."

A parchment manuscript is preserved in the Royal Library of Copenhagen, No. 2087, 4to, old collection, which contains the annals known as Annales regii. These are written in various hands, and are brought down to the year 1341. From the first entry down to the year 1306 the hand is the same, and from this fact the conclusion has been drawn that this portion of the manuscript was completed not later than 1307. Against the year 1121 we find the entry: "Bishop Eric of Greenland went in search of Wineland."

Similar entries to these occur in two other collections of Icelandic Annals, which may be mentioned here, for while these are, in their present form, of much more recent creation than those already noticed, they still seem to have drawn their material from elder lost vellums. One of these, Henrik Hoyer's Annals, derives its name from its first owner, who died in Bergen in the year 1615. It is a paper manuscript contained in AM. 22, fol., and bears strong internal evidence of having been copied from an Icelandic original, which has since disappeared. The entry in this manuscript under the year 1121 is: "Bishop Eric sought Wineland."

The other modern collection, known as Gottskalk's Annals, is contained in a parchment manuscript in the Royal Library of Stockholm, No. 5, 8vo., which it is believed was chiefly written by one Gottskalk Jonsson, a priest, who lived in the north of Iceland in the sixteenth century, and it has been conjectured, from internal evidence, that the portion of the compilation prior to the year 1394 was copied from a lost manuscript. The entry under the year 1121 corresponds with those already quoted: "Eric, the Greenlanders' bishop, sought Wineland."

From these different records, varying slightly in phra-

seology, but all of the same purport, we may safely conclude that, in the year 1121, a certain Bishop of Greenland, called Eric Uppsi, went upon a voyage in search of
Wineland. It is the sum of information which the Annals have to give concerning that country, and is meagre
enough, for we are not only left unenlightened as to why
the voyage was undertaken, but we are not even informed
whether the bishop succeeded in finding the country of
which he went in search. It is not possible to obtain
much additional knowledge concerning this Bishop Eric
elsewhere. It seems altogether probable that he was the
"Greenlanders' Bishop Eric Gnup's son," mentioned in a
genealogical list in Landnama, and it is clear that if this
be the same Eric, he was by birth an Icelander. This
view is in a slight measure confirmed by an entry in the
Lawman's Annals under the year 1112 [in the Annals of
the Flatey Book under the year 1113] wherein the journey of Bishop Eric is recorded, a "journey" presumably
undertaken away from Iceland, and probably to Greenland. In the ancient Icelandic scientific work called
Rimbegla, in a list of those men who had been bishops
at Gardar, the episcopal seat in Greenland, Eric heads the
list, while in a similar list of Greenland bishops in the
Flatey Book, Eric's name is mentioned third. No record
of Bishop Eric's ordination has been preserved, and none
of his fate, unless indeed it be written in the brief memorial of his Wineland voyage. It has been conjectured
that this voyage to Wineland was undertaken as a missionary enterprise, a speculation which seems to have
been suggested solely by the ecclesiastical office of the

chief participant. It has been further conjectured, since we read in the Annals of the ordination of a new bishop for Greenland in 1124, that Eric must have perished in the undertaking. The date of his death is nowhere given and it is possible that the entry in the Annals, under the year 1121, is a species of necrological record. It is, in any event, the last surviving mention of Wineland the Good in the elder Icelandic literature.

Although no subsequent visit to Wineland is recorded, a portion of the American coastland, seen by the original explorers, does appear to have been visited by certain of the Greenland colonists, more than a hundred years after Bishop Eric's Wineland voyage.

A parchment manuscript, AM. 420 *a,* 4to, contains a collection of Annals, known as the Elder Skalholt Annals not heretofore cited because of a lacuna covering the year 1121. This manuscript, which Arni Magnusson obtained from Skalholt, in the south of Iceland, and which he conjectures may have belonged to Skaholt church, or to Bishop Bryniolf's private library, is believed to have been written about the year 1362. We find in this, against the year 1347, the following record: "There came also a ship from Greenland, less in size than small Icelandic trading vessels. It came into the outer Stream-firth. It was without an anchor. There were seventeen men on board, and they had sailed to Markland, but had afterwards been driven hither by storms at sea." The Annals of Gottskalk record the simple fact in the same year: "A ship from Greenland came into the mouth of Stream-firth." On the other hand the Annals of the Flatey

Book, under the year 1347, have the following more particular record: "A ship came then from Greenland, which had sailed to Markland, and there were eighteen men on board."

This scanty record is the last historical mention of a voyage undertaken by Leif's fellow-countrymen to a part of the land which he had discovered three hundred years before. The nature of the information indicates that the knowledge of the discovery had not altogether faded from the memories of the Icelanders settled in Greenland. It seems further to lend a measure of plausibility to a theory that people from the Greenland colony may, from time to time, have visited the coast to the southwest of their home for supplies of wood, or for some kindred purpose. The visitors in this case had evidently intended to return directly from Markland to Greenland, and had they not been driven out of their course to Iceland, the probability is that this voyage would never have found mention in Icelandic chronicles, and all knowledge of it must have vanished as completely as did the colony to which the Markland visitors belonged.

CHAPTER VI.

NOTICES OF DOUBTFUL VALUE; FICTIONS.

IT will be remembered that a passage in the Book of Settlement [Landnamabok] recites the discovery, by one Ari Marsson, of a country lying westward from Ireland, called White-men's-land, or Ireland the Great. This White-men's-land is also mentioned in the Saga of Eric the Red, and in both places is assigned a location in the vicinity of Wineland the Good. Many writers have regarded this White-men's-land as identical with a strange country, the discovery of which is recounted in the Eyrbyggja Saga, having been led to this conclusion, apparently, from the fact that both unknown lands lay to the "westward," and that there is a certain remote resemblance between the brief particulars of the Eric's Saga and the more detailed narrative of Eyrbyggja.

It is related in the Eyrbyggja Saga that a certain Biorn Asbrandsson became involved in an intrigue with a married woman named Thurid, which resulted in his wounding the affronted husband and slaying two of the husband's friends, for which he was banished from Iceland for the term of three years. Biorn went abroad, led an adventurous life, and received the name of "kappi" [champion, hero] on account of his valorous deeds. He subsequently returned to Iceland, where he was afterwards known as the Broadwickers'-champion. He brought with him on his return not only increase of fame,

but the added graces of bearing due to his long fellow-
ship with foreign chieftains, and he soon renewed his at-
tentions to his former mistress. The husband, fearing to
cope alone with so powerful a rival, invoked the aid of
one skilled in the black art to raise a storm, which should
overwhelm the object of his enmity. The hero, however,
after three days of exposure to the preternaturally-agita-
ted elements, returned exhausted, but in safety, to his
home. The husband then prevailed upon his powerful
brother-in-law, the godi (72) Snorri, to come to his assistance, and as a result of Snorri's intervention, Biorn
agreed to leave the country. He accordingly rode "south,
to a ship in Laga-haven, in which he took passage that
same summer, but they were rather late in putting to sea.
They sailed away with a north-east wind, which prevailed far into the summer, but nothing was heard of this
ship for a long time afterwards."

Further on in the same saga we read of the fortuitous
discovery of this same Biorn by certain of his fellow-
countrymen, and as the account of their strange meeting
contains the sole description of this unknown land, it may
best be given in the words of the saga. "It was in the
latter days of Olaf the Saint that Gudleif engaged in a
trading voyage westward to Dublin, and when he sailed
from the west it was his intention to proceed to Iceland.
He sailed to the westward of Ireland, and had easterly
gales and winds from the northeast, and was driven far
to the westward over the sea and toward the southwest,
so that they had lost all track of land. The summer was
then far spent, and they uttered many prayers that they

might be permitted to escape from the sea, and it befell thereupon that they became aware of land. It was a great country, but they did not know what country it was. Gudleif and his companions determined to sail to the land, for they were weary with battling with the tempestuous sea. They found a good harbour there, and they had been alongside the land but a short time when men came toward them. They did not recognize a single man, but it rather seemed to them that they were speaking Irish; soon so great a throng of men had drawn about them that they amounted to several hundreds. These people thereupon seized them all and bound them, and then drove them up upon the land. They were then taken to a meeting, at which their case was considered. It was their understanding that some [of their captors] wished them to be slain, while others would have them distributed among the people and thrown into bondage. While this was being argued they descried a body of men riding, and a banner was carried in their midst, from which they concluded that some manner of chieftain must be in the company; and when this band drew near they saw a tall and warlike man riding beneath the banner; he was far advanced in years, however, and his hair was white. All of the people assembled bowed before this man, and received him as he had been their lord; they soon observed that all questions and matters for decision were submitted to him. This man then summoned Gudleif and his fellows, and when they came before him he addressed them in the Northern tongue [i. e., Icelandic], and asked them to what country they belonged. They responded that they were, for the most part, Icelanders. This man asked which of them were the Icelanders. Gudlief then advanced before this man, and greeted him worthily, and he received his salutations graciously, and asks from what part of Iceland they came, and Gudleif replied that he came from Borgarfirth. He then enquired from what part of Borgarfirth he came, and Gudleif informs him. After this he asked particularly after every one of the leading men of Borgarfirth and Breidafirth, and in the course of the conversation he asked after Snorri Godi and Thurid, of Froda, his sister, and he enquired especially after all details concerning Froda, and particularly regarding the boy Kiartan,[1] who was then the master at Froda. The people of the country, on the other hand, demanded that some judgment should be reached concerning the ship's crew. After this the tall man left them, and called about him twelve of his men, and they sat together for a long time in consultation, after which they betook themselves to the [general] meeting. Thereupon the tall man said to Gudleif and his companions: 'We, the people of this country, have somewhat considered your case, and the inhabitants have given your affair into my care, and I will now give you permission to go whither ye list; and even though it may seem to you that the summer is far spent, still I would counsel you to leave here, for the people here are untrustworthy and hard to deal with, and have already formed the belief that their laws have been broken.' Gudleif replied: 'If it be vouchsafed us to reach our native land, what shall we say

---

*This Kiartan was Thurid's son.

concerning him who has granted us our freedom.' He answered: 'That I may not tell you, for I cannot bear that my relatives and foster-brothers should have such a voyage hither as ye would have had if ye had not had my aid; but now I am so advanced in years,' said he, 'that the hour may come at any time when age shall rise above my head; and even though I should live yet a little longer, still there are those here in the land who are more powerful than I who would offer little mercy to strangers, albeit these are not in this neighbourhood where ye have landed.' Afterward this man aided them in equipping their ship, and remained with them until there came a fair wind, which enabled them to put to sea. But before he and Gudleif parted, this man took a gold ring from his hand and handed it to Gudleif, and with it a goodly sword; and he then said to Gudleif: 'If it be granted thee to come again to thy father-land, then do thou give this sword to Kiartan, the master at Froda, and the ring to his mother.' Gudleif said: 'What shall I reply as to who sends these precious things?' He answered: 'Say that he sends them who was more of a friend of the mistress at Froda than of the Godi at Helgafell, her brother. But if any persons shall think they have discovered from this to whom these treasures belonged, give them my message, that I forbid any man to go in search of me, for it would be a most desperate undertaking, unless he should fare as successfully as ye have in finding a landing-place; for here is an extensive country with few harbours, and over all a disposition to deal harshly with strangers, unless it befall as it has in this case.' After this they parted. Gudleif and his men put to sea, and arrived in Ireland late in the autumn, and passed the winter in Dublin; but in the summer they sailed to Iceland, and Gudleif delivered the treasures, and all men held of a verity that this man was Biorn Broadwickers'-champion; but people have no other proof of this, save these particulars, which have now been related."

It will be observed that the narrator of the saga does not in this incident once connect this unknown land with White-men's-land, nor does he offer any suggestion as to its situation. The work of identifying this strange country with White-men's-land, and so with Wineland the Good, has been entirely wrought by the modern commentator. If we accept as credible a meeting so remarkable as the one here described, if we disregard the statements of the narrative showing the existence of horses in this unknown land, which the theorist has not hesitated to do, and, finally, if we assume that there was at this time an Irish colony or one speaking a kindred tongue in North America, we may conclude that Biorn's adopted home was somewhere on the eastern North-American coast. If, however, we read the statements of the saga as we find them, they seem all to tend to deny this postulate, rather than to confirm it. The entire story has a decidedly fabulous appearance, and, as has been suggested by a learned editor of the saga, a romantic cast, which is not consonant with the character of the history in which it appears. A narrative, the truth of which the narrator himself tells us had not been ratified by collateral evidence, and whose details are so vague and indefinite, seems to afford historical evidence of a character so equivocal that it may well be dismissed without further consideration.

Of an altogether different nature from the narrative of discovery above recited is the brief notice of the finding of a new land, set down in the Icelandic Annals toward the end of the thirteenth century. In the Annales regii, in the year 1285, the record reads: "Adalbrand and Thorvald, Helgi's sons, found New-land;" in the Annals of the Flatey Book, under the same year, "Land was found to the westward off Iceland;" and again in Gottskalk's Annals an entry exactly similar to that of the Flatey Book. In Hoyer's Annals the entry is of a different character: "Helgi's sons sailed into Greenland's uninhabited regions."

In the parchment manuscript AM. 415, 4to, written, probably, about the beginning of the fourteenth century, is a collection of annals called "Annales vetustissimi," and here, under the year 1285, is an entry similar to that of the Flatey Book: "Land found to the westward off Iceland." In the Skalholt Annals, on the other hand, the only corresponding entry against the year 1285 is: "Down-islands discovered."

It required but the similarity between the names Newland and Newfoundland to arouse the effort to identify the two countries; and the theory thus created was supposed to find confirmation in a passage in a copy of a certain document known as Bishop Gizur Einarsson's Register [brefa-bok], for the years 1540-47, which is contained in a paper manuscript of the seventeenth century, AM. 266, fol. This passage is as follows: "Wise men

have said that you must sail to the southwest from Krisuvik mountain to Newland." Krisuvik mountain is situated on the promonotory of Reykianess, the southwestern extremity of Iceland, and, as has been recently pointed
out, to sail the course suggested by Bishop Gizur would
in all probability land the adventurous mariner in south-
eastern Greenland. The record of the Annals, however,
is so explicit, that in determining the site of "Newland"
we do not need to orient ourselves by extraneous evidence. We are informed, that, in 1285, Helgi's sons
sailed into Greenland's "obygdir," the name by which
the Greenland colonists were wont to designate the uninhabited east coast of Greenland; and as it is elsewhere
distinctly stated that the "Newland," which these men
discovered in the same year, lay to the "westward off Iceland," there can be little room for hesitancy in reaching
the conclusion that "Newland," and the "Down-islands"
all lie together, and are probably only different names for
the same discovery. However this may be, it is at least
manifest, from the record, that if Newland was not a
part of the eastern coast of Greenland, there is nothing
to indicate that it was anywhere in the region of Newfoundland.

A few years after this discovery is recorded, namely in
1289, we find the following statement in the Flatey Annals: "King Eric sends Rolf to Iceland to seek Newland;" and again in the next year: "Rolf travelled about
Iceland soliciting men for a Newland voyage." No additional information has been preserved touching this enterprise, and it therefore seems probable that if the voy-

age was actually undertaken, it was barren of results.
The Flatey Annals note the death of Rolf, Land-Rolf, as
he was called, in 1295, and as no subsequent seeker of
Newland is named in Icelandic history, it may be assumed that the spirit of exploration died with him.

This brief record of the Annals is unquestionably historically accurate; moreover there may be somewhat of an
historical foundation for the adventures of the Broadwickers'-champion recounted in the Eyrbyggja Saga;
neither of these notices of discovery, however, appears to
have any connection with the discovery of Wineland;
they have been considered here chiefly because of the fact
that they have been treated in the past as if they had a
direct bearing upon the Wineland history.

The historical and quasi-historical material relating to
the discovery of Wineland has now been presented. A
few brief notices of Helluland, contained in the later Icelandic literature, remain for consideration. These notices necessarily partake of the character of the sagas in
which they appear, and as these sagas are in a greater or
less degree pure fictions, the references cannot be regarded as possessing much historical value.

First among these unhistorical sagas is the old mythical tale of Arrow-Odd, of which two recensions exist;
the more recent and inferior version is that which contains the passages where Helluland is mentioned, as follows: " 'But I will tell thee where Ogmund is; he is come
into that firth which is called Skuggi, it is in Helluland's
deserts ....; he has gone thither because he does not
wish to meet thee; now thou mayest track him home, if

thou wishest, and see how it fares.' Odd said thus it should be. Thereupon they sail until they come into Greenland's sea, when they turn south and west around the land..... They sail now until they come to Helluland, and lay their course into the Skuggi-firth. And when they had reached the land the father and son went ashore, and walked until they saw where there was a fortification, and it seemed to them to be very strongly built."

In the same category with Arrow-Odd's Saga may be placed two other mythical sagas, the Saga of Halfdan Eysteinsson, and the Saga of Halfdan Brana's-fostering; in the first of these the passage containing the mention of Helluland is as follows: "Raknar brought Helluland's deserts under his sway, and destroyed all the giants there." In the second of these last-mentioned sagas the hero is driven out of his course at sea, until he finally succeeds in beaching his ship upon "smooth sands" beside "high cliffs;" "there was much drift-wood on the sands, and they set about building a hut, which was soon finished. Halfdan frequently ascended the glaciers, and some of the men bore him company. . . . The men asked Halfdan what country this could be. Halfdan replied that they must be come to Helluland's deserts."

Belonging to a class of fictitious sagas known as "land-vættasogur" [stories of a country's guardian spirits], is the folk-tale of Bard the Snow-fell god. The first chapter of this tale begins: "There was a king named Dumb, who ruled over those gulfs, which extend northward around Helluland and are now called Dumb's sea." Subsequently we find brief mention of a king of Helluland, of whom Gest, the son of the hero of the saga, says: "I have never seen him before, but I have been told by my relatives that the king was called Rakin, and from their account I believe I recognize him; he at one time ruled over Helluland and many other countries, and after he had long ruled these lands he caused himself to be buried alive, together with five hundred men, at Raknslodi; he murdered his father and mother, and many other people; it seems to me probable, from the reports of other people, that his burial-mound is northward in Helluland's deserts." Gest goes in quest of this mound, sails to Greenland's deserts, where, having traversed the lava-fields [!] for three days on foot, he at length discovers the burial-mound upon an island near the sea-coast; "some men say that this mound was situated to the northward off Helluland, but wherever it was, there were no settlements in the neighbourhood."

The brief extracts here quoted will suffice to indicate not only the fabulous character of the sagas in which they appear, but they serve further to show how completely the discoveries of Leif, and the exploration of Karlsefni had become distorted in the popular memory of the Icelanders at the time these tales were composed, which was probably in the thirteenth or fourteenth century. The Helluland of these stories is an unknown region, relegated, in the popular superstition, to the trackless wastes of northern Greenland.

CHAPTER VII.

THE PUBLICATION OF THE DISCOVERY.

THE earliest foreign mention of Wineland appears in the work of the prebendary, Adam of Bremen, called *Descriptio insularum aquilonis.* The material for this work was obtained by its author during a sojourn at the court of the Danish king, Svend Estridsson, after the year 1069, and probably very soon thereafter, for his history appears to have been completed before the year 1076, the date of king Svend's death. The most important manuscript of Adam's longer work, the *Gesta Hammaburgensis ecclesiæ pontificum,* is the Codex Vindobonensis deposited in the Imperial Library of Vienna under the number 413. This manuscript, written in the thirteenth century, contains also the complete "description of the Northern islands," which is partially lacking in the fine manuscript of the same century, contained in the Royal Library of Copenhagen. This "description" was first printed in Lindenbruch's edition of Adam's work, published in 1595, and is the first printed reference to Wineland, being as follows: "Moreover he spoke of an island in that ocean discovered by many, which is called Wineland, for the reason that vines grow wild there, which yield the best of wine. Moreover, that grain unsown grows there abundantly is not a fabulous fancy, but from the accounts of the Danes we know to be a fact. Beyond this island, it is said, there is no habitable land in

119

that ocean, but all those regions which are beyond are filled with insupportable ice and boundless gloom, to which Martian thus refers: "One day's sail beyond Thile the sea is frozen." This was essayed not long since by that very enterprising Northmen's prince, Harold, who explored the extent of the northern ocean with his ship, but was scarcely able by retreating to escape in safety from the gulf's enormous abyss, where before his eyes the vanishing bounds of earth were hidden in gloom."

The learned cleric, it will be observed, is very careful to give his authority for a narrative which evidently impressed him as bordering sharply upon the fabulous. The situation which he would ascribe to the strange country is inaccurate enough, but the land where vines grow wild and grain self-sown, stripped of the historian's adornments, would accord sufficiently well with the accounts of the discoverers of Wineland to enable us to identify the country, if Adam had not himself given us the name of this land, and thus arrested all uncertainty. It is not strange, however, that with the lapse of time the knowledge of such a land should have been erased from the recollection of the outer world. The author of the so-called "Breve Chronicon Norvegiæ" is, therefore, constrained to omit all reference to this wonderful land, although his reference to Greenland indicates an acquaintance with that tradition, which in Icelandic geographical notices, already cited, would ascribe Wineland to a more southerly clime, bordering indeed upon Africa. The manuscript of this history, which has been preserved, belongs to the Earl of Dalhousie, and was probably written between the years 1443 and 1460. The passage mentioned, while it is not strictly pertinent, in a measure indicates, perhaps, the information accessible at this period to an author who must have been more or less acquainted with the current lore of the land in which the Wineland history was still preserved. Greenland, this author writes, "which country was discovered and settled by the inhabitants of Thule [Telensibus], and strengthened by the Catholic faith, lies at the western boundary of Europe, almost bordering upon the African isles, where the overflowing sea spreads out." No quickening evidence came from Iceland until long afterward, and those who saw Adam's Wineland recital probably regarded it as the artless testimony of a too-credulous historian.

After the publication of Adam of Bremen's work, in 1595, the name of Wineland next recurs in print in a poem written by the Danish clergyman, Claus Christoffersson Lyschander, called the Chronicle of Greenland, which was published in Copenhagen in 1608. Founded, apparently, upon the scantiest of historical material, which material was treated with the broadest of poetic license, the Chronicle is devoid of historical value. Lyschander seems to have derived from Icelandic Annals the knowledge of Bishop Eric's Wineland voyage, and to have elaborated this entry, with the aid of his vivid imagination, into three lines of doggerel in somewhat the following manner:

> And Eric of Greenland did the deed,
> Planted in Wineland both folk and creed,
> Which are there e'en now surviving.

A few years prior to this rhapsody of Lyschander's, the geographer Ortelius had ascribed to the Northmen the credit of the discovery of America. According to Alexander von Humboldt, Ortelius announced this opinion in 1570, and he cites Ortelius' work, "Theatrum orbis terrarum," in the edition of 1601. The edition of 1584 of Ortelius' work does not so credit the discovery, but the English edition of 1606 does explicitly, and clearly sets forth upon what foundation the author rests his statement. Ortelius does not seem to have had, and could not well have had at the time he wrote, any acquaintance with Icelandic records; his opinion, as he himself tells us, was based upon the marvellous relation of the voyages of the brothers Zeni, first published in 1558. It is not pertinent to dwell here upon the authenticity of the Zeni discoveries, and while it is true that Ortelius stated the fact, when he announced that the "New World was entered upon many ages past by certain 'islanders' of Greenland and Iceland," he travelled to it by a circuitous route, and hit upon it, after all, by a happy chance.

The debased taste in Iceland, which followed the age when the greater sagas were committed to writing, found its gratification in the creation of fictitious tales, in recounting the exploits of foreign heroes, and for a time the garnered wealth of their historical literature was disregarded or forgotten by the people of Iceland. With the revival of learning, which came in post-Reformation times, after a long period of comparative literary inactivity, came a reawakening of interest in the elder literature, and the Icelandic scholars of this era heralded abroad the great wealth of the discarded treasures which their ancestors had amassed.

The first writer in modern times to glean from Icelandic records, and to publish, as thus established, the discovery made by his countrymen, was Arngrim Jonsson [Arngrimr Jonsson], who was born in Iceland in 1568. His various historical works, published during his life-time, were written in Latin, and all, with the exception of the first edition of a single work, issued from presses on the Continent. His writings were, for the most part, devoted to the history of his fatherland and to its defence, but incidentally two of these, at least, refer to the Wineland discovery. The first of these works, "Crymogœa, sive Rerum Islandicarum," was published in Hamburg in 1610, 1614, 1630. The notice in this book refers to the discovery of "New Land" in 1285, and Land-Rolf's expedition to Iceland [undertaken with a view to the exploration of this land], diverges into a consideration of the Frislanda of the Zeni narrative, which the author regards as Iceland, and concludes: "In truth we believe the country which Land-Rolf sought to be Wineland, formerly so-called by the Icelanders, concerning which island of America, in the region of Greenland, perhaps the modern Estotelandia, elsewhere;" a statement chiefly interesting from the fact that it is the first printed theory as to the location of Wineland.

In a second book, written *ca.* 1635, but not published until 1643, Arngrim refers at some length to Karlsefni and his Wineland voyage, which information he states he draws from Hauk's history, and also makes mention of Bishop Eric's Wineland voyage, noting incidentally Adam of Bremen's reference to that country.

Arngrim died in 1648, leaving behind him an unprinted Latin manuscript, which was subsequently translated into Icelandic and published in Iceland under the title "Gronlandia." In this treatise he deals more minutely with the Wineland discovery, but it is probable that this book failed to obtain as wide a circulation among the scholars of Europe as his earlier works, and even though it had become well known, it was destined to be followed, a few years later, by a much more exhaustive work, which must have supplanted it.

Although the Icelandic discovery had now been published, the chief documents from which the knowledge of the discovery was drawn, remained for many years in Iceland, where they were practically inaccessible to the foreign student. Arngrim Jonsson was himself, probably, the first to set the example, which, actively followed after his death, soon placed the Icelandic manuscripts within comparatively easy reach of the students of the Continent. We have already seen, incidentally, how certain of these codices were exported; it remained for the tireless bibliophile, Arni Magnusson, to complete the deportation of manuscripts from his fatherland, so that early in the eighteenth century all of the more important early vellums containing the Wineland narrations were lodged in the libraries of Copenhagen. The hugest of all these manuscripts, the Flatey Book, had been brought by the talented Icelander, Thormod Torfæus, from Iceland to Denmark, as a gift to King Frederick the Third.

In the year 1715 Torfæus published the first book devoted exclusively to the discovery of Wineland. In this little work the place of priority is assigned to the account of the discovery as unfolded in the Flatey Book; this is followed by a compendium of the Saga of Eric the Red [Thorfinns Saga], with which the author seems to have become acquainted through a transcript of the Hauk's Book Saga, made by Biorn of Skardsa. The interest which Torfæus' little book elicited was of such a character that the general dissemination of the knowledge of the discovery may almost be said to date from its appearance; the publication of texts of the sagas upon which Torfæus' book was based was not accomplished, however until the present century.

In 1837 the sumptuous work entitled "Antiquitates Americanæ" was published by the Royal Society of Northern Antiquaries of Copenhagen. The book was edited by Carl Christian Rafn, with whom were associated Finn Magnusen and Sveinbiorn Egilsson; the associate editors, however, especially the last-named, seem to have shared to a very limited extent in the preparation of the work; all were scholarly men, well versed in the literature of Iceland. This book was by far the most elaborate which had been published up to that time upon the subject of the Icelandic discovery of America, and in it the texts of the sagas relating to the discovery were first printed, and with these the lesser references bearing upon the discovery, which were scattered through other Icelandic writings. Side by side with the Icelandic texts, Latin and Danish versions of these texts were presented, and along with these the interpretations and theories of the gifted editor, Rafn. The book obtained a wide circulation, and upon it have been based almost all of the numerous treatises upon the same subject which have since appeared. Rafn's theories touching the Old Stone Tower at Newport, R. I., and the Dighton Picture Rock near Taunton, Mass., have latterly fallen into disfavour, but others of his errors, less palpable than these, if we may judge by recent publications, still exercise potent sway. While the editor of the "Antiquitates Americanæ" deserves great praise for having been the first to publish to the world the original records, he has seriously qualified the credit to which he is entitled by the extravagant theories and hazardous statements to which he gave currency, and which have prejudiced many readers against the credibility of the records themselves.

Since the publication of the "Antiquitates Americanæ" the most important and original treatise upon the Wineland discovery which has appeared, is that recently published by Dr. Gustav Storm, Professor of History in the University of Christiania, entitled, "Studies relating to the Wineland voyages, Wineland's Geography and Ethnography." These "Studies" appear to have been the natural sequence of an article upon the vexed question, affecting the site of Wineland, to which reference has already been made. Professor Storm's method of treatment is altogether different from that of Rafn; it is philosophical, logical, and apparently entirely uninfluenced by preconceived theories, being based strictly upon the records. These records of the Icelandic discovery have now been presented here. They clearly establish the fact that some portion of the eastern coast of North America was visited by people of Iceland and the Icelandic colony in Greenland early in the eleventh century. In matters of detail, however, the history of the discovery leaves wide the door to conjecture as to the actual site of Wineland. It was apparently not north of the latitude of northern Newfoundland; present climatic conditions indicate that it was situated somewhat south of this latitude, but how far south the records do not show.

NOTES.

(1) It has been claimed that the Icelandic discovery attained a practical result through the imparting of information to those to whom the discovery of America has been generally ascribed, and notably to Columbus and the Cabots. The tendency to qualify Columbus' fame as the original discoverer dates from the time of Ortelius, while the effort to show that his first voyage was influenced by information which he received from Icelandic sources was, perhaps, first formulated in extenso within the present century. The theory that Columbus obtained definite information from Icelandic channels, rests, after all, upon the following vague letter, which is cited by Columbus' son in the biography of his father, as follows:

"In the month of February, of the year 1477, I sailed one hundred leagues beyond the island of Tile, the southern portion of which is seventy-three degrees removed from the equinoctial, and not sixty-three, as some will have it; nor is it situated within the line which includes Ptolemy's west, but is much further to the westward; and to this island, which is as large as England, the English come with their wares, especially those from Bristol. And at the time when I went thither the sea was not frozen, although the tides there are so great that in some places they rose twenty-six fathoms, and fell as much. It is, indeed, the fact that that Tile, of which Ptolemy makes mention, is situated where he describes it, and by the moderns this is called Frislanda."

John and Sebastian Cabot are supposed, by similar theorists, to have derived knowledge of the Icelandic discovery through the English, and especially the Bristol trade with Iceland. These theories do not require further consideration here, since they have no bearing on the primitive history of the Wineland discovery.

(2) Lit. law-saying men, publishers of the laws. The office was introduced into Iceland contemporaneously with the adop-

tion of the law code of Ulfliot, and the establishment of the Althing [Popular Assembly] in the year 930, and was, probably, modelled after a similar Norwegian office. It was the duty of the "law-sayer" to give judgment in all causes which were submitted to him, according to the common law established by the Althing. The "law-sayer" appears to have presided at the Althing, where it was his custom to regularly announce the laws. From this last, his most important, function called "law-saying" [logsaga], the office received its name. From the time of its adoption, throughout the continuance of the Commonwealth, the office was elective, the incumbent holding office for a limited period [three years] although he was eligible for reelection.

(3) Rafn was distantly related to Ari Marsson and Leif Ericsson. His ancestor, Steinolf the Short, was the brother of Thorbiorg, Ari Marsson's grandmother, and through the same ancestor, Steinolf, Rafn was remotely connected with Thiodhild, Leif Ericsson's mother.

(4) By this Thorfinn, the second earl of that name, is probably meant, i. e., Thorfinn Sigurd's son. "He was the most powerful of all the Orkney earls. * * * Thorfinn was five years old when the Scotch king, Malcolm, his maternal grandfather, gave him the title of earl, and he continued earl for seventy years. He died in the latter days of Harold Sigurdsson," [ca. A. D. 1064].

(5) It is recorded in Icelandic Annals that King Olaf Tryggvason effected the Chrisitanization of Halogaland in the year 999.

(6) Lit. "house-neat-wood." May be rendered either brown, weather vane, or gable decoration of a house. That the names should have been used interchangeably for the similar object, in both house and ship, is the less remarkable, since we read of a portion of a ship's prow having been removed from a vessel and placed above the principal entrance of a house, that is, in some part of the gable-end of the dwelling.

(7) If the meaning is, as suggested in this passage, that the "house-neat" was hewed to the northward of Hóp, the only intelligible interpretation of the following clause would seem to be that although Karlsefni attained the region which corres-

ponded with Leif's accounts of Wineland, he did not succeed, on account of the hostility of the natives which compelled him to beat a retreat, in accomplishing a thorough exploration of the country, nor was he able to carry back with him any of the products of the land.

(8) Lit. the Uplanders, i. e., the people of the Norwegian Oplandene; a name given to a district in Norway comprising a part of the eastern inland counties.

(9) Olaf the White is called in the Eyrbyggja Saga "the greatest warrior-king in the western sea." This expedition, in which he effected the capture of Dublin, appears to have been made about the year 852. As the forays of these "warrior-kings" were mainly directed against the people living in and about the British Isles, and hence to the westward of Norway, the expression, "at herja í vestrvíking," "to engage in a westerly foray," came to be a general term for a viking descent upon some part of the coast of Great Britain, Ireland, or the adjacent islands. These free-booting expeditions began on the Irish coasts, perhaps as early as 795. In 798 the Norsemen plundered the Hebrides, and in 807 obtained a lodgment upon the mainland of Ireland.

(10) Aud, or as she is also called Unnr, the Enormously-wealthy or Deep-minded, was one of the most famous of the Icelandic colonists. She was one of the few colonists who had accepted the Christian religion before their arrival in Iceland. Her relatives, however, seemed to have lapsed into the old faith soon after her death, for on the same hill on which Aud had erected her cross, they built a heathen altar, and offered sacrifices, believing that, after death, they would pass into the hill.

(11) [Sodor], lit. the southern islands; a name applied specifically, as here, to the Hebrides.

(12) Knorr, a kind of trading-ship. It was in model, doubtless, somewhat similar to the modern typical sailing craft of northern Norway. It was, probably, a clinker-built ship, pointed at both ends, half-decked [fore?] and aft, and these half-decks were in the larger vessels connected by a gangway along the gunwale. The open space between the decks was reserved for

the storage of the cargo, which, when the ship was laden, was protected by skins or some similar substitute for tarpaulins. The vessel was provided with a single mast, and was propelled by a rude square sail, and was also supplied with oars. The rudder was attached to the side of the ship, upon the starboard quarter, and the anchor, originally of stone, was afterward supplanted by one of iron, somewhat similar in form to those now in use. When the vessel was in harbour a tent was spread over the ship at both ends. The vessel was supplied with a large boat, called the "after-boat," sometimes large enough to hold twenty persons [Egils Saga Skallagrímssonar, ch. 27], which was frequently towed behind the ship; in addition to this, a smaller boat often appears to have been carried upon the ship. Upon Queen Aud's vessel there were twenty freemen, and besides these there were probably as many more women and children, perhaps forty or fifty persons in all. As Aud was going to a new country to make it her permanent home, she took with her, no doubt, a considerable cargo of household utensils, timber, grain, live-stock, etc.

(13) Frjáls, a freedman, from frí-háls, i. e., having the neck free; a ring worn about the neck having been a badge of servitude. Slaves were called thralls. The thrall was entirely under the control of his master, and could only obtain his freedom by purchase, with the master's approval. He was occasionally freed by his lord, as a reward for some especial act of devotion, for a long period of faithful service, or, in Christian times, as an act of atonement or propitiation on the part of the master. The early settlers of Iceland brought with them many of their thralls from Norway; others were captured in the westerly forays, or purchased in the British Isles,—indeed the ranks of the slaves would appear, both from actual record and from their names, to have been mainly recruited from the British Isles. The majority of these were probably not serfs by birth, but by conquest, as witness the case of Vifil in this saga. The freeing of thralls was very common in Iceland, and there are frequent references in the saga to men who were themselves, or whose fathers had been freedmen. The master could kill his own thrall without punishment; if he killed the slave of another he was required to pay to the master the value of the slave,

within three days, or he laid himself liable to condemnation to
the lesser outlawry. The thralls were severely punished for
their misdeeds, but if one man took into his own hands the punishment of the thralls of another, it was held to be an affront
which could be, and usually was, promptly revenged by their
master. It was this right of revenge for such an affront which
led Eric the Red to kill Eyiolf Saur, who had punished Eric's
thralls for a crime committed against Eyiolf's kinsman, Valthiof. The master, however, was made liable for the misdeeds
of his thrall, and could be prosecuted for these; the offense in
Eyilof's case was, that he took the execution of the law into his
own hands.

(14) Dalalend, lit. the Dale-lands. The region of which Aud
took possession is in the western part of Iceland, contiguous to
that arm of the Breidafirth [Broad-firth] which is known as
Hvamms-firth. Hvammr is on the northern side of this firth at
its head, and Krosshólar [Cross-hill is hard by. Both Hvammr
and Krosshólar still retain their ancient names.

(15) [Vifilsdale] unites with Laugardalr to form the Hörd-
adalr, through which the Hörda-dale river flows from the south
into Hvamms-firth, at the south-eastern bight of that firth.

(16) Jæderen was a district in south-western Norway, in
which the modern Stavanger is situated.

(17) Drangar on Horn-strands, where Eric and his father
first established themselves, is on the northern shore of the
north-west peninsula of Iceland. Erics-stead, to which Eric
removed after his father's death and his own marriage to Thorhild, was in Haukadalr, in western Iceland, in Queen Aud's
"claim."

(18) Brokey [Brok-island, which receives its name from a
kind of grass called "brok"] is the largest of the numerous
islands at the mouth of Hvamms-firth, where it opens into
Breida-firth. It is claimed that Eric's home was upon the northern side of the island, at the head of a small bay or creek,
called Eiríksvágr, and it is stated that low mounds can still be
seen on both Öxney and Sudrey, which are supposed to indicate
the sites of Eric's dwellings.

(19) In the skáli, which was, perhaps, at the time of which this saga treats, used as a sleeping-room, there was a raised daïs or platform, called the "set," on either side of what may be called a nave of the apartment, extending about two-thirds the length of the room. This "set" was used, as a sleeping-place by night.

(20) Drangar [Monoliths] and Broad-homestead were both situated on the mainland, a short distance to the southward of the islands on which Eric had established himself.

(21) One of the famous "settlers" of Iceland, named Thorolf Moster-beard, like many another "settler," because he would not acknowledge the supremacy of king Harold Fairhair, left his home in the island of Moster, in south-western Norway, and sailed to Iceland, where he arrived about the year 884. He was a believer in the "old" or heathen faith, and when he reached the land, he cast the pillars of the "place of honour" of his Norwegian home into the sea; upon these the figure of the god Thor was carved, and where these penates were cast up by the sea, according to the custom of men of his belief, he established himself.

(22) Dímunarvágr [Dimun-inlet] was, probably, in that group of small islets called Dímun, situated north-east of Brokey at the mouth of Hvamms-firth.

(23) Very little information has been preserved concerning Gunnbiorn, or his discovery. His brother, Grimkell, was one of the early Icelandic colonists, and settled on the western coast of Snowfells-ness, his home being at Saxahóll. It is not known whether Gunnbiorn ever lived in Iceland, but it would seem to be probable that it was upon a voyage to western Iceland, that he was driven westward across the sea between Iceland and Greenland, and discovered the islands which received his name, and likewise saw the Greenland coast.

(24) Blacksark and Whitesark may have been either on the eastern or the south-eastern coast of Greenland. It is not possible to determine from the description here given whether Blacksark was directly west of Snæfellsjökull, nor is it clear whether Blacksark and Whitesark are the same mountain, or

133

whether there has been a clerical error in one or the other of the manuscripts.

(25) The principal Norse remains [i. e., remains from the Icelandic colony in Greenland] have been found in two considerable groups; one of these is in the vicinity of the modern Godthaab, and the other in the region about the modern Julianehaab [the famous Kakortok church ruin being in the latter group]. It may be, that the first or Godthaab ruins, are upon the site of the Western Settlement, and the second, or Julianehaab group, upon that of the Eastern Settlement.

(26) This Ingolf was called Ingolf the Strong. He was probably a son of the Icelandic colonists, named Thorolf Sparrow. His home was on the southern side of Hvamms-firth.

(27) Thorbiorn's and Thorgeir's father was the same Vifil who came out to Iceland with Queen Aud, and who received from her the land which is settled, Vifilsdale, as has been narrated in this saga.

(28) Thorgeirsfell was upon the southern side of Snowfellsness, to the eastward of Arnarstapi.

(29) The simple fact that Thorgeir was a freedman would seem to have offered no valid reason for Thorbiorn's refusal to consider his son's offer for Gudrid's hand, since Thorbiorn was himself the son of a man who had been a thrall; the ground for his objection was, perhaps, not so much the former thraldom of Einar's father, as the fact that he was a man of humble birth, which Thorbiorn's father, although a slave, evidently was not.

(30) Hraunhöfn [Lava-haven] was on the southern side of Snowfells-ness, nearly midway between Laugarbrekka and Thorgeirsfell. It was this harbour from which Biorn Broadwickers'-champion set sail, as narrated in Eyrbyggja.

(31) The word velva signifies a prophetess, pythoness, sibyl, a woman gifted with the power of divination. The characterization of the prophetess, the minute description of her dress, the various articles of which would seem to have had a symbolic meaning, and the account of the manner of working the spell, whereby she was enabled to forecast future events, form

one of the most complete pictures of a heathen ceremony which has been preserved in the sagas.

(32) The expression "Leif had sailed," would seem to refer to an antecedent condition, possibly to the statement concerning the arrival of Thorbiorn and his daughter at Brattahlid; i. e., "Leif had sailed" when they arrived. If this be indeed the fact, it follows that Thorbiorn and his daughter must have arrived at Brattahlid during Leif's absence in Norway, and obviously before his return to Greenland, in the autumn of the year 1000. Upon this hypothesis, it is clear, that Thorbiorn and Gudrid must have been converted to Christianity before its legal acceptance in Iceland; that is to say, before the year 1000; and further, that Thorstein Ericsson may have been married to Gudrid in the autumn after his return from his unsuccessful voyage, namely, in the autumn of the year 1001; accordingly Karlsefni may have arrived in the following year, have been wedded to Gudrid at the next Yule-tide, 1002-3, and have undertaken his voyage to Wineland in the year 1003. This chronology is suggested with the sole aim of fixing the earliest possible date for Karlsefni's voyage or exploration.

(33) The expression "margkunnig," conveys the impression that Thorgunna was gifted with preternatural wisdom.

(34) It has been suggested, that this Thorgunna is the same woman of whom we read in the Eyrbyggja Saga: "That summer, when Christianity was accepted by law in Iceland, a ship arrived out of Snowfells-ness; this was a Dublin ship. . . . Thorgunna was a large woman, tall, and very stout; with dark brown eyes set close together, and thick brown hair; she was for the most part pleasant in her bearing, attended church every morning before she went to her work, but was not, as a rule, easy of approach nor inclined to be talkative. It was the common opinion that Thorgunna must be in the sixties." In the autumn after her arrival Thorgunna died, and strange events accompanied her last illness. As she approached her end, she called the master of the house to her, and said: "It is my last wish, if I die from this illness, that my body be conveyed to Skálholt, for I foresee that it is destined to be one of the most famous spots in this land, and I know that there must be

priests there now to chant my funeral service. I have a gold ring, which is to go with my body to the church, but my bed and hangings I wish to have burned, for these will not be of profit to any one; and this I say, not because I would deprive any one of the use of these things, if I believed that they would be useful; but I dwell so particularly upon this," says she, "because I should regret, that so great affliction should be visited upon any one, as I know must be, if my wishes should not be fulfilled."

(35) The Fródá-wonder is the name given to the extraordinary occurrences which befell at the farmstead of Fródá soon after Thorgunna's death. The "wonder" began with the appearance of a "weird-moon," which was supposed to betoken the death of some member of the family. This baleful prophecy was followed by the death of eighteen members of the household, and subsequently by the nightly apparitions of the dead. The cause of this marvel was attributed to the fact that the Mistress of Fródá had prevailed upon her husband to disregard Thorgunna's injunction to burn the drapery of her bed; and not until these hangings were burned was the evil influence exorcised, and the ghostly apparitions laid, the complete restoration of the normal condition of affairs being further facilitated by the timely recommendations of a priest, whose services had been secured to that end.

(36) It is not certain what variety of wood is meant; the generally accepted view has been that it was some species of maple. That the tree called mosurr was also indigenous in Norway is in a manner confirmed by a passage in the Short Story of Helgi Thorisson, contained in Flatey Book (vol. i, p. 359): "One summer these brothers engaged in a trading voyage to Finmark in the north, having butter and pork to sell to the Finns. They had a successful trading expedition, and returned when the summer was far-spent, and came by day to a cape called Vimund. There were very excellent woods here. They went ashore, and obtained some 'mosurr' wood." It is reasonably clear, however, that the wood was rare and, whether it grew in Finmark or not, it was evidently highly prized.

(37) Thiodhild is also called Thorhild, and similarly Gudrid

is called Thurid. It has been conjectured that Thorhild and Thurid were the earlier names, which were changed by their owners after their conversion to Christianity, because of the suggestion of the heathen god in the first syllable of their original names.

(38) Such a fall as this of Eric's does not seem to have been generally regarded as an evil omen, if we may be guided by the proverb: "A fall bodes a lucky journey from the house but not toward it."

(39) The display of an axe seems to have been peculiarly efficacious in laying such fetiches. From among numerous similar instances the following incident may be cited: "Thorgils heard a knocking outside upon the roof; and one night he arose, and taking an axe in his hand went outside, where he saw a huge malignant spectre standing before the door. Thorgils raised his axe, but the spectre turned away, and directed itself toward the burial-mound, and when they reached it the spectre turned against him, and they began to wrestle with each other, for Thorgils had dropped his axe."

(40) Thorfinn Karlsefni's ancestral line was of rare excellence; it is given in Landnáma at rather greater length, but otherwise as here: "Thord was the name of a famous man in Norway, he was a son of Biorn Byrdusmior," etc. His grandmother's father, Thord the Yeller, was one of the most famous men in the first century of Iceland's history; he it was who established the Quarter-courts.

(41) Swan-firth is on the southern side of Hvamms-firth, near its junction with Breida-firth, in western Iceland. It is not improbable that the two ships sailed from Breida-firth, the starting-point for so many of the Greenland colonists.

(42) It has been claimed that this Thorhall, Gamli's son, was no other than the Thorhall Gamli's son, of Grettis Saga. It would appear, however, to be pretty clearly established, that the Thorhall, Gamli's son of Grettis Saga, was called after his father Vindlendingr [Wendlander], and that he was an altogether different man from the Thorhall, Gamli's son, of the Saga of Eric the Red.

(43) The celebration of Yule was one of the most important festivals of the year, in the North, both in heathen and in Christian times. Before the introduction of Christianity it was the central feast of three, which were annually held. Of the significance of these three heathen ceremonials, we read: "Odin established in his realm those laws which had obtained with the Ases. . . At the beginning of winter a sacrificial banquet was to be held for a good year, in mid-winter they should offer sacrifice for increase, and the third [ceremonial], the sacrifice for victory, was to be held at the beginning of summer."

(44) Freydis also accompanied the expedition, as appears further on in the saga.

(45) This passage is one of the most obscure in the saga. If the conjecture as to the probable site of the Western Settlement in the vicinity of Godthaab is correct, it is not apparent why Karlsefni should have first directed his course to the north-west, when his destination lay to the south-west. It is only possible to explain the passage by somewhat hazardous conjecture. Leif may have first reached the Western Settlement on his return from the voyage of discovery, and Karlsefni, reversing Leif's itinerary, may have been led to make the Western Settlement his point of departure; or there may have been some reason, not mentioned in the saga, which led the voyagers to touch first the Western Settlement.

(46) Dœgr is thus defined in the ancient Icelandic work on chronometry called Rímbegla: "In the day there are two 'dœgr;' in the 'dœgr" twelve hours." This reckoning, as applied to a sea-voyage, is in at least one instance clearly confirmed, namely in the Saga of Olaf the Saint, wherein it is stated that King Olaf sent Thorarin Nefiolfsson to Iceland: "Thorarin sailed out with his ship from Dorntheim, when the King sailed, and accompanied him southward to Mœri. Thorarin then sailed out to sea, and he had a wind which was so powerful and so favorable, that he sailed in eight 'dœgr' to Eyrar in Iceland, and went at once to the Althing." The meaning of the word is not so important to enable us to intelligently interpret the saga, as is the determination of the distance, which was reckoned to an average "dœgr's" sail; that is to say, the

distance which, we may safely conclude, was traversed, under average conditions, in a single "dœgr" by Icelandic sailing craft. Having regard to the probable course sailed from Norway to Iceland, it would appear that a "dœgr's" sail was approximately one hundred and eight miles. This result precludes the possibility that any point in Labrador could have been within a sailing distance of two "dœgr" from the Western Settlement. The winds appear to have been favorable to the explorers; the sail of seven "dœgr" "to the southward," from Greenland with the needful westering, would have brought Karlsefni and his companions off the Labrador coast. Apart from this conjecture, it may be said that the distance sailed in a certain number of "dœgr" (especially where such distances were probably not familiar to the scribes of the sagas), seem in many cases to be much greater than is reconcilable with our knowledge of the actual distances traversed, whether we regard the "dœgra" sail as representing a distance of one hundred and eight miles or a period of twenty-four hours.

(47) This may well have been the keel of one of the lost ships belonging to the colonists who had sailed for Greenland with Eric the Red a few years before; the wreckage would naturally drift hither with the Polar current.

(48) Lit. Scotch. This word seems to have been applied to both the people of Scotland and Ireland. The names of the man and woman, as well as their dress, appear to have been Gaelic, they are, at least, not known as Icelandic; the minute description of the dress, indeed, points to the fact that it was strange to Icelanders.

(49) i. e. Thor. It has been suggested, that Thorhall's persistent adherence to the heathen faith may have led to his being regarded with ill-concealed disfavor.

(50) There can be little doubt that this "self-sown wheat" was wild rice. The habit of this plant, its growth in low ground as here described, and the head, which has a certain resemblance to that of cultivated small grain, especially oats, seem clearly to confirm this view. The explorers probably had very slight acquaintance with cultivated grain, and might on this account more readily confuse this wild rice with wheat.

There is not, however, the slightest foundation for the theory that this "wild wheat" was Indian corn, a view which has been advanced by certain writers. Indian corn was a grain entirely unknown to the explorers, and they could not by any possibility have confused it with wheat, even if they had found this corn growing wild, a conjecture for which there is absolutely no support whatever. The same observation as that made by the Wineland discoverers was recorded by Jacques Cartier five hundred years later, concerning parts of the Canadian territory which he explored. It is no less true that this same explorer found grapes growing wild, in a latitude as far north as that of Nova Scotia, and, as would appear from the record, in considerable abundance. Again, in the following century, we have an account of an exploration of the coast of Nova Scotia, in which the following passage occurs: "All the ground between the two Riuers was without Wood, and was good fat earth hauing seueral sorts of Berries growing thereon, as Gooseberry, Straw-berry, Hyndberry, Rasberry, and a kinde of Red-wine-berry: As also some sorts of Graine, as Pease, some eares of Wheat, Barley, and Rye, growing there wild," etc. [Purchas his Pilgrimes, London, 1625.]

(51) Lit. "holy fish." The origin of the name is not known. Prof. Maurer suggests that it may have been derived from some folk-tale concerning St. Peter, but adds that such a story, if it ever existed, has not been preserved.

(52) It is not clear what the exact nature of these staves may have been. These "staves" may have had a certain likeness to the long oars of the inhabitants of Newfoundland, described in a notice of date July 29th, 1612: "They haue two kinde of Oares, one is about foure foot long of one peece of Firre; the other is about ten foot long made of two peeces, one being as long, big and round as a halfe Pike made of Beech wood, which by likelihood they made of a Biskin Oare, the other is the blade of the Oare, which is let into the end of the long one slit, and whipped very strongly. The short one they use as a Paddle, and the other as in Oare." [Purchas his Pilgrimes, London, 1625.]

(53) The white shield, called the "peace-shield," was displayed by those who wished to indicate to others with whom

they desired to meet that their intentions were not hostile, as in Magnus Barefoot's Saga, "the barons raised aloft a white peace-shield." The red shield, on the other hand, was the war-shield, a signal of enmity, as Sinfiotli declares in the Helgi song, "Quoth Sinfiotli, hoisting a red shield to the yard, . . . 'tell it this evening, . . . that the Wolfings are come from the East, lusting for war.'" The use of a white flag-of-truce for a purpose similar to that for which Snorri recommended the white shield, is described in the passage quoted in note 52, "Nouember the sixt two Canoas appeared, and one man alone coming towards vs with a Flag in his hand of a Wolfes skin, shaking it and making a loud noise, which we took to be for a parley, where-upon a white Flag was put out, and the Barke and Shallop rowed towards them." [Purchas his Pilgrimes.]

(54) The natives of the country here described were called by the discoverers, as we read, Skrælingjar; since this was the name applied by the Greenland colonists to the Eskimo, it has generally been concluded that the Skrælingjar of Wineland were Eskimo. Prof. Storm has recently pointed out that there may be sufficient reason for caution in hastily accepting this con-clusion, and he would identify the inhabitants of Wineland with the Indians, adducing arguments philological and ethnographical to support his theory. The description of the savages of New-foundland, given in the passage in Purchas' "Pilgrims," already cited, offers certain details which coincide with the description of the Skrellings, contained in the saga. These savages are said by the English explorers to be "full-eyed, of black colour; the colour of their hair was diuers, some blacke, some browne, and some yellow, and their faces something flat and broad." Other details, which are given on the same authority, have not been noted by the Icelandic explorers, and one statement, at least, "they haue no beards," is directly at variance with the saga statement concerning the Skrellings seen by the Icelanders on their homeward journey. The similarity of description may be a mere accidental coincidence, and it by no means follows that the English writer and Karlsefni's people saw the same people, or even a kindred tribe.

(55) John Guy, in a letter to Master Slany, the Treasurer and

"Counsell" of the New-found-land Plantation writes: "The doubt that haue bin made of the extremity of the winter season in these parts of New-found-land are found by our experience causelesse; and that not onely men may safely inhabit here without any neede of stoue, but Nauigation may be made to and fro from England to these parts at any time of the yeare. . . . Our Goates haue liued here all this winter; and there is one lustie kidde, which was yeaned in the dead of winter." [Purchas his Pilgrimes, vol. iv, p. 1878.]

(56) i. e., a One-footer, a man with one leg or foot. In the Flatey Book Thorvald's death is less romantically described. The mediæval belief in a country in which there lived a race of one-legged men, was not unknown in Iceland, for mention is made in Rímbegla, of "a people of Africa called One-footers, the soles of whose feet are so large that they shade themselves with these against the heat of the sun when they sleep." It is apparent from the passages from certain Icelandic works already cited, that, at the time these works were written, Wineland was supposed to be in some way connected with Africa. Whether this notice of the finding of a Uniped in the Wineland region may have contributed to the adoption of such a theory, it is, of course, impossible to determine. The reports which the explorers brought back of their having seen a strange man, who, for some reason not now apparent, they believed to have but one leg, may, because Wineland was held to be contiguous to Africa, have given rise to the conclusion that this strange man was indeed a Uniped, and that the explorers had hit upon the African "land of the Unipeds." It has also been suggested that the incident of the appearance of the "One-footer" may have found its way into the saga to lend an additional adornment to the manner of Thorvald's taking-off. It is a singular fact that Jacques Cartier brought back from his Canadian explorations reports not only of a land peopled by a race of one-legged folk, but also of a region in those parts where the people were "as white as those of France."

(57) These words, it has been supposed, might afford a clue to the language of the Skrellings, which would aid in determining their race. In view not only of the fact, that they probably

passed through many strange mouths before they were committed to writing, but also that the names are not the same in the
different manuscripts, they appear to afford very equivocal testimony. . . . Especially is the soft melody of these Skrelling-
words altogether different from the harsh guttural sounds of the
Eskimo language. We must therefore refer for the derivation
of these words to the Indians, whom we know in this region
in later times. The inhabitants, whom the discoverers of the
sixteenth century found in Newfoundland, and who called themselves "Beothuk" [i. e., men], received from the Europeans the
name of Red Indians, because they smeared themselves with
ochre; they have now been exterminated, partly by the Europeans, partly by the Micmac Indians, who in the last century
wandered into Newfoundland from New Brunswick. Of their
language only a few remnants have been preserved, but still
enough to enable us to form a tolerably good idea of it.

"Even as there are on the north-western coast of North
America races which seem to me to occupy a place between the
Indian and Eskimo, so it appears to me not sufficiently proven,
that the now extinct race on America's east coast, the Beothuk,
were Indians. Their mode of life and belief have many points
of resemblance, by no means unimportant, with the Eskimo and
especially with the Angmagsalik. It is not necessary to par-
ticularize these here, but I wish to direct attention to the possibility, that in the Beothuk we may perhaps have one of the
transition links between the Indian and the Eskimo."

(58) The sum of information which we possess concerning
White-men's-land or Ireland the Great, is comprised in this
passage and in the quotation from Landnáma. It does not
seem possible from these very vague notices to arrive at any
sound conclusion concerning the location of this country. Rafn
concludes that it must have been the southern portion of the
eastern coast of North America. Vigfusson and Powell suggest that the inhabitants of this White-men's-land were "Red
Indians;" with these, they say, "the Norsemen never came into
actual contact, or we should have a far more vivid description
than this, and their land would bear a more appropriate title."
Storm, in his "Studier over Vinlandsreiserne," would regard

"Greater Ireland" as a semi-fabulous land, tracing its quasi-historical origin to the Irish visitation of Iceland prior to the Norse settlement. No one of these theories is entirely satisfactory, and the single fact which seems to be reasonably well established is that "Greater Ireland" was to the Icelandic scribes terra incognita.

(59) The modern Reynistadr is situated in Northern Iceland, a short distance to the southward of Skaga-firth. Glaumbœr, as it is still called, is somewhat farther south, but hard by.

(60) Thorlak Runolfsson was the third bishop of Skálholt. He was consecrated bishop in the year 1118, and died 1133. Biorn Gilsson was the third bishop of Hólar, the episcopal seat of northern Iceland; he became bishop in 1147, and died in the year 1162. Bishop Biorn's successor was Brand Sæmundsson, "Bishop Brand the Elder," who died in the year 1201.

(61) We read concerning the introduction of Christianity into Iceland: "Thorvald [Kodransson] travelled widely through the southern countries; in the Saxon-land [Germany] in the south, he met with a bishop named Frederick, and was by him converted to the true faith and baptised, and remained with him for a season. Thorvald bade the bishop accompany him to Iceland, to baptise his father and mother, and others of his kinsmen, who would abide by his advice; and the bishop consented." According to Icelandic annals, Bishop Frederick arrived in Iceland, on this missionary enterprise, in the year 981; from the same authority we learn that he departed from Iceland in 985.

(62) Heriulf or Heriolf, who accompanied Eric the Red to Greenland, was not, of course, the same man to whom Ingolf allotted land between Vág and Reykianess, for Ingolf set about the colonization of Iceland in 874, more than a century before Eric the Red's voyage to Greenland. The statement of Flatey Book is, therefore, somewhat misleading, and seems to indicate either carelessness or a possible confusion on the part of the scribe. Heriulf, Eric the Red's companion, was a grandson of the "settler" Heriulf, as is clearly set forth in two passages in Landnáma.

(63) In the "King's Mirror," an interesting Norwegian work of the thirteenth century, wherein, in the form of a dialogue, a

father is supposed to be imparting information to his son concerning the physical geography of Greenland, he says: "Now there is another marvel in the Greenland Sea, concerning the nature of which I am not so thoroughly informed; this is that which people call 'Sea-rollers.' This is likest all the sea-storm and all the billows, which are in the sea, gathered together in three places, from which three billows form; these three hedge in the whole sea, so that no break is to be seen, and they are higher than tall fells, are like steep peaks, and few instances are known of persons who, being upon the sea when this phenomenon befell, have escaped therefrom." There can be little question that Heriulf experienced a perilous voyage, since out of the large number of ships, which set sail for Greenland at the same time, so few succeeded in reaching their destination.

(64) This has been assumed by many writers to have been Labrador, but the description does not accord with the appearance which the country now presents.

(65) Certainly a marvellous coincidence, but it is quite in character with the no less surprising accuracy with which the explorers, of this history, succeed in finding "Leif's-booths" in a country which was as strange to them as Greenland to Biarni.

(66) This statement has attracted more attention, perhaps, than any other passage in the account of the Icelandic discovery of America, since it seems to afford data which, if they can be satisfactorily interpreted, enable us to determine approximately the site of the discovery. The observation must have been made within the limits of a region wherein, early in the eleventh century, the sun was visible upon the shortest day of the year between dagmálastadr and eyktarstadr; it is, therefore, apparent that if we can arrive at the exact meaning of either dagmálastadr or eykarstadr, or the length of time intervening between these, it should not be difficult to obtain positive information concerning the location of the region in which the observation was made.

The result of the application of Professor Storm's simple and logical treatment to this passage in Flatey Book, "the sun had there Eyktarstad," etc., is summed up in Capt. Pythian's statement, "the explorers could not have been, when the record was made, farther north than Lat. [say] 49°;" that is to say, Wineland may have been somewhat further to the south than northern Newfoundland or the corresponding Canadian coast, but, if we may rely upon the accuracy of this astronomical observation, it is clear that thus far south it must have been.

(67 A wooden granary. The word "hjálmr" appears to have a double significance. In the passage in the Saga of King Olaf the Saint: "Wilt thou sell us grain, farmer? I see that there are large 'hjálmar' here,' the word 'hjálmar' may have the meaning of stacks of grain. The use of the word as indicating a house for the storage of grain is, however, clearly indicated in the Jydske Lov of 1241, wherein we read: "But if one build upon the land of another either a 'hialm' or any other house," etc. As there is no suggestion in the saga of the finding of cultivated fields, it is not apparent for what uses a house for the storage of grain could have been intended.

(68) Lit. war-hurdle. This was a protection against the missiles of the enemy raised above the sides of the vessel. In this instance, as perhaps generally on ship-board, this protecting screen would appear to have been formed of shields attached to the bulwarks, between these the arrow, which caused Thorvald's death, doubtless, found its way.

(69) The Landnámabók makes no mention of this Thori; its language would seem to preclude the probability of a marriage between such a man and Gudrid; the passage with reference to Gudrid being as follows: "His son was Thorbiorn, father of Gudrid who married Thorstein, son of Eric the Red, and afterwards Thorfinn Karlsefni; from them are descended bishops Biorn, Thorlak and Brand.

(70) Námkrytill [namkirtle] is thus explained by Dr. Valtýr Gudmundsson, in his unpublished treatise on ancient Icelandic dress: "Different writers are not agreed upon the meaning of 'námkrytill;' " Sveinbjörn Egilsson interprets it as signifying a kirtle made from some kind of material called "nám." In this definition he is followed by Keyser. The Icelandic painter, Sigurdr Gudmundsson has, on the other hand, regarded the word as allied to the expression: "Fitting close to the leg, nar-

row," and concludes that "námkyrtill" should be translated, "narrow kirtle."

(71) A "Mark" was equal to eight "aurar;" an "eyrir" [plur. "aurar"] of silver was equal to 144 skillings. An "eyrir" would, therefore, have been equal to three crowns [kroner], modern Danish coinage, since sixteen skillings are equal to one-third of a crown [33⅓ ore], and a half "mark" of silver would accordingly have been equal to twelve crowns, Danish coinage. As the relative value of gold and silver at the time described is not clearly established, it is not possible to determine accurately the value of the half "mark" of gold. It was, doubtless, greater at that time, proportionately, than the value here assigned, while the purchasing power of both precious metals was very much greater then than now.

(72) At the time of the "settlement" of Iceland the homestead of the more prominent "settler" became the nucleus of a little community. The head of this little community, who was the acknowledged leader in matters spiritual and temporal, was called the "godi." With the introduction of Christianity the "godi" lost his religious character though he still retained his place of importance in the Commonwealth.

BOOK II.

By North Ludlow Beamish.

ARGUMENTS and evidences respecting the claim that America was discovered by Norsemen about A. D. 1000, and colonized about A. D. 1003, with proofs submitted as to occupation of a part of the country, known as Irland in Mikla, or Great Ireland, by the Irish, in the Eleventh Century.

Introduction to a Study of Icelandic Records.

BY N. L. BEAMISH.

SKETCH OF THE RISE, EMINENCE, AND EXTINCTION OF
ICELANDIC HISTORICAL LITERATURE.

THE national literature of Iceland holds a distinct and eminent position in the literature of Europe. In that remote and cheerless isle, separated by a wide and stormy ocean from the more genial climates of southern lands, religion and learning took up their tranquil abode, before the south of Europe had yet emerged from the mental darkness which followed the fall of the Roman Empire. There the unerring memories of the Skalds and Sagamen were the depositories of past events, which, handed down from age to age in one unbroken line of historical tradition, were committed to writing on the introduction of Christianity, and now come before us with an internal evidence of their truth, which places them among the highest order of historical records.

To investigate the origin of this remarkable advancement in mental culture, and trace the progressive steps by which Icelandic literature attained an eminence which even now imparts a lustre to that barren land, is an object of interesting and instructive inquiry, and will, it is presumed, form an acceptable introduction to the perusal of the ancient Icelandic manuscripts, which constitute the text of the present volume.

149

The author has, therefore, availed himself of an able essay by Bishop Muller on this interesting subject, to put before his readers, in a concise form, the leading characteristics of that peculiar state of society, which generated these evidences of peaceful and civilized pursuits, and gave birth to productions, which, like their own Aurora, stood forth the Northmen's meteor in the shades of night!

Among no other people of Europe can the conception and birth of historical literature be more clearly traced than amongst the people of Iceland. Here it can be shown how memory took root, and gave birth to narrative; how narrative multiplied and increased until it was committed to writing; how the written relation became eventually sifted and arranged in chronological order, until at length, in the withering course of time, the breath which had given life and character to the whole fled hence, and only the dead letter remained behind.

But why was it Icelanders, in particular, who kindled the torch of history in the North. How came its light to spread so far from this remote and unimportant island? What cause led Icelanders more than any other people to a minute observation of both the present and the past? How came they to clothe these recollections in connected narratives, and eventually to commit them to writing?— are questions which first naturally present themselves, and the true solution of which can alone lead to a correct estimate of the value of Icelandic annals.

It is well known, that when towards the end of the ninth century Iceland had been discovered by the roving northern Vikings, the imperious sway of Harald Haarfager led many Norwegians to seek safety and independence in that distant island. But its remote position rendered the voyage thither both difficult and dangerous; not one amongst hundreds of fugitives,—scarcely the chiefs themselves, who possessed large ships,—could provide the necessary outfit for a voyage, which often lasted for half the year; and the colonization of the new country was necessarily slow and progressive, and confined, at first, to the high-minded and more wealthy chieftains of the western coast. But the intelligence was soon abroad that brave and daring men had established themselves in a new country, where the cattle could provide for themselves in winter, where the waters were full of fish, and the land abounding in wood; and many therefore determined upon removing to this favoured region. The tide of emigration from Norway progressively increased, and soon became so great that Harald, fearing that his kingdom would, eventually, be left desolate, prohibited it altogether, and laid a tax upon every voyager to Iceland.

The chiefs took their families, servants, slaves, and cattle; and many kinsmen and relatives, who were accustomed to follow the fortunes of the chief, accompanied him also on this new venture. The particular locality of their future residence was determined by the wind and weather, united with an implicit faith in the superintending guidance of the tutelary idol, under whose invocation the seat-posts were cast into the sea, and wherever these happened to be washed ashore was the dwelling raised.

In the course of sixty years the whole island had become thus colonized. Meantime the first settlers had acquired no means of circumscribing the movements of the last, who with the same independent spirit as their predecessors, took possession of that particular tract of country which appeared to them most eligible; and the extent of the land, the difficulties of the voyage, and the limited number of the population, admitted, for some time, the continuance of this arbitrary appropriation. Amicable restrictions were the only checks that could be at first opposed to such unconstrained and uncertain movements, and these were all either of Norwegian origin, or brought directly from Norway. For many of the settlers were related by ties of blood; the greater number had made common cause against Harald; in their native land they had been accustomed to meet together at the Court (Thing), in the temple, at the great feast of Yule, at the periodical offerings to their idols —and thus, naturally, and with one accord, they were led to establish a form of self-government somewhat similar to that under which they had lived in Norway. The absence of any despotic ruler gave, however, the new community a great advantage over the parent state, and hence arose a constitution more free than the model upon which it had been formed.

This little republic was held together solely by moral laws. Some of the richer emigrants had slaves, which after putting to cultivate some particular lands, they liberated; all others were free; the sturdy yeoman was the unrestricted lord of his own soil; if he came into collision with his neighbour, and thought himself more powerful, he slew him without scruple, but thereupon immediately endeavoured either through the intercession of the chief of the district or some other influential person, to screen himself from reproach, or effect a reconciliation with the friends of the deceased, by the payment of a fine.

The situation of chief generally arose from the relative position of the ship's-company in the mother country, which led to one particular individual among the crew taking possession of the new district in his own name; but it oftener depended upon property or personal bravery. Was he a gallant warrior, or could afford to keep more servants and slaves than his neighbors, his assistance became of importance in settling disputes: and the same cause produced a reciprocal feeling in support of the chief, on the part of those whom he assisted.

Before a certain number of statutes had been collected and formally established, the people followed the old customs of their native land, the parties themselves naming their judges from amongst the neighbouring yeomen; but although there was no want of legal forms to which they could appeal, or chicanery by which justice could be evaded, the result more often depended upon the relative strength and influence of the party than upon the merits of the case. At the district courts (Herredsthinget), the influence of the Chief was considerable, but not altogether paramount; many of the more wealthy yeomen could offer him effective resistance: his influence at the superior court (Althinget), depended upon his personal reputation, the power of his friends, and the number of his followers.

The income of the Chief was principally derived from the tract of land, of which he had taken possession on his arrival; he was also, in most cases, the Hofgode, or priest of the temple; and for the duties of this office, in which providing the altar with offerings was included, he received a small contribution (hoftollr) from every farm in the neighbourhood. To this was afterwards added compensation for journeys to the Althing, and he also received fees from those whose causes he conducted, as well as a small payment from the ships which landed their cargoes on his ground. But all these various sources did not furnish him

153

with any considerable income, and his land remained his principal means of support. The office was hereditary, as in Norway, but it could also be sold or resigned, and sometimes was lost by being appropriated to the payment of a judicial fine.

Notwithstanding this elevated position of the chief, it not unfrequently happened that a powerful individual in the province acquired a higher reputation, and obtained more clients than his superior. Thus after Olaf Paa had returned from his celebrated expedition to Ireland, married the daughter of the powerful Egil Skalagrim, and became possessed of his father-in-law's property, many people flocked around him, and he became a great chief, without being actually a Godordsman, or pontiff.

So long as the colonization continued, the extent of the island secured internal peace; the Landnamsmen, as the first settlers were called, had few disputes amongst themselves, for every one was taken up with his own affairs and although it might sometimes happen, that a quarrelsome individual by single combat (Holmgang*) or the threat of personal encounter, would drive another from his farm, disputes and contests were of rare occurrence. Another local circumstances of no inconsiderable importance as connected with the tranquillity of the country, was the diminutive character of the forests in Iceland. These consisted of dwarf trees, ill suited to ship building, and therefore only small vessels could be built upon the island; whoever wished to trade with Norway, entered into partnership with some Norwegian merchant, or bought a vessel which had been already brought out from the parent state. Such vessels

---

*From *holm,* a small island. So called in consequence of these duels generally taking place upon one of the small neighbouring islands, from whence the combatants could not so easily escape.

could not, however, be used for piratical expeditions, and
those who wished to engage in such adventures were
obliged to join some kindred spirits in Norway who possessed what was called a long ship (Langskip). These difficulties of outfit, connected with the want of sufficient
hands for warlike purposes, and the long distance from the
coasts, where they were accustomed to carry on their piratical proceedings, was doubtless the cause of so few of the
new settlers being concerned in sea-roving, while in all
other matters they followed the customs of their ancestors.

Thus did this remote and comparatively barren island
give freedom and peace to many of Norway's bravest sons,
far from their native land. Instead of participating in the
dangers of the perilous voyage, or aiding in the obstinate
encounter, or sharing in the lawless spoil, when plunder
conferred upon the Sea-King both a fortune and a name,
they now sat down peacefully in their tranquil homes, or
directed the agricultural labours of their servants and de-
pendants. And now did faithful memory carry them back
in imagination to the old and warlike time, which appeared
the more attractive when contrasted with the tranquility
of their present pursuits; personal deeds led to the
remembrance of those of the father, for it was often in
avenging his death that their prowess had been first called
forth, or from his kinsmen or associates that they had received the first assistance. The colonists were, besides,
men of high family; the Scandinavians were accustomed
to set great weight upon this circumstance; the fewer were
the outward distinctions that characterized the individual,
the more important was that prerogative considered which
promised magnanimity and valour. The stranger was
therefore minutely questioned about his family, and even

the peasant girl despised the suitor whose lineage was unknown. In the mother country the remembrance of the old families lived amongst the people of the district; they had travelled together to the national assembly; the paternal barrow, and the ancient hall bore testimony to their noble birth,—but of this, nothing save the relation could accompany them to Iceland, and therefore was the new settler so careful in detailing to his sons and posterity the history and achievements of their kinsmen in Norway. The son equally tenacious of ancestral fame failed not to propagate the same minute details amongst his immediate descendants, and thus was insensibly formed, among the Icelanders, connected oral narratives of the families, fortunes, and actions of their ancestors.

These Sagas, or traditions, did not generally go further back than the time of the father and grandfather; but the recollections preserved in the songs of the Skalds were of much older date, and a number of historical songs can be pointed out which the Icelanders must have brought with them to the new country. Others were historical in a more limited sense, being thrown into rhyme for the occasion, to flatter the vanity of some powerful chief, by a poetical representation of his genealogy; but the more numerous were those in which all the achievements of a hero were specifically enumerated.

These compositions bore little evidence of Brage's* favour. Under the jingle of rude rhymes and alliteration a pictorial expression was given to sword-cuts and slaughter, which brought to remembrance the order in which the several achievements had succeeded each other. The poetical form is more visible in the earlier songs, such as: Hornk-

---

*Brage, the fourth son of Odin and Frigga, was the Apollo of the Northern Mythology; he chaunted the exploits of the Gods and heroes to the tones of a golden harp, and was represented by the figure of an old man with a snow-white beard.

love's Ode on Harald Haarfager, particularly his description of the battle of Hafursfjord* than in the later, such as Ottar Svartes Ode on the combats of Olaf the Saint; and those compositions have still more poetical worth in which, like Eyvind Skialdespilders Ode in praise of the fallen king Hakon Adelsteen, the writers express the feeling which the events call forth.

It may be readily supposed that heroic verses, sung by the Skalds themselves in the courts of heroes, were committed to memory, and that at a time when this was the only means of recording their achievements such verses would pass orally through many generations. The memory was also sometimes aided by carving the verses in Runic letters† upon a staff. The dying Halmund is introduced in Gretter's Saga, saying to his daughter:—"Thou shalt now listen whilst I relate my deeds, and sing thereof a song, which thou shalt afterwards cut upon a staff." In Egil's Saga, also, Thorgerd, addressing her father Egil Skalagrimson, whose grief for the loss of his son Bodvar had made him resolve on putting an end to his existence, says:—"I wish, father, that we might live long enough for you to sing a funeral song upon Bodvar, and for me to cut it upon a staff."

Sometimes verses were immediately committed to memory by a number of persons. When King Olaf the Saint drew up his army for the battle of Stikklestad (1030), he directed the Skalds to stand within the circle (Skioldborg), which the bravest men had formed around the king. "Ye shall," said he, "stand here, and see what passes, and thus

---

*The famous naval engagement in the Bay of Hafursfjord, now called Stavangerfjord. (A. D. 875), made Harald Haarfager master of the entire kingdom of Norway.

†The word Rune is said to be derived from *ryn* a furrow or channel; the invention is attributed to Odin and his Aser, or Gods; the alphabet consists of sixteen letters, which, like the Hiberno-Celtic, claims Phœnician origin.

will ye not require to depend on the sagas of others for
what ye afterwards relate and sing." The Skalds **now**
consulted with each other, and said that it would be fitting
to indite some memorial of that which was about to happen,
upon which each improvised a strophe, and the historian
adds: "these verses the people immediately learned." In the
same manner much older songs were held in remembrance,
and there is still extant in that part of Snorre's Edda, called
Kenningar, a fragment of Brage the Skald's ode on Ragnor
Lodbrok, by means of which he, in the 7th century, moderated the anger of Bjorn Jernside against himself. In the
same poem are fragments of an old ode on the fall of Rolf
Krake, which St. Olaf directed the Skald, Thormod Kol-
bran, to sing when the battle of Stikklestad was to com-
mence. The whole army, says the Saga, was pleased at
hearing this old song, which they called the Soldier's Whet-
stone, and the king thanked the bard, and gave him a gold
ring that weighed half a mark.

But it was more particularly the Skalds themselves who
preserved the older songs in remembrance. By hearing
these, their own poetical character had been formed, their
memories sharpened; and a knowledge of the past was
necessary for the acquisition of those mythic and historical
allusions which were considered indispensable to poetical
expression. An instance of their historical knowledge is
thus mentioned in the Landnamabok:* when King Harald

---

*The Landnamabok or Book of the first Norwegian settlers in Ice-
land, is the most complete national record that has, perhaps, ever been
compiled. It contains the names of about 3000 persons, and 1400 places,
and forms a minute genealogical register of the colonists, their properties,
kinsmen, and descendants, together with short notices of their achievements. The compilation was the work of several authors, beginning with
Are, surnamed Hinns Frode, or the learned (b. 1067, d. 1148), continued
by Kolsteg, Styrmer, and Thordsen, and ending with Hauk Erlendson, for
many years Lagman, or Governor of Iceland, who died A. D. 1334. The
Landnamabok is considered the first authority in all matters connected
with the early history of the island, and will be often found quoted in the
present volume.

Haardraade lay with his army in Holland, two large bar-
rows were observed on the edge of the strand, but no one
knew who was interred there; however, on the return of the
army to Norway, Kare the black, a kinsman of the famous
Skald Theodolf of Hvine, was enabled to state that the
graves contained the bodies of Snial and Hiald, the two
warlike sons of the old Norwegian King Vatnar. This
historical knowledge of the Skalds led to their being held
in high respect throughout Scandinavia, and we find them
allotted the first place at the courts of Kings. Harald
Haarfager is stated to have had more respect for the Skalds
than for all the rest of his courtiers, and more than a century later they appear to have been held in equal estimation by the Swedish King, Olaf Skiodkonning, who is
stated to have taken great delight in their freedom of
speech.

The northern pagan Skalds must not however be looked
upon as the Grecian Aonides, whose only province was to
sing; they bear a nearer resemblance to the Provencal
Knights, who were also Troubadours. The Scandinavian
bards were besides of goodly lineage, for only the higher
and more independent conditions of life could call forth
Brage's favour; they were also well versed in warlike exercises; the song was the accompaniment to the combat,
and we have nearly as many records of their heroic deeds
as of their poetical effusions. They were also, at times, the
favourites or confidants of kings, like Theodolf of Hvine,
who was the bosom friend of Harald Haarfager, and Flein,
to whom the Danish King, Eisteen, gave his daughter in
marriage.

Thus were the Skalds well furnished with knowledge
of both the present and the past, and therefore has the

sagacious Snorre Sturleson truly said, in the Preface to his work:—"The principal foundation is taken from the songs that were sung before the chiefs, or their children, and we hold all that to be true, which is there stated, of their deeds and combats. It was, no doubt, the practice of the Skalds to praise those the most in whose presence they stood, but no one even so circumstanced would venture to tell of actions which both he and all those who heard him knew to be false, for that would be an affront instead of a compliment."

Besides heroic songs, or Drapas, single strophes were often improvised, not only by Skalds but by many other individuals, of both sexes, in a critical moment; and these, by being committed to memory, preserved the remembrance of the occasion which called them forth. Like the Orientalists, the Northmen loved to shew their wit by an enigmatical and antithetical mode of speaking, and from thence, the ear having been once accustomed to the simple measure, the transition was easy to the formation of a strophe, by means of alliteration or rhyme.

The means of preserving the recollections of past events, which have been here pointed out, were for the most part common both to those who remained in Norway and those who emigrated to the new country; but in the parent state the stream of present events carried away and obscured the recollections of the past. The changes which came upon the whole nation from Harald Haarfager's time were naturally looked upon by the Norwegians as more important than the events in which only individual persons or families had been previously concerned. The Icelanders, on the other hand, viewed the one as affecting their home, while the other appeared to be the transactions of a foreign country, and thus the recollections which up to the time of the migration had been preserved in the several detached districts of Norway were transferred to and became united in Iceland, as the one settler enumerated to the other the valorous deeds and achievements of his forefathers.

Besides, it was amongst the families of high birth that these ancient traditions were best preserved. Such families maintained an unbroken succession in Iceland, whereas in Norway they became extinct, first, in consequence of the many events under the immediate successors of Harald Haarfager, and next, from the furious zeal of Olaf in the propagation of Christianity, which brought ruin to the more tenacious adherents of the old faith, and these were just the individuals amongst whom the ancient Sagas were best preserved. Not less destructive to the old families was the unfortunate expedition to England and Ireland under Harald Haardraade and Magnus Barfoot, in the 11th century, as also the long civil wars in the 12th century, which ended with the fall of the Optimists.

The other parts of Scandinavia also produced Skalds, and several, both Danish and Swedish, are mentioned in the ancient Sagas; but these countries were of much greater extent, and ruled by much more powerful monarchs, than Norway, previous to the 9th century; and thus did the heroic age terminate and the songs of the Skalds become silent at an earlier period there than in the neighbouring kingdom.

SECOND PERIOD.

WE have thus seen how the desire to tell of old times arose and was propagated amongst the inhabitants of the new colony. But the remembrance and relation of individual exploits, and the transmission of these records from one generation to the other, would perhaps have never led to the Icelanders becoming historians had not such habits been united with a strong feeling for poetry, a desire for fame, and that peculiar state of society which had been formed amongst them.

The Island had been colonized in peace; each enterprising navigator as he touched its shore took possession of a tract of land without impediment, and became the independent proprietor of his small estate; but now these settlements approached each other; interests began to clash; individual demeanour to become developed. The social bonds had been too loosely attached to keep within due limits the wild self will of so many impetuous Northmen. True, their ancient Norwegian customs had been spontaneously resumed on their arrival, and fifty years later (A. D. 928), the laws of Ulfliot had given a form and consistency to the moral code; but these checks had little weight when individual power or interest were enabled to oppose them. Personal strength was necessary for personal safety; and the many narratives which have been preserved, detailing the untimely fate of the most respectable families in the course of the first two centuries, exhibit a long list of feuds and deeds of violence unchecked by the laws or the judicial authority of the land.

These civil broils were not, however, in general, of a very sanguinary character, and often consisted of individual encounters, where courage and presence of mind were equally exhibited on both sides, and the contest was obstinate: in a more general fray the loss was looked upon as considerable if ten men fell.

The time of feud was also a time of re-union: the object of the individual was spread abroad; discussion was created, sympathy was awakened; the relative merits of the contending parties became the theme of conversation, and the Skalds were stimulated to the composition of new specimens of their inspiring art. On particular occasions they improvised. Hate as well as love formed the theme of these effusions, and the same means were employed to give a graceful form to satire, in which style of composition these ancient poets were remarkably successful: in fact, so cutting were these sallies, and of so much weight among a people peculiarly under the influence of public opinion, that they often became the causes of bloodshed, and were looked upon as a ground of complaint before the Courts.* For the most part, however, the songs were of an historical character; sometimes the Skald sang of his own exploits, sometimes of those of his friends, who upon such occasions were accustomed to present him with costly gifts: After the Norwegian Skald, Eyvind Skialdespilder, had sung a Drapa or ode in praise of the Icelanders, every peasant in the island contributed three pieces of silver, which were applied to the purchase of a clasp or ornament for a mantel

---

*"As an instance of the effect produced by these satirical songs, it is related that Harold Blaatand, King of Denmark, was so incensed at some severe lines which the Icelanders had made upon him for seizing one of their ships, that he sent a fleet to ravage the island, which occurrence led them to make a law subjecting any one to capital punishment who should indulge in satire against the Sovereigns of Norway, Sweden and Denmark!"

that weighed 50 marks and this they sent to the bard, as an acknowledgment of his poetic powers.

The climate and mode of living contributed to keep alive this taste for poetry, which the Icelanders had inherited from their Norwegian ancestors. Agriculture was almost entirely confined to the care of pasture and meadow land; fishing could only be carried on at certain seasons, and the feeding of cattle required little attention. Their hostile proceedings were also soon concluded; but was a reprisal apprehended, it became necessary for the chief to retain his followers at the farm until a reconciliation was brought about, and these assemblages in the common room, during the long winter evenings, contributed to increase the social union and reciprocal communication of past events. Public amusements also brought the people frequently together: besides the great feasts, which lasted from eight to fourteen days, sports and games, such as bowls or wrestling, were carried on in the several districts for many weeks in succession; and still more attractive was the Heste-thing, where stallions were made to fight against each other, to the great amusement of both old and young. To these reunions must be added those caused by attendance at the different courts, and particularly at the Althing* or general Assizes, where all the first men of the island met annually, with great pomp and parade. It was looked upon as a disgrace to be absent from this meeting, which was held in the open air on the banks of the Thingvalla Vatn, the largest lake in Iceland, a natural hill or mount forming the court.

To figure here with a display and retinue that drew upon him the eyes of all beholders, was the great ambition of the

*Ting or Thing signifies in the old Scandinavian tongue *to speak*, and hence a popular assembly, or court of justice. The national assembly of Norway still retains the name of Stor-thing, or great meeting, and is divided into two chambers called the Lag-thing, and Odels-thing.

Chief, whose power and influence depended much upon the number of friends and followers he could produce on such occasions. These were again determined by the degree of support and assistance which they could calculate on obtaining from him in the hour of need; and hence the anxiety on the part of the Icelandic yeoman to be fully acquainted with the character and circumstances of his chief, to which cause may be more immediately attributed the interest which he took in all new Sagas or narratives of remarkable individuals.

In the Laxdæla Saga* it is related that, after a brave Icelander, named Bolle Bolleson, had gallantly defeated an assailant, by whom he had been attacked in the course of a journey through the island, his exploit became the subject of a new Saga, which quickly spread over the district and added considerably to his reputation. In Gisle Sursens Saga, a stranger is introduced, saying to his neighbours at the court—"Shew me the men of great deeds, those from whom the Sagas proceed."

The greater number of the remaining Sagas bear what may be called a political stamp; they contain a detail of the most important disputes between individual families, or districts, painted in the most minute manner, and followed by a general description of the most important personages in the narrative. How much weight was attached to these personal descriptions is shewn by the nature of the Icelandic language, which is richer than any other European tongue in words that express those various qualities and shades of character which are of the most importance in society. The exterior of the chief person in the Saga is

---

*The annals of a particular family, as the Eyrbiggia Saga is of a particular district in Iceland. The former has been translated into Latin by Mr. Repp, and Sir Walter Scott has given a brief account of the other.

also painted with equal accuracy, especially his features, in which the richness of the language is also observable; and even the particulars of the dress are not omitted. This was of importance in a country where it was not always easy to determine whether the stranger who made his appearance was friend or foe, and a remarkable instance is mentioned in the Laxdæla Saga of a chief named Helge Hardbeinsen identifying some stranger knights, whom he had never seen, solely from the accurate description of their personal appearance, which was brought to him by the messenger who communicated the intelligence of their approach.

The same characteristics are imprinted on the Sagas. The peculiarities of the narrator never appear; it is as if one only heard the simple echo of an old tradition; no introductory remarks are made, but the history begins at once abruptly with:—"There was a man called so and so, son of so and so," etc.: no judgment is pronounced upon the transaction, but it is merely added that *this* deed increased the hero's reputation, or *that* was considered bad. In most Sagas the dialogistic form prevails, particularly in those of more ancient date, for this form was natural to the people, who insensibly threw their narratives into dialogue, and thus they acquired a more poetical colouring; for not only were the conversations related which had actually taken place, but also those which from the nature of the subject it might have been concluded had been held; and the general mode of expression being simple and nearly uniform, and the character being best developed in this definite form, those imaginary conversations were, for the most part, not inconsistent with truth.

The talent for narrating was naturally generated by the desire of hearing these narratives. Those Skalds who remembered the old Sagas, and whose imagination was lively, were best enabled to adopt the dramatic form, and now, independent of their local or political interest, the narratives became interesting on their own account. Scarce a century after the colonization of the country we find that the people took great pleasure in this amusement. "Is no one come," asks Thorvard, at a meeting of the people mentioned in Viga Glums Saga, "who can amuse us with a new story?" They answered him: "There is always sport and amusement when thou are present." He replied: "I can think of nothing better than Glum's songs," upon which he sang one of those which he had learned. In the Sturlunga Saga a certain priest, named Ingemund, is mentioned as a man rich in knowledge, who told good stories, afforded much amusement, and indited good songs for which he obtained payment abroad. Such a narrator was called a Sagaman.

Thus did oral tradition, beginning with the mythic, proceed thence to the historical and end with the fabulous. We have now come to the period when books were written and collected in the island; but in order to trace the cause of that peculiar fondness for their own history, which led the Icelanders not only to become the historians of Iceland but of the whole North, it is necessary to go back to the earlier condition of the country and the people.

It may at first sight appear that the local position of this remote island would be alone sufficient to prevent the inhabitants from taking any interest in the affairs of other countries; but the communication with Norway continued; the migration from thence lasted for many generations, even after the island was colonized, and many merchant ships passed annually between Iceland and the parent state. They brought with them meal, building-timber, leather, fine cloth and tapestry, taking in exchange silver, skins, coarse cloth (Wadmel), and other kinds of wollens, as well as dried fish.

As soon as it was known that a merchant had brought a cargo to the Icelandic coast the chief of the temple, and in later times the governor of the province, rode down immediately to the ship and asked for news; he then fixed the price at which the various goods were to be sold to the people of the district, chose what he wanted for himself, and invited the captain of the vessel to stop at his house for the winter. The visitor was now looked upon as one of the family, he entered into their amusements, and disputes, entertained them at Yule with his stories, and presented his host at parting with a piece of English tapestry, or some other costly gift, in return for the hospitality which he had received. Piratical expeditions had at this time given place to trading voyages, and the merchant or ship's captain was often a person of good family sometimes attached to the Norwegian Court, and hence well acquainted with all that was passing there. How much this intercourse tended to the increase of historical material is shown by an old MS. of St. Olafs Saga, wherein is stated that:—"In the time of Harald Haarfager there was much sailing from Norway to Iceland; every summer was news communciated between the two countries, and this was afterwards remembered, and became the subject of narratives."

The Icelanders not only received intelligence from Norway, but brought it away themselves. They were led to undertake these voyages as well from the desire to see their relations, and claim inheritances, as for the purpose of procuring more valuable building-timber than the merchant could bring them. The chief considered that his reputation

PLATE 2.

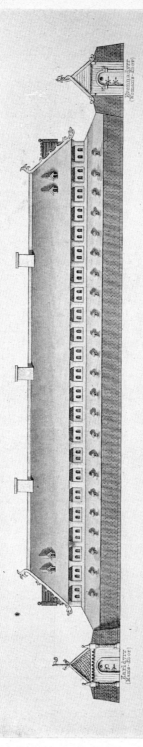

Engraved by Gudbrandson, del't Reykjavik

FRONT VIEW OF THE OLD ICELANDIC SKÁLI OR HALL.

depended much upon the number of persons he could entertain, and for this purpose a spacious hall was required.
This formed a separate building, in the midst of which the
cheerful wood fire blazed upwards to an aperture in the
roof, unchecked by ceilings or partition walls:—

> The drinking hall, a separate house, was built
> Of heart of fir; not twice three hundred men
> Could fill that hall, when gather'd there at Yule.
>
> * * * * * * * *
>
> The cheerful faggot on the straw-strewn floor
> Unceasing blazed, gladdening its stony hearth,
> While downwards through the dense smoke shot the stars,
> Those heavenly friends, upon the guests below.*

The adventurous stripling, on the other hand, sailed to
Norway for the purpose of there engaging in a sea-roving
expedition, or seeking advancement amongst his influential
kinsmen; and thus many earned renown at the courts of
the Norwegian kings, or entered into mercantile pursuits in
order to obtain wealth, or experience and consideration.
For the old Northern maxim of "a fool is the home-bred
child," also held good in Iceland, and therefore do we
find Bolle Bollesen saying to his father-in-law Snorre Gode,
who wished to dissuade him from going abroad: "Little
do I think he knows who knows no more than Iceland."
Trading was often undertaken by young men solely as the
means of acquiring knowledge, which being accomplished,
the pursuit was given up.

After the lapse of a few centuries this passion for travelling was increased by a new cause which had more immediate influence upon the collection of historical materials.

---

*Frithiof's Saga.

The Skalds passed over to England, the Orkneys, and the Norwegian courts, seeking rewards and reputation. They neither required the aid of friends nor money for such expeditions, but boldly entering the drinking hall of the kings craved permission to sing a drapa in praise of the monarch, which was always granted, and the bard received handsome presents, such as weapons, clothes, gold rings, together with an honourable reception at the court, in return for his exertions.

The Icelandic Skalds, favoured by the independent position of their country, and a superior knowledge of the Scandinavian mythology, acquired a marked pre-eminence over their competitors in other parts of the North. The praises of a stranger bard, from a free country, were more flattering to a king or chieftain than the more servile adulation of his own laureate; and it was but reasonable, as well as politic, to reward him well who had come from so great a distance, and who, travelling from land to land, could sound the king's praise and tell of the royal bounty. The odes thus sung were all of an historical character; and it was therefore necessary for the Skald to be well acquainted with the deeds of the monarch and his ancestors. It was also required of him that he should be able to repeat the national ballads; and the extraordinary power of the Skalds in this particular is shown in the saga of the blind Skald Stuf, who one evening sang sixty songs before Harald Haardraade, and could repeat four times as many longer poems!

But if a knowledge of history was of importance to the Skald, it was absolutely indispensable to the Sagaman. A remarkable anecdote of one of these narrators is contained in the Saga of Thorstein Frode, preserved in the Arne-Mag-

GROUND PLAN OF THE INTERIOR OF THE OLD ICELANDIC SKÁLI OR HALL.

EAST   NORTH   WEST   SOUTH

0 1 2 3 4 5 6 7 8 9 10   15   20   30   40

Dönsk Alin or Danish Ells, about two English Feet.

a. High Seat on the Lower Bench (Öndvegi á hinu úœðra bekk)
b High Seat on the Upper Bench (Öndvegi á hinn œðra bekk)
c High Seat on the Dais or Cross Bench (Öndvegi á palli)
d Hearths on which the Fires were lighted
e Table on which the Drinking Cups stood
f Doors of the Hall

g Passages *
h Porch or outer Hall (Anddyri Forskáli)
i Store-rooms for Ale and Food
k The Pillar-door, or Man's-door: The Main Door of the House (Karldyrr or Brandadyrr)
l The Lower-door for Women and Servants (Kvennadyrr)
l The Shut Beds (Lokrekkjur) with chairs and tables for the Heads of the Family
m Shut Beds (Lokrekkjur)   p Stools (Forsæti)
n Tables (Borð)   o Benches (Bekk)

* Between the rows of Pillars and Posts which supported the centre and side Roofs. A restricted Forsæti ran all round the Hall between the pillars and the...
In the Passages between the Pillars were Sleeping places for the Household. The Women slept in the recesses of the passage behind the Dais.

Sigurdr Gudmundsson, del.t Reykjavik

Bartholomew, Edinr

næan collection of Icelandic MSS.;* a certain Sagaman, called Thorstein, repaired to King Harald of Norway. The king asked him "whether he knew anything that would amuse." He replied that he knew a few sagas. "I will receive thee," said the king, "and thou shalt entertain whoever requires it of thee." Thorstein became favoured by the courtiers, and obtained clothes from them; the king also gave him a good sword.

Towards Yule† he became sorrowful; the king guessed the cause, namely, that his Sagas were at an end, and that he had nothing for Yule. He answered that so it was; he had one remaining, and that he durst not tell, for it was about the king's journeys. The king said that he should begin with that the first day of Yule, and he (the king) would take care

---

*Arne Magnussen, a learned Icelander and ardent patriot, devoted his time, talents, and fortune to the national literature of his country. Filling the situation of Professor of Northern Antiquaries at the University of Copenhagen, in the beginning of the 18th century, he amassed the largest collection of books and manuscripts that has, perhaps, ever been brought together by one individual. Amongst these are the rarest and most ancient vellum MSS. in the old northern tongue, relating to the history, laws, manners, and customs of the ancient Scandinavians. The great fire of Copenhagen, in 1728, robbed the devoted antiquary of many of these often dearly-purchased treasures; but he recommenced his labours with undiminished zeal, and although then in his 65th year, was enabled to leave to his country, at his death (A. D. 1730), nearly 2000 Icelandic MSS., together with a fund of 10,000 rix dollars for their publication. Little progress was made towards carrying the testator's wishes into effect until a commission, called the Arne-Magnæan commission, was instituted by the King of Denmark, in 1772, soon after which the publication commenced, and all the most important MSS. have been given to the public by this society. The collection is called the Arne-Magnæan collection, and is preserved in the University Library of Copenhagen.

†Yule was a pagan festival, celebrated in honor of Thor, at the beginning of February, when the Northmen's year commenced, and they offered sacrifices for peace and fruitful seasons to this deity, who presided over the air, launched the thunder, and guarded mankind from giants and genii; it lasted 14 days. Etymologists differ as to the derivation of the name, but the most probable seems to be the supposition that it was so called from *Jolner*, one of the many names for Odin, the father of Thor. After the introduction of Christianity, the anniversary of Yule was transferred to Christmas, which is still called by that name throughout Scandinavia. The word Yule is also used in many parts of Scotland to denote the same festive period, shewing the early connection of the Caledonians with their more northern neighbours, and tending to confirm the conjecture of Tacitus, as well as the accounts of ancient English chroniclers, that the Picts were of northern descent, or as Moore expressively says, "from the same hive of northern adventurers, who were then pouring forth their predatory swarms over Europe."

that it should last to the end of the festival. The thirteenth day Thorstein's Saga came to an end, and now he looked anxiously for the judgment of the king who said smiling: "It is not the worse told because thou hast a talent therefor, but where didst thou get it?" Thorstein answered: "It is my custom to repair every summer to the Althing in our land, and there I learn the sagas which Haldor Snorreson relates." The king said: "Then it is no wonder thou knowest them so well," and upon this, gave him a good ship load; and now Thorstein passed often between Norway and Iceland.

To comprehend how such a narrative could have lasted thirteen days, we must presume that the dialogistic form was freely used, and that the story was interrupted and decorated with verses and poetical allusions to a considerable extent. The anecdote also shows that while Sagamen were of later origin than Skalds, they also stood in lower estimation; the Skald was enrolled amongst the courtiers; the Sagaman was only looked upon as an amusing visitor.

In the 11th century, the Icelanders ceased to engage in piratical expeditions; the chiefs, whose power and riches had increased, looked with contempt on trading voyages; but on the other hand it was often a result of their feuds, that one of the parties was obliged to leave the country for a few years. Sometimes also they engaged in a voluntary pilgrimage to Rome. Such an expedition went first to Denmark, where it was always well received by the Danish kings, and more particularly in the 13th century we find the Icelandic chiefs drawing forth expressions of respect and esteem at the court of Valdemar II.

All these travellers were sure to return home after a few years and establish themselves in Iceland, nor could the most flattering reception at foreign courts abate their inherent love of country. Thus King Harald Gormson could not prevail upon Gunnar of Hlidarende to remain at his court, although he held out the temptations of a wife and fortune; and hence says Hakon to Finboge Ramme, "That is just the way with you Icelanders! the moment you are valued and favoured by princes, you want to get away." When the travelled man came home he was received with the greatest attention; he was instantly sought out at the Althing, and now he must make a public statement of his travels and adventures. The curiosity of Icelanders is proverbial, and seems to be in proportion to their distance from the continent. If a ship arrived, the people instantly ran down to the shore to ask for news, unless the chief of the district (Herredsforstanderen) had ruled that he should be the first. Thorstein Ingemundson, a hospitable man, who lived in the 10th century, looked upon it as the duty of every stranger to visit him first; and he was once highly exasperated with some strangers who neglected this courtesy. When Kiartan, mentioned in the history of Olaf Tryggveson, had returned from Norway, and was grieving over the infidelity of his betrothed, his father was most distressed at the people thus losing the benefit of his stories; and when he was afterwards married, and a splendid wedding took place on the island, nothing amused the guests more than the bridegroom's narratives of his services under the great King Olaf Tryggveson. However desirous the new comer might be to learn what had happened during his absence from home, he was always first obliged to tell his countrymen the news from abroad. A remarkable illustration of this is given in the life of Bishop Magnus, who returned from Saxony by Norway (A. D. 1135), just as the people were assembled at the Althing, and were loudly contending upon a matter respecting which no unanimity could be obtained. A messenger suddenly appears among the crowd, and states that the Bishop is riding up. Upon this they all become so pleased that they instantly leave the court, and the Bishop is obliged to parade on a height near the church, and tell all the people what had happened in Norway whilst he was abroad!

Such a narrative, told by a person of veracity, went from mouth to mouth, under the name of the first narrator, which was looked upon as a security for the truth of the Saga.

THIRD PERIOD.

It has thus been shewn how the materials for history had been collected in Iceland, and how these materials were moulded into the form of narrative by oral tradition; it now remains to be seen how the traditions became the subjects of written documents, and historical literature assumed a definite and permanent form.

Snorre Sturleson says in the preface to the Heimskringla that Are Frode (b. 1067, d. 1148) was the first who committed to writing, in the northern tongue, historical narrations both of the present and past. Soon afterwards Sæmund Frode wrote of the Norwegian kings. Both these authors finished their works at a late period of life, and after the year 1120; hence it has been inferred that no history was written in Iceland before the time of Are Frode, and consequently that such historical writing was the fruit of a taste for literature generated by the introduction of Christianity.

This important event occurred in the year 1000. New ideas and new writings were now, doubtless, introduced, but a considerable time must have elapsed before these civilizing effects became general. Christianity was not propagated in Iceland by force, but was the result of the example of the mother country, the adhesion of individual chiefs to the new religion, and the indifference of many to the old. No violent persecution was awakened against the followers of the old idolatry, nor was the influence of the new religion upon morals and customs very visible at first. Sixteen years had elapsed from the introduction of Christianity, before an injunction from Olaf the Saint forbade the Icelanders to expose their children and eat horse-flesh. The first bishop (Isleif) was consecrated in 1056, but the influence of the priestly character depended, like that of the Hofgode in former times, on his personal qualities, and the power of his kinsmen. The oligarchy checked the growth and influence of the hierarchy. Even in the beginning of the 13th century, interdicts were little attended to, and we find the Archbishop of Throndhjem so late as A. D. 1213, obliged to shew great indulgence to the chiefs, who had cruelly maltreated Bishop Jodmund Aresen. With Christian worship came also frankincense, clerical robes, bells and books. Previous to this, the Icelanders were only acquainted with Runes, Runic stones, and Staves, and such small articles, upon which single words or sentences were inscribed. Individuals may, doubtless, have met with books, upon or near the island, just as Irish books were found there by the first settlers, but so long as Roman letters and the language in which they were written were unknown, such books could only have been looked upon as foreign novelties. Now the priests brought Latin breviaries, and the new alphabet could not be found very difficult after the use of Runes. Fifty years after the introduction of Christianity, Bishop Isleif established the first school, which was soon followed by many others. The previous state of society had awakened a greater taste for reading and knowledge in Iceland, than in the rest of the North, and the tranquil habits of the people being favourable to the cultivation of letters, it was not long before many of them applied themselves ardently to literature. The Kristni Saga relates that towards the end of the 11th century there were many chiefs so learned that they might have been priests, and many were actually appointed to the sacred office. In the beginning of the 12th century, Ovid's Epistles and *Amores* were read in the schools, and in the course of the same century we find mention made of many who possessed collections of books.

For some time reading and literature were closely connected with the new religion. A knowledge of Latin letters was acquired in order to sing the Psalter, to which, without well understanding it, some magical influence was ascribed, and the young priest applied himself to Latin, in order that he might becomingly celebrate the Mass. For records of daily life, the Icelander needed not the foreign character; his Runes afforded him a readier medium, and their use was continued for a long period. On the other hand an acquaintance with the Latin language became of the greatest importance to his whole being; for thus an inexhaustible source of knowledge had been opened to him, and the travelling Icelander could now, in foreign schools, become endowed with all the learning of the age, and by means of Latin books transfer this learning to his own country. Of these, the historical were the most congenial to his taste and habits, and the annalistic form was best suited to retain the fruits of his reading; hence came Icelanders to copy and afterwards to compile annals embracing long periods of time, and hence to treat Northern history in the same simple manner.

But peculiar difficulties presented themselves to the correct arrangement of these records. Much as had been related in Iceland of the events of the past, their chronological order was not preserved, and the only guide to this indispensable element of history were the long genealogical details of the individuals whose actions were recorded. To ascribe these different events to particular years, and arrange them in chronological order, required much time, trouble and investigation, yet under all these difficulties a book was completed which must excite the surprise and admiration of all the modern literati.

This book was written by Are Frode, under the title of Book of the Icelanders (Islendingabok) and contained a dry and condensed, but at the same time well arranged and conmprehensive, view of the most important events in the history of the country. It has often been regretted that a larger work by the same author has been lost. The former, with good reason, was highly prized, for it laid the foundation of all northern history, determining many important epochs, and shewing their connexion and succession with minor events. But Snorre's expression about Are Frode has been misunderstood, when he is made to say that Are was the first Icelander who wrote anything historical. Snorre says that Are was the first Icelander who was *a historian,* but by this he could not mean to say that no one had ever put a Saga upon paper before Are Frode; for this, after Icelanders had been educated in schools, could not be well maintained.

The preceding shows that a number of narratives, thrown into an agreeable form, were current throughout Iceland, and that these, favoured by a free constitution, were increased by all the remarkable events that took place either in the island or the neighbouring kingdoms. The transition to written documents was now easy and natural: he who was accustomed to read and write, and who perhaps relied less upon his memory than others, was readily led to take down in writing that which he was desirious to retain, and thus he constructed a Saga. But the writer of such a Saga would never think of appending his name to it, and thereby seeking the honours of authorship, for he merely wrote down what he had heard others say, and exactly as he had heard it. Hence are the greater number of Icelandic Sagas anonymous; the date must be determined by the contents, and it is very possible that many of these narratives, such as Vigastrys and Heidarviga Saga were written earlier than the *Schedæ* of Are Frode. The other principal Icelandic historian was Are's friend, Sæmund, also surnamed Frode, or the learned, whose work on the Norwegian kings, from Harald Haarfager to Magnus the Good, is now lost: it is quoted less frequently than that of Are, the most important events having probably been already determined by him.

The peculiar nature of the settlement, and the circumstances under which it had been formed, directed the attention of the Icelandic historians of the 12th century more particularly to details connected with the colonization of the island: the order in which families had become established, their genealogy, territory, how they were allied etc.; and the fruit of these enquiries was the celebrated Landnamabok. Next to these local matters came the reigns of the two Olafs, of whose achievements many narratives were in circulation and whose zeal in the propagation of Christianity caused them to be surrounded with a sacred halo. The life of Olaf Tryggveson was written in Latin by two monks, named Gunlaug and Odd, who gave as authorities the oral relations of men from the middle of the same century, at the end of which they wrote; their labour consisted in little more than translating into Latin, and accompanying with a few remarks that which had been communicated to them by others, for both these notices of Olaf's life shew that neither of the authors related anything on his own personal knowledge. About the same period a diffuse compilation was made, recording the achievements of St. Olaf during his life, and his miracles after his death; this was afterwards employed by Snorre, and his contemporary Styrmer, but the nature of both these works renders it probable that many parts had been already written in detached narratives before the whole was collected.

These lives of the Olafs are, in all probability, the earliest regularly arranged written record of a narrative which had been orally related, and they form a connecting link between historical writing and tradition. The achievements of Harald Haarfager, also, which are mentioned in so many narratives of the Icelandic colonists, as having been sung by so many Skalds, whose songs were remembered, and which besides contained events of such great general importance to the Icelanders, were no doubt committed to writing in the course of the 12th century

From such lives of individual kings, the Sagas of the

Kings of Norway could easily be compiled, for just as the isolated deeds of an Icelander were put together to form the history of his life, and thereto were added the achievements of his forefathers and children, so by uniting the lives of Harald Haarfager and the two Olafs, a Saga of Norwegian Kings was already formed. But he who collected or transcribed such a history in the 12th century never thought of writing a book, still less of being looked upon as an author; he wrote either because he wished to note down certain events for his own satisfaction, or in order to have a good collection of entertaining narratives to relate to his friends. The first attempts were naturally imperfect and unequal, for the materials were casually collected, and the most disproportionate brevity and prolixity is to be observed amongst them; but these became better after a time, and only the most deserving were eventually transcribed.

Next to the Olafs, Harald Haardraade was the Norwegian King who furnished the richest materials to the historian, and already during his life time, and with his cognizance, a romantic complimentary Saga, of his residence at Constantinople, founded upon Haldor Snorreson's prolix narrative, was in circulation. There was another class of Saga which must have led the admirers of the bardic art to collect them into a united form, namely, the celebrated mythic Sagas of the Volsunger and Ginkunger, whose deeds formed the theme of the oldest songs of the Skalds, and from whence so many poetical images are taken. No Icelander who either ventured to indite a strophe himself, or made any pretensions to poetic taste, could be ignorant of these. The Volsunga Saga is supposed to have been written either at the end of the 12th or beginning of the 13th century.

That the Icelanders who thus, in the 12th century, committed to paper for their own information the achievements of foreign kings, were not unmindful of the transactions of their own island, may be easily believed; nor did they fail to note down carefully the concerns of their own families and the valorous deeds of their kinsmen and forefathers. But of these narratives, there was scarcely one that could be properly called a book, that is to say, a work published for the information of others; they could only be looked upon as records for personal use, or echoes of the living narrative and assistants to its propagation.

The first real writers of history that Iceland produced—those, namely, who collected historical materials, which they individually worked out with the view of communicating the knowledge of remarkable events to their fellow men,—were those who wrote the history of their own times. The first of these was Erik Oddson, who, according to Snorre, wrote from the testimony of eye-witnesses, and from what he himself had learned from Harald Gille and his sons in the middle of the 12th century. This book is used by Snorre, and still more literally by the author of the MS. Morkinskinna. Next to him comes Carl Jonson, who was Abbot of Thingore Monastery in 1169, and wrote the first part of the history of King Sverre, under the personal inspection of the monarch himself: the succeeding part was finished by Styrmer, in the first half of the 13th century. These authors followed exactly the historical style which had been formed by oral relation. The circumstance of King Sverre, who carefully employed every means of leading public opinion in his favour, having sought to influence the Abbot while writing his history, proves that already at that time a feeling for literature had been awakened.

Thus in the 12th century, when the night of ignorance and barbarism still hung over the rest of Europe, narratives which had previously been transmitted by oral tradition were taken down with the pen, and the writing of books was commenced in Iceland. The following century was the golden age of Icelandic historical literature, for in that age lived Snorre Sturleson.* His mode of writing history was to collect the Sagas that had been written before his time, to strike out whatever displeased him, make abstracts of what he considered too diffuse, and enliven the recital by the introduction of a few strophes from the old Skalds. He states nothing for which he has not good authority; he rejects whatever was too trifling to be consistent with the dignity of history, as well as the greater part of those legends which several of the copyists have inserted in his work: but, on the other hand, he does not pass by a single illustrative feature, and has faithfully preserved the lively character of the ancient Saga.

Between 1264 and 1271, being some years after Sverres Saga had been completed, Sturle Thordson wrote the history of Hakon Hakonson, at the instigation of Magnus Lagebæter, and according to the materials which he had collected at the Norwegian court. His work is therefore to be looked upon as an independent performance, and both

---

*Son of the wealthy and powerful Chief Sturle Thordson, and Lagman or governor of Iceland in 1213. "His countrymen," says an eloquent writer, "love to compare him with the most celebrated of the Roman orators, to whom both in character and fortune he bore a striking resemblance. Both were called to the highest offices in their native land by the voice of their admiring countrymen—both amidst the cares and distractions of political life, soothed their labours by literature, and won its brightest honors from their less busy contemporaries,—both lived at a time when the bulwarks of freedom were crumbling into fragments around them,—and both, taking an active share in the unnatural conflict, fell victims to the success of their enemies. Like Cicero, too, Snorre was distinguished for his powerful, fervid eloquence, and by his rank, wealth and talents. was entitled to the highest place in the state. But his character was stained by avarice and ambition, and he is accused of having often failed to perform boldly what he had prudently contrived."

as regards its comprehensiveness and historical arrangement, must be classed amongst the best of the Icelandic historical works.

The Sagas which embrace that period of time, extending from the death of Sverre to the birth of Hakon Hakonson, are probably written later than Hakon Hakonson's Saga, for as they just fill up the space between these two great historical works, the want of this link would not clearly appear until the latter had been completed. The fragment which remains of Magnus Lagebæter's Saga, shews that it was intended to continue the series of Royal Narratives, but these could scarcely have been of much interest, as no MSS. are extant.

A Jarls Saga was also compiled in the 13th century, being a collection of ancient Narratives relating to the Jarls of the Orkneys, which were united and continued under the name of the Orkneyinga Saga. The civil disturbances in Iceland at this period were described by Sturle Thordson, and besides this many were employed in writing Annals.

In the 16th century, although the decline of learning had commenced much literary activity was still visible in Iceland; but the independent compilation or composition of history had ceased, and only a few Bishop Sagas were still written. On the other hand copying was carried on with great industry, older Sagas were transcribed, the Landnamabok completed, and the Kristnisaga, or description of the introduction of Christianity into the country, was extracted from the older writings: the copious MSS. called Flatobogen,* still shews with what industry individual ecclesiastics

---

*The book of Flat island (codex Flateyensis), so called from having been found in a monastery on the island of Flato (Flat island) situated north of the Breida Fjord in Iceland. It is a vellum MS. containing copies of a number of Sagas, executed between 1387 and 1395, and is preserved in the Royal Library of Copenhagen.

collected and transcribed the older historical Sagas towards the end of this century.

LAST PERIOD.

WE have now seen how Icelandic historical literature, after having blossomed and borne good fruit, began at last to wither and decay; and the cause of its origin and bloom leads us also to the cause of its decline and extinction. The old state of society had called forth individual action and heroic deeds, and awakened a feeling for their representation; but now the power of the petty chief over his Thingmen had become diminished, and the equilibrium had been removed from amongst the chieftains themselves. Already in the beginning of the 11th century had Gudmund the Powerful one hundred servants at his farm, and he was accustomed to travel through his district like a petty king, with a retinue of thirty men, to judge the disputes of his Thingmen. He did not, however, venture to combat the general dissatisfaction caused by the increased expense to the individuals where he lodged, which this practice occasioned, and eventually contented himself with six attendants. As long as public opinion had so much weight, the voice of the Saga was also influential, but when powerful families intermarried, their influence invariably increased as well as the number of their followers and constituents. In the beginning of the 12th century Haflide Marson had a dispute with Thorgill Oddeson, and rode to the Thing with 1200 men, while 700 accompanied his antagonist. No individual yeoman could oppose such an armament, either with his own force or that of his kinsmen, and the field of domestic narrative was therefore reduced from the multiplicity of characters and events which the time of the colonists brought forth, to the more serious feuds of a few powerful chiefs.

From the middle of the 12th century all power and influence was divided between the three warlike sons of Sturle— the historian—Snorre, Thord, and Sigvat. Avarice, ambition, and revenge generated implacable hatred between these, and brought on the destruction of their race; and the history of the independent age of Iceland may be said to end with the feuds of this family, which lasted one hundred years, and gave to that period the name of "the time of the Sturlungers" (Sturlungatiden). Although the history of this period has been written in a good style, with the greatest accuracy, and rare impartiality by an eye-witness and participator in the events—Sturle Thordson; nothwithstanding the much more important occurrences which are here narrated, as compared with the former periods, and which, it might therefore be supposed, would awaken greater interest, —the Sturlunga Saga does not present that attraction to the reader which is afforded by the narratives of less important periods.

Mere numerical force, and not the personal strength or ability of the individual now determined the result. The question was no longer about defending a cause at the Court, but assembling an army; the old thirst for revenge had not vanished, but honourable feeling had given place to treachery, and the power of numbers. No distinguished individual appeared whose deeds could awaken sympathy. Snorre Sturleson was talented and eloquent, but at the same time ambitious, avaricious, and not very celebrated for his personal prowess; his nephew, Sturle Sigvatson, was full of energy, but imperious, violent, and faithless; Kolbein the younger, and Gissur, authors of Snorre's murder, were only clever partisans; Thord Kakal, who revenged the fall of the Sturlungers, awakened more sympathy, but he did not possess energy enough either to overcome his enemies or sincerity enough to be reconciled to them, and hastened the submission of the island to Norway

The submission of the Icelanders to the sway of the Norwegian Kings was a natural consequence of these domestic dissensions; there was no end to the wars of the chiefs; not a single house, as formerly, was burned down, but whole provinces were laid waste. The chiefs themselves also looked to Norway for assistance as well as to their bishops, who were dependant on the see of Throndhjem; Hakon Hakonson well knew how to avail himself of this internal weakness, and hastening on a crisis, which was the necessary consequence of the natural course of events, secured the allegiance of the island in 1261.

Thus did all the noble sentiments generated by equal laws, an independent position, high descent and intellectual endowment, sink beneath the angry and narrow-minded conflicts of private interest and personal animosity. Party feeling,—that curse of a nation,—fell upon the land; the Norwegian monarch, availing himself of the weakness which ever accompanies disunion, accomplished the subjection of the island, and as in a more southern and greener isle, the intestine dissensions of his own excited sons affixed the badge of vassalage upon Iceland!

What theme could now animate the lyric muse, or give interest and distinction to the annals of the historian? The flame of discord lighted by the chiefs, and fanned into destructive extension by the Norwegian King, had carried with it the last spark of freedom from the exhausted land, and with freedom fled the spirit which had breathed life into the songs of the Skalds and given force and character to the records of the Saga!

After a short time the Sagas ceased to be produced, for nothing occurred that was worthy of being committed to writing; the dry annalist alone could fill his note book with the successions of Lagmen or chief magistrates, the wedings of the chiefs, law suits, and solitary deeds of violence, or more destructive still, with details of the ravages of the pestilential diseases which now spread death and desolation throughout the land.

But even more injurious to the historical literature of Iceland than these depopulating effects was the taste for romance which arose about this period, and weakened the feeling for pure history. We have already seen that in the 12th century, fabulous or poetical ornament was given to historical narrative, in order to increase the gratification of the hearer; and by such embellished adventures Sturle Thordson obtained so much favour with Magnus Lagebæter; but so long as real acts of heroism were performed, and recorded, and the Sagas were connected with the songs of the Skalds and the genealogy of families, such narratives justly attained the preference; it was otherwise, however, when the public interest in domestic events had subsided, or rather when the altered condition of society produced nothing to call it forth, and the romances of chivalry were opened like a new world before the admiring eyes of the Icelanders. This was particularly apparent in the reign of Hakon Hakonson, by whose orders several of the most popular foreign romances were translated into Icelandic.

To these may be added the copious Vilkina Saga, a romance of Didrik of Bern and his champions, which was probably written by Icelanders in Bergen in the 14th century from the narratives of Hanseatic merchants.

The passion for hearing and reading foreign romances injured historical literature in two ways; first, by corrupting the pure taste for true history; and secondly, by leading many to exaggerate, and deck out facts with imaginative features borrowed from these fables. Public interest in the history of the neighbouring countries also ceased to be longer entertained; some considerable properties fell to the Norwegian crown; the riches of the chiefs passed away, and the island sank fast into an abject and unimportant condition. Journeys to foreign courts, and consequently the knowledge of foreign events became more rare; the complimentary verses of the subject poet to his monarch were naturally less valued than those sung by the travelling bard in honour of a stranger king; they were no longer liberally rewarded, and soon both Skald and Sagaman ceased to sing and to narrate. With good reason therefore does Torfæus observe that Hakon Hakonson, by subjecting Iceland, left a larger kingdom to his successors, but at the same time diminished their glory by depriving them of the men who could have immortalized their name.

In the 14th and 15th centuries the voyages of the Icelanders altogether ceased. The stranger who landed on their coast, unlike the old skipper of wide experience and goodly lineage and connexion, was now the paltry trader or ordinary seaman from whom little could be learned; and if an Icelander went abroad, he found himself a stranger in Scandinavia. In the course of the 13th century, the old language, by mixture with the German, and a careless

188

manner of speaking, had become quite altered in Denmark, and the same change appeared in the following century in Norway, these two languages becoming nearly similar; so that the old *Danske Tunge,* together with the Saga, was no longer heard in Scandinavia, while in remote Iceland the ancient songs of the Skalds, and stories of the Sagamen, secured its preservation there.

Thus separated from the rest of the world, as well by language as locality, the Icelanders could only gratify their taste for reading in the books of their own country. The value of oral tradition, and therewith its power had gradually diminished and died away as books and reading became more general; but the old supply of true and poetical narratives became corrupted by legends of foreign and native saints, adventures with ghosts and spirits, and traditions from foreign romances, which were written in the 15th, 16th and 17th centuries. Meantime the feeling for the old Saga was still kept alive by historical songs (Rimar) and the labours of the genealogist; the latter has been a favourite pursuit with Icelanders in all ages, and by these means have the principal families been enabled to trace their descent, from the 10th and 11th centuries, with far greater accuracy than the most ancient nobility of the rest of Europe. The Rimar had much resemblance to the Champion songs (Kæmpe viser), traces of which are to be found in the Sturlunga Saga, and which were composed in great numbers in the following century. Of the seventy-eight Icelandic poets that are enumerated by Einarm, as having flourished from the Reformation to the end of the 18th century, the greater number have composed such rhymes, and in many of these the old traditions are included.

In the 16th century still fewer Sagas were written than in the 15th, not so much because people began to get acquainted with printed works, which took place slowly, but because the Reformation at first operated against the reading of Sagas: they were said to contain Popery.

It was, therefore, fortunate for history that from the 17th century the attention of the literati, both in Sweden and Denmark, was turned to the importance of Icelandic manuscripts. Arngrim Johnson, author of Crymogæa, assisted by King Christian IV. of Denmark (1643), collected several of them, and Bishop Brynjulf Svendson sent some of the most important Icelandic codices to Frederic III. (1670), who was a zealous promoter of all intellectual advancement. The Icelander Rugman who, taken prisoner in the wars of Charles X. of Sweden, had awakened the attention of the Sweedish literati to the literary treasures of his own country, was sent to the island in 1661 to purchase manuscripts for the Antiquarian Museum of Stockholm, and many were afterwards sent thither on the same errand; but Christian V. of Denmark, whose dominion, including Norway, extended to Iceland, issued a prohibition in 1685 against any manuscripts being disposed of to strangers, nor was it until the eminent antiquary Professor Arnas Magnussen was placed at the head of a royal commission in Iceland, which carried on its labours with unwearied assiduity from 1702 to 1712, that the remaining manuscripts were collected and lodged in the libraries of Copenhagen.

SAGA OF ERIK THE RED.

DISCOVERY AND COLONIZATION OF GREENLAND.
A. D. 985.

In presenting the historical evidences, and results that attended the independent investigations of Professors Reeves, Rafn and Beamish, there is necessarily much repetition, but it is nevertheless essential, because not only are the translations, in many instances, different, but the interpretations of text, and the conclusions reached therefrom are at times widely dissimilar. The importance of bringing the relations, arguments, and proofs of these distinguished authorities into apposition will, therefore, readily appear. The value of the submitted record from so many sources will be appreciated by those who have a sincere desire to know all the grounds upon which are based the claim that Norsemen discovered and made a settlement upon what are now America's shores as early as about the year 1000-3.

The first important document that appears in Professor Rafn's collection, is the Saga or narrative of Erik the Red, the first settler in Greenland. This manuscript forms part of the celebrated Flatobogen, or Codex Flateyensis, and the language, construction and style of the narrative, together with other unerring indications, prove it to have been written in the 12th century.

Although the main object of the writer of this narrative appears to have been to enumerate the deeds and adventures of Erik and his sons, short accounts are also given of the discoveries of succeeding voyagers, the most distinguished of whom was Thorfinn Karlsefne; but as a more detailed narrative of the discoveries of this remarkable personage is contained in the manuscript entitled the Saga of Thorfinn Karlsefne, which is also translated, the following selections are principally confined to the voyages of Erik and his immediate followers.

Thorvald hight (name) a man, a son of Osvald, a son of Ulf-Oxne-Thorersson. Thorvald and his son Erik the Red removed from Jæder* to Iceland, in consequence of murder. At that time was Iceland colonized wide around.† They lived at Drange on Hornstand; there died Thorvald. Erik then married Thorhild, the daughter of Jærunda and Thorbjorg Knarrarbringa, who afterwards married Thorbjorn of Haukadal.

Then went Erik northwards and lived at Erikstad near Vatshorn. The son of Erik and Thorhild hight Leif. But after Eyulf Soers and Rafn the duellists' murder, was Erik banished from Haukadal, and he removed westwards to Breidafjord, and lived at Oexney at Erikstad. He lent Thorgest his seat-posts, and could not get them back again; he then demanded them; upon this arose disputes and frays between him and Thorgest, as is told in Erik's saga. Styr Thorgrimson, Eyulf of Svinoe, and the sons of Brand of Alptafjord, and Thorbjorn Vifilson assisted Erik in this matter, but the sons of Thorgeller and Thorgeir of Hitardal stood by the Thorgestlingers. Erik was declared outlawed by the Thornesthing, and he then made ready his ship in Erik's creek, and when he was ready, Styr and the others followed him out past the is-

---

*S. W. coast of Norway.

†Iceland was colonized by Ingolf, a Norwegian, in 874. The discovery of the island has been erroneously given to Nadodd in 862, but Finn Magnusen and Rafn have shewn that it had been previously visited by Gardar, a Dane of Swedish descent about the year 860, and was first called Gardarsholm (Gardar's island), nor can the arrival of Nadodd, who called it Sneeland (Snowland) be fixed at an earlier period than 864. But both the Norwegian and Swedo-Dane must give place to the Irish monks, who, it will be shewn, visited and resided in Iceland *sixty-five years* before the discovery of Gardar.

lands. Erik told them that he intended to go in search
of the land, which Ulf Krages son Gunnbjorn saw, when
he was driven out to the westward in the sea, the time
when he found the rocks of Gunnbjorn.* He said he
would come back to his friends if he found the land. Erik
sailed out from Snæfellsjokul; he found land, and came in
from the sea to the place which he called Midjokul; it is
now hight Blaserkr. He then went southwards to see
whether it was there habitable land. The first winter he
was at Eriksey, nearly in the middle of the eastern settlement; the spring after repaired he to Eriksfjord, and
took up there his abode. He removed in summer to the
western settlement, and gave to many places names. He
was the second winter at Holm in Hrafnsgnipa, but the
third summer went he to Iceland, and came with his ship
into Breidafjord. He called the land which he had
found Greenland, because, quoth he, "people will be attracted thither, if the land has a good name." Erik was
in Iceland for the winter, but the summer after, went he
to colonize the land; he dwelt at Brattahlid in Eriksfjord.
Informed people say that the same summer Erik the Red
went to colonize Greenland, thirty-five ships sailed from
Breidafjord and Borgafjord, but only fourteen arrived;
some were driven back, and others were lost. This was
fifteen winters before Christianity was established by law
in Iceland. The following men who went out with Eirik
took land in Greenland: Herjulf took Herjulfsfjord (he
lived at Herjulfsness), Ketil Ketilsfjord, Rafn Rafnsf-

*Gunnbjarnasker, stated by Bjorn Johnson to have been about midway
between Iceland and Greenland, but now concealed, or rendered inaccessible
by the descent of Arctic ice.

jord, Sœlve Sœlvedal, Helge Thorbrandsson Alptefjord, Thorbjornglora Siglefjord, Einar Einarsfjord, Hafgrim Hafgrimsfjord and Vatnahverf, Arnlaug Arnlaugsfjord, but some went to the western settlement.

BJARNE SEEKS OUT GREENLAND.

A. D. 986.

Herjulf was the son of Bard Herjulfson; he was kinsman to the colonist Ingolf. To Herjulf gave Ingolf land between Vog and Reykjaness. Herjulf lived first at Drepstock; Thorgerd hight his wife, and Bjarne was their son, a very hopeful man. He conceived, when yet young, a desire to travel abroad, and soon earned for himself both riches and respect, and he was every second winter abroad, every other at home with his father. Soon possessed Bjarne his own ship, and the last winter he was in Norway, Herjulf prepared for a voyage to Greenland with Erik. In the ship with Herjulf was a Christian from the Hebrides, who made a hymn respecting the whirlpool, in which was the following verse:—

O thou who triest holy men!
 Now guide me on my way,
Lord of the earth's wide vault, extend
 Thy gracious hand to me!

Herjulf lived at Herjulfsness; he was a very respectable man. Erik the Red lived at Brattahlid; he was the most looked up to, and every one regulated themselves by him. These were Erik's children: Leif, Thorvald and Thorstein, but Freydis hight his daughter; she was mar-

194

ried to a man who Thorvard hight; they lived in Garde, where is now the Bishop's seat; she was very haughty, but Thorvard was narrow-minded; she was married to him chiefly on account of his money. Heathen were the people in Greenland at this time. Bjarne came to Eyrar with his ship the summer of the same year in which his father had sailed away in spring. These tidings appeared serious to Bjarne, and he was unwilling to unload his ship. Then his seamen asked him what he would do; he answered that he intended to continue his custom, and pass the winter with his father; "and I will," said he, "bear for Greenland if ye will give me your company." All said that they would follow his counsel. Then said Bjarne: "Imprudent will appear our voyage since none of us has been in the Greenland ocean." However, they put to sea so soon as they were ready and sailed for three days, until the land was out of sight under the water; but then the fair wind fell, and there arose north winds and fogs, and they knew not where they were, and thus it continued for many days. After that saw they the sun again, and could discover the sky; they now made sail, and sailed for that day, before they saw land, and counselled with each other about what land that could be, and Bjarne said that he thought it could not be Greenland. They asked whether he wished to sail to this land or not. "My advice is," said he, "to sail close to the land;" and so they did, and soon saw that the land was without mountains, and covered with wood, and had small heights. Then left they the land or their larboard side, and let the stern turn from the land. Afterwards they sailed two days before they saw another land. They asked if Bjarne thought that this was Greenland, but he said that he as little believed this to be Greenland as the other; "because in Greenland are said to be very high ice hills." They soon approached the land, and saw that it was a flat land covered with wood. Then the fair wind fell, and the sailors said that it seemed to them most advisable to land there; but Bjarne was unwilling to do so. They pretended that they were in want of both wood and water. "Ye have no want of either of the two," said Bjarne; for this, however, he met with some reproaches from the sailors. He bade them make sail, and so was done; they turned the prow from the land, and, sailing out into the open sea for three days, with a southwest wind, saw then the third land; and this land was high, and covered with mountains and ice-hills. Then asked they whether Bjarne would land there, but he said that he would not: "for to me this land appears little inviting." Therefore did they not lower the sails, but held on along this land, and saw that it was an island; again turned they the stern from the land, and sailed out into the sea with the same fair wind; but the breeze freshened, and Bjarne then told them to shorten sail, and not sail faster than their ship and ship's gear could hold out. They sailed now four days, when they saw the fourth land. Then asked they Bjarne whether he though that this was Greenland or not. Bjarne answered: "This is the most like Greenland, according to what I have been told about it, and here will we steer for land." So did they, and landed in the evening under a ness; and there was a boat by the ness, and just here lived Bjarne's father, and from him has the ness taken its name, and is since called Herjulfs-ness. Bjarne now repaired to his father's, and gave up seafaring, and was with his father so long as Herjulf lived, and afterwards he dwelt there after his father.

Such is the simple detail of the first voyage of the North-men to the western hemisphere, and Professor Rafn shews that there are sufficient data in the ancient Icelandic geo-graphical works to determine the position of the various coasts and headlands thus discovered by Bjarne Herjulfson. A day's sail was estimated by the Northmen at from twenty-seven to thirty geographical miles, and the knowledge of this fact, together with that of the direction of the wind, the course steered, the appearance of the shores, and other details contained in the narrative itself, together with the more minute description of the same lands given by suc-ceeding voyagers,—leave no doubt that the countries thus discovered by Bjarne Herjulfson, were Connecticut, Long Island, Rhode Island, Massachusetts, Nova Scotia, and Newfoundland, and the date of the expedition is deter-mined by the passage in the preliminary narrative which fixes the period of Herjulf's settlement at Herjulfsness in Iceland.

It may, perhaps, be urged in disparagement of these discoveries that they were *accidental,*—that Bjarne Her-julfson set out in search of Greenland, and fell in with the eastern coast of North America; but so it was, also, with Columbus.—The sanguine and skilful Genoese navigator set sail in quest of Asia, and discovered the West Indies; even when in his last voyage, he did reach the eastern shore of Central America, he still believed it to be Asia, and continued under that impression to the day of his death* Besides, how different were the circumstances under which the two voyages were made? The Northmen, without compass or quadrant, without any of the advantages of science, geographical knowledge, personal experience, or previous discoveries,—without the support of either kings or governments,—which Columbus, however discouraged at the outset, eventually obtained,—but guided by the stars, and upheld by their own private resources, and a spirit of adventure which no dangers could deter—cross the broad northern ocean, and explore these distant lands! Columbus, on the other hand, went forth with all the advantages of that grand career of modern discovery which had been commenced in the preceding century, and which, under Prince Henry of Portugal, had been pushed forward to an eminent position in the period immediately preceding his first voyage.

The compass had been discovered and brought into general use; maps and charts had been constructed; astronomical and geographical science had become more diffused, and the discoveries of the African coast from Cape Blanco to Cape de Verde, together with the Cape de Verde and Azore Islands, had produced a general excitement amongst all who were in any way connected with a maritime life, and filled their minds with brilliant images of fairer islands and more wealthy shores amidst the boundless waters of

---

*"With all the visionary fervour of his imagination, its fondest dreams fell short of reality. He died in ignorance of the real grandeur of his discovery. Until his last breath, he entertained the idea that he had merely opened a new way to the old resorts of opulent commerce, and had discovered some of the wild regions of the East. He supposed Hispaniola to be the ancient Ophir, which had been visited by the ships of King Solomon, and that Cuba and Terra Firma were but remote parts of Asia."— Irving's Columbus, Fam. Lib. No. XI, p. 353.

"He imagined that the vast stream of fresh water which poured into the gulf of Paria, issued from the fountain of the tree of life, in the midst of the Garden of Eden."—Ib. p. 219.

"He fancied that he had actually arrived at the Aurea Chersonesus, from whence, according to Josephus, the gold had been procured for the building of the Temple of Jerusalem."—Ib. p. 291.

the Atlantic. It should also be recollected that Columbus ever ready to gather information from veteran mariners, had heard of land seen far to the west of Ireland and of the island of Madeira; had been assured that, four hundred and fifty leagues east of Cape St. Vincent, carved wood, not cut with iron instruments, had been found in the sea, and that a similar fragment, together with reeds of an immense size, had drifted to Porto Santo from the west: added to this, was the fact of huge pine trees, of unknown species, having been wafted by westerly winds to the Azores, and human bodies of wondrous form and feature cast upon the island of Flores. Nor should it be forgotten that Columbus visited Iceland in 1477,* when, having had access to the archives of the island, and ample opportunity of conversing with the learned there, through the medium of the Latin language, he might easily have obtained a complete knowledge of the discoveries of the Northmen, sufficient at least to confirm his belief in the existence of a western continent. How much the discoveries of the distinguished Genoese navigator were exceeded by those of the Northmen, will appear from the following narratives.

---

*"While the design of attempting the discovery in the west was maturing in the mind of Columbus, he made a voyage to the northern seas, to the island of Thule, to which the English navigators, particularly those of Bristol, were accustomed to resort on account of its fishery. He even advanced, he says, one hundred leagues beyond, penetrated the polar circle, and convinced himself of the fallacy of the popular belief, that the frozen zone was uninhabitable. The island thus mentioned by him as Thule is generally supposed to have been Iceland."

VOYAGE OF LEIF ERIKSON.

A. D. 1008.

THE next thing now to be related is that Bjarne Herj-ulfson went out from Greenland and visited Erik Jarl, and the Jarl received him well. Bjarne told about his voyages, that he had seen unknown lands, and people thought he had shown no curiosity, when he had nothing to relate about these countries, and this became somewhat a matter of reproach to him. Bjarne became one of the Jarl's courtiers, and came back to Greenland the summer after. There was now much talk about voyages of discovery. Leif, the son of Erik the Red, of Brattahlid, went to Bjarne Herjulfson, and bought the ship of him, and engaged men for it, so that there were thirty-five men in all. Leif asked his father Erik to be the leader on the voyage, but Erik excused himself, saying that he was now pretty well stricken in years, and could not now, as formerly, hold out all the hardships of the sea. Leif said that still he was the one of the family whom good fortune would soonest attend; and Erik gave in to Leif's request, and rode from home so soon as they were ready; and it was but a short way to the ship. The horse stumbled that Erik rode, and he fell off, and bruised his foot. Then said Erik, "It is not ordained that I should discover more countries than that which we now inhabit, and we should make no further attempt in company." Erik went home to Brattahlid, but Leif repaired to the ship, and his com-

rades with him, thirty-five men. There was a southern*
on the voyage, who Tyrker hight (named). *Now prepared they their ship, and sailed out into the sea when they
were ready, and then found that land first which Bjarne
had found last.* There sailed they to the land, and cast
anchor, and put off boats, and went ashore, and saw there
no grass. Great icebergs were over all up the country,
but like a plain of flat stones was all from the sea to the
mountains, and it appeared to them that this land had no
good qualities. Then said Leif, "We have not done like
Bjarne about this land, that we have not been upon it;
now will I give the land a name, and call it Helluland."
Then went they on board, and after that sailed out to
sea, and found another land; they sailed again to the land,
and cast anchor, then put off boats and went on shore.
This land was flat, and covered with wood, and white
sands were far around where they went, and the shore
was low. Then said Leif, "This land shall be named after its qualities, and called Markland† (woodland.)" They
then immediately returned to the ship. Now sailed they
thence into the open sea, with a northeast wind, and were
two days at sea before they saw land, and they sailed

---

*Sudrmadr, supposed to mean a German, as the terms Sudrmenn and Thydverskirmenn are used promiscuously to distinguish the natives of Germany, by old northern writers.

†"The land about the Harbour of Halifax, and a little to the south-ward of it, is, in appearance, rugged and rocky, and has on it, in several places, scrubby withered wood. Although it seems bold, yet it is not high." Columbian Navigator, Vol. I. P. i. p. 17. *"The land is low in general,* and not visible twenty miles off, except from the quarter-deck of a seventy-four. Apostogon Hills have a long level appearance. Between Cape le Have and Port Medway, the coast *to the seaward* being *level* and *low,* and the shores *with white rocks,* and *low barren* points; from thence to Shel-burne and Port Roseway are woods. Near Port Haldimand are several *barren* places, and thence to Cape Sable, which makes the S. W. point into Barrington Bay, is a *low woody* island, at the S. E. extremity of a range of *sandy cliffs,* which are very remarkable at a considerable distance in the offing."

thither and came to an island (Nantucket?) which lay to the eastward of the land,* and went up there, and looked round them in good weather, and observed that there was dew upon the grass; and it so happened that they touched the dew with their hands, and raised the fingers to the mouth, and they thought that they had never before tasted anything so sweet.

After that they went to the ship, and sailed into a sound, which lay between the island and a ness (promontory), which ran out to the eastward of the land; and then steered westwards past the ness. It was very shallow at ebb tide, and their ship stood up, so that it was far to see from the ship to the water.

But so much did they desire to land, that they did not give themselves time to wait until the water again rose under their ship, but ran at once on shore, at a place where a river flows out of a lake; but so soon as the waters rose up under the ship, then took they boats, and rowed to the ship, and floated it up to the river, and thence into the lake, and there cast anchor, and brought up from the ship their skin cots,† and made their booths.

After this took they counsel, and formed the resolution of remaining there for the winter, and built there large houses. There was no want of salmon either in the river or in the lake, and larger salmon than they had

---

*Literally "northward of the land," but the Editor shows that the Northmen placed this point of the compass nearly in the position of our east."

†*Hudfot*, from *hud*, skin, and *fat*, a case or covering, being strictly speaking, a skin bag or pouch, in which the ancients were accustomed to keep their clothes and other articles on a journey; the same was used for a bed on ship-board, as appears in the Laxdæla Saga, p. 116, where Thurid says, "she went to the couch, where Geirmund slept." It thus answers to the *uter* of the Romans.

NORSEMEN CELEBRATING THEIR DISCOVERY.

(From a drawing by Russell.)

LEIF ERICKSON, with his companions, found the country about Vinland so fertile and attractive that sailing up the River St. Charles a short distance they landed at a site suitable for a settlement and there erected booths. These booths were built after the primitive fashion, by driving sharpened posts into the ground, which with forked tops supported cross pieces on which were then laid boughs and a covering of grass and earth. These temporary structures answered very well for shelter during the summer, and until more substantial buildings could be erected, which was done the following spring

NORSEMEN CELEBRATING THEIR DISCOVERY.

(From a drawing by Russell.)

LEIF ERICKSON, with his companions, found the country about Vinland so fertile and attractive that sailing up the River St. Charles a short distance they landed at a site suitable for a settlement and there erected booths. These booths were built after the primitive fashion, by driving sharpened posts into the ground, which with forked tops supported cross pieces on which were then laid boughs and a covering of grass and earth. These temporary structures answered very well for shelter during the summer, and until more substantial buildings could be erected, which was done the following spring.

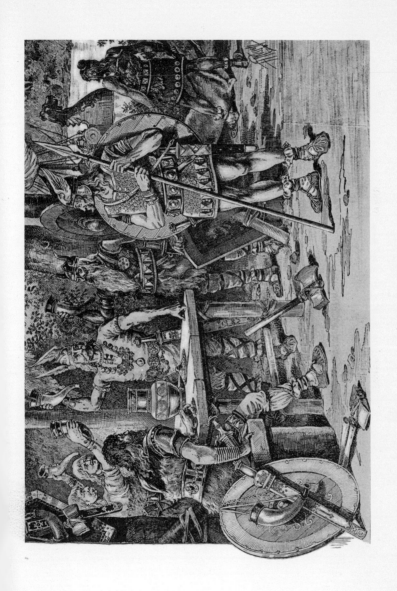

before seen. The nature of the country was, as they thought, so good that cattle would not require house feeding in winter, for there came no frost in winter, and little did the grass wither there. Day and night were more equal than in Greenland or Iceland, for on the shortest day was the sun above the horizon from half-past seven in the forenoon till half-past four in the afternoon, hence Prof. Rafn makes the latitude 41°, 24′, 10″.

This would give very nearly the latitude of Mount Hope Bay, which locality is previously pointed out by the details relating to the soil and climate, and fully corresponds with the descriptions of modern travellers.

But when they had done with the house building, Leif said to his comrades :—"Now will I divide our men into two parts, and have the land explored, and the half of the men shall remain at home at the house, while the other half explore the land; but however, not go further than that they can come home in the evening, and they should not separate." Now they did so for a time, and Leif changed about, so that the one day he went with them, and the other remained at home in the house. Leif was a great and strong man, grave and well favoured, therewith sensible and moderate in all things.

It happened one evening that a man of the party was missing, and this was Tyrker the German. This took Leif much to heart, for Tyrker had been long with his father and him, and loved Leif much in his childhood. Leif now took his people severely to task, and prepared to seek for Tyrker, and took twelve men with him. But when they had gotten a short way from the house, then came Tyrker towards them, and was joyfully received. Leif soon saw that his foster-father was not in his right senses. Tyrker had a high forehead, and unsteady eyes, was freckled in the face, small and mean in stature, but excellent in all kinds of artifice. Then said Leif to him: "Why wert thou so late my fosterer, and separated from the party?" He now spoke first, for a long time, in German, and rolled his eyes about to different sides, and twisted his mouth, but they did not understand what he said. After a time he spoke Norse. "I have not been much further off, but still have I something new to tell of; I found vines and grapes." "But is that true, my fosterer?" quoth Leif. "Surely is it true," replied he, "for I was bred up in a land where there is no want of either vines or grapes." They slept now for the night, but in the morning, Leif said to his sailors: "We will now set about two things, in that the one day we gather grapes, and the other day cut vines and fell trees, so from thence will be a loading for my ship," and that was the counsel taken, and it is said their long boat was filled with grapes. Now was a cargo cut down for the ship, and when the spring came they got ready and sailed away, and Leif gave the land a name after its qualities, and called it Vinland, or Wineland.

They sailed now into the open sea, and had a fair wind until they saw Greenland, and the mountains below the joklers. Then a man put in his word and said to Leif: "Why do you steer so close to the wind?" Leif answered: "I attend to my steering, and something more, and can ye not see anything?" They answered that they

could not observe anything extraordinary. "I know not,"
said Leif, "whether I see a ship or a rock." Now looked
they, and said it was a rock. But he saw so much
sharper than they that he perceived there were men
upon the rock. "Now let us," said Leif, "hold our wind
so that we come up to them, if they should want our assistance, and the necessity demands that we should help
them; and if they should not be kindly disposed, the
power is in our hands, and not in theirs." Now sailed
they under the rock, and lowered their sails, and cast anchor, and put out another little boat, which they had
with them. Then asked Tyrker who their leader was?
He called himself Thorer, and said he was a Northman;
"but what is *thy* name?" said he. Leif told his name.
"Art thou a son of Erik the Red, of Brattahlid?" quoth
he. Leif answered that so it was. "Now will I," said
Leif, "take ye all on board my ship, and as much of the
goods as the ship can hold." They accepted this offer,
and sailed thereupon to Eriksfjord with the cargo, and
thence to Brattahlid, where they unloaded the ship. After
that, Leif invited Thorer and his wife Gudrid, and three
other men to stop with him, and got berths for the other
seamen, as well Thorer's as his own, elsewhere. Leif
took fifteen men from the rock; he was, after that, called
Leif the Lucky. Leif had now earned both riches and
respect. The same winter came a heavy sickness among
Thorer's people, and carried off as well Thorer himself as
many of his men. This winter died also Erik the Red.
Now was there much talk about Leif's voyage to Vinland, and Thorvald, his brother, thought that the land

had been much too little explored. Then said Leif to
Thorvald: "Thou can'st go with my ship, brother! if
thou wilt, to Vinland, but I wish first that the ship
should go and fetch the timber, which Thorer had upon
the rock;" and so was done.

THORVALD REPAIRS TO VINLAND.

A. D. 1002.

Now Thorvald made ready for this voyage with 30
men, and took counsel thereon with Leif his brother.
Then made they their ship ready, and put to sea, and
nothing is told of their voyage until they came to Leif's
booths in Vinland. There they laid up their ship, and
spent a pleasant winter, and caught fish for their support. But in the spring, said Thorvald, that they should
make ready the ship, and that some of the men should
take the ship's long boat round the western part of the
land, and explore there during the summer. To them
appeared the land fair and woody, and but a short distance between the wood and the sea, and white sands;
there were many islands, and much shallow water. They
found neither dwellings of men nor beasts, except upon
an island, to the westward, where they found a corn-
shed of wood, but many works of men they found not;
and they then went back and came to Leif's booths in the
autumn. But the next summer, went Thorvald eastward
with the ship, and round the land to the northward.
Here came a heavy storm upon them when off a ness,
so that they were driven on shore, and the keel broke off
from the ship, and they remained here a long time, and

repaired their ship. Then said Thorvald to his companions: "Now will I that we fix up the keel here upon the ness, and call it Keelness (Kjalarness), and so did they. After that they sailed away round the eastern shores of the land, and into the mouths of the firths, which lay nearest thereto, and to a point of land which stretched out, and was covered all over with wood. There they came to, with the ship, and shoved out a plank to the land, and Thorvald went up the country with all his companions. He then said: "Here it is beautiful, and here would I like to raise my dwelling." Then went they to the ship, and saw upon the sands within the promontory three elevations, and went thither, and saw there three skin boats (canoes), and three men under each. Then divided they their people, and caught them all, except one, who got away with his boat. They killed the other eight, and then went back to the cape, and looked round them, and saw some heights inside of the frith, and supposed that these were dwellings. After that, so great a drousiness came upon them that they could not keep awake, and they all fell asleep. Then came a shout over them, so that they all awoke. Thus said the shout: "Wake thou! Thorvald! and all thy companions, if thou wilt preserve life, and return thou to thy ship, with all thy men, and leave the land without delay." Then rushed out from the interior of the frith an innumerable crowd of skin boats, and made towards them. Thorvald said then: "We will put out the battle-skreen, and defend ourselves as well as we can, but fight little against them." So did they, and the Skrælings shot at them for a time, but afterwards ran away, each as fast as he could. Then asked Thorvald his men if they had gotten any wounds; they answered that no one was wounded. "I have gotten a wound under the arm," said he, "for an arrow fled between the edge of the ship and the shield, in under my arm, and here is the arrow, and it will prove a mortal wound to me. Now counsel I ye, that ye get ready instantly to depart, but ye shall bear me to that cape, where I thought it best to dwell; it may be that a true word fell from my mouth, that I should dwell there for a time; there shall ye bury me, and set up crosses at my head and feet, and call the place Krossaness for ever in all time to come." Greenland was then Christianized, but Erik the Red died before Christianity was introduced. Now Thorvald died, but they did all things according to his directions, and then went away, and returned to their companions, and told to each other the tidings which they knew, and dwelt there for the winter, and gathered grapes and vines to load the ship. But in the spring they made ready to sail to Greenland, and came with their ship in Eriksfjord, and could now tell great tidings to Leif.

UNSUCCESSFUL VOYAGE OF THORSTEIN ERIKSON.

A. D. 1005.

THORSTEIN ERIKSON DIES IN THE WESTERN SETTLEMENT.

MEANTIME it had happened in Greenland that Thorstein in Eriksfjord married Gudrid, Thorbjorn's daughter, who had been formerly married to Thorer the Eastman, as is before related. Now Thorstein Erikson conceived a desire to go to Vinland after the body of Thorvald his brother, and he made ready the same ship, and chose great and strong men for the crew, and had with him 25 men, and Gudrid his wife. They sailed away so soon as they were ready, and came out of sight of the land. They drove about in the sea the whole summer, and knew not where they were; and when the first week of winter was past, then landed they in Lysefjord in Greenland, in the western settlement. Thorstein sought shelter for them and procured lodging for all his crew; but he himself and his wife were without lodging, and they, therefore, remained some two nights in the ship. Then was Christianity yet new in Greenland. Now it came to pass one day that some people repaired, early in the morning, to their tent, and the leader of the party asked who was in the tent. Thorstein answered: "Here are two persons, but who asks the question?" "Thorstein is my name," said the other, "and I am called Thorstein the Black, but my business here is to bid ye both,

thou and thy wife, to come and stop at my house."
Thorstein said that he would talk the matter over with
his wife, but she told him to decide, and he accepted the
bidding. "Then will I come after ye in the morning with
horses, for I want nothing to entertain ye both; but it is
very wearisome at my house, for we are there but two, I
and my wife, and I am very morose; I have also a different religion from yours, and yet hold I that for the better
which ye have." Now came he after them in the morning with horses, and they went to lodge with Thorstein
the Black, who shewed them every hospitality. Gudrid
was a grave and dignified woman, and therewith sensible,
and knew well how to carry herself among strangers.
Early that winter came sickness amongst Thorstein Erikson's men, and there died many of his people. Thorstein
had coffins made for the bodies of those who died, and
caused them to be taken out to the ship, and there laid;
"for I will," said he, "have all the bodies taken to Eriksfjord in the summer." Now it was not long before the
sickness came also into Thorstein's house, and his wife,
who hight Grimhild took the sickness first; she was very
large, and strong as a man, but still did the sickness master her. And soon after that, the disease attacked Thorstein Erikson, and they both lay ill at the same time, and
Grimhild, the wife of Thorstein the Black, died. But
when she was dead, then went Thorstein out of the
room, after a plank to lay the body upon. Then said
Gudrid: "Stay not long away, my Thorstein!" he answered that so it should be. Then said Thorstein Erikson: "Strangely now is our house-mother* going on,

*Husfreyju.

210

for she pushes herself up on her elbows, and stretches her feet out of bed, and feels for her shoes." At that moment came in the husband Thorstein, and Grimhild then lay down, and every beam in the room creaked. Now Thorstein made a coffin for Grimhild's body, and took it out, and buried it; but although he was a large and powerful man, it took all his strength to bring it out of the place. Now the sickness attacked Thorstein Erikson and he died, which his wife Gudrid took much to heart. They were then all in the room; Gudrid had taken her seat upon a chair beyond the bench upon which Thorstein her husband, had lain; then Thorstein the host took Gudrid from the chair upon his knees, and sat down with her upon another bench, just opposite Thorstein's body. He comforted her in many ways, and cheered her up, and promised to go with her to Eriksfjord, with her husband's body, and those of his companions; "and I will also," added he, "bring many servants to comfort and amuse thee." She thanked him. Then Thorstein Erikson sat himself up on the bench, and said: "Where is Gudrid?" Three times said he that, but she answered not. Then said she to Thorstein the host: "Shall I answer his questions or not?" He counselled her not to answer. After this, went Thorstein the host across the floor, and sat himself on a chair, but Gudrid sat upon his knees, and he said: "What wilt thou, Namesake?" After a little he answered: "I wish much to tell Gudrid her fortune, in order that she may be the better reconciled to my death, for I have now come to a good resting place; but this can I tell thee, Gudrid! that thou wilt be married to an Icelander, and ye shall live long together, and have a numerous posterity, powerful, distinguished, and excellent, sweet and well favoured; ye shall remove from Greenland to Norway, and from thence to Iceland; there shall ye live long, and thou shalt outlive him. Then wilt thou go abroad, and travel to Rome, and come back again to Iceland, to thy house; and then will a church be built, and thou wilt reside there, and become a nun, and there wilt thou die." And when he had said these words, Thorstein fell back, and his corpse was set in order, and taken to the ship. Now Thorstein the host kept well all the promises which he had made to Gudrid; in the spring (1006) he sold his farm, and his cattle, and betook himself to the ship, with Gudrid, and all that he possessed; he made ready the ship, and procured men therefor, and then sailed to Eriksfjord. The bodies were now buried by the Church. Gudrid repaired to Leif in Brattahlid, but Thorstein the Black made himself a dwelling at Eriksfjord, and dwelt there so long as he lived, and was looked upon as a very able man.

This prophetic announcement of Thorstein Erikson is highly characteristic of the superstition of the times, and although pertaining to the marvellous, is not the less corroborative of the authenticity of the narrative. "Such incidents," says Sir Walter Scott, "make an invariable part of the history of a rude age, and the chronicles which do not afford these marks of human credulity, may be greviously suspected as being deficient in authenticity."

From the Heimskringla, or History of the Norwegian Kings, According to the 2nd Vellum Codex of the Arnae-Magnaean Collection, No. 45 Folio.

VINLAND THE GOOD IS DISCOVERED.

The same winter was Leif, the son of Erik the Red, with King Olaf, in good repute, and embraced Christianity. But the summer that Gissur went to Iceland, King Olaf sent Leif to Greenland, in order to make known Christianity there; he sailed the same summer to Greenland. He found, in the sea, some people on a wreck, and helped them; the same time discovered he Vinland the Good; and came in harvest to Greenland. He had with him a priest, and other clerks, and went to dwell at Brattahlid with Erik, his father. Men called him afterwards Leif the Lucky; but Erik his father said that these two things went one against the other, inasmuch as Leif had saved the crew of the ship, but brought evil men to Greenland, namely the priests.

SAGA OF THORFINN KARLSEFNE.

Next in importance and interest to the Saga of Erik the Red, is that of Thorfinn, with the significant surname of Karlsefne, *i. e.,* destined to become a great man. This distinguished individual was a wealthy and powerful Icelandic merchant, descended from an illustrious line of Danish, Swedish, Norwegian, Irish, and Scottish ancestors, some of whom were kings, or of royal blood. The narrative of his exploits is taken from two ancient Icelandic MSS. not previously known to the literati, and one of which, there is every reason to believe, is a genuine autograph of the celebrated Hauk Erlendson, who was Lagman or Chief Governor of Iceland in 1295, and one of the compilers of the Landnamabok; he was also a descendant of Karlsefne in the ninth generation. This very remarkable Saga forms part of the Arnæ-Magæan collection, and besides short notices of the discoveries of the earlier voyagers, which are more fully described in the Saga of Erik the Red, gives detailed accounts of voyages to and discoveries in America, carried on by Karlsefne and his companions for a period of three years, commencing in 1007. Some discrepancies and misnomers appear in those parts of the narrative, which treat of the personages and events recorded in the preceding Saga, but they are only such as to preclude all suspicion of confederacy or fraud on the part of the writers, as all the *main facts* are substantially the same in both; and the circumstance of the Saga of Erik having been written in Greenland, while that of Karlsefne was written in Iceland, is sufficient to account for these variations. The same circumstance, also, renders the former the best authority in all matters of detail connected with Greenland, while the other must be considered more correct respecting occurrences relating to Iceland. These differences are pointed out in the notes, and where any minor points of interesting detail connected with the voyage of Karlsefne appear in the Saga of Erik the Red, while they are absent in Karlsefne's saga, they have been supplied from that of Erik, the interpolation being pointed out.

Torfæus imagined that the Saga of Thorfinn Karlsefne was lost, and the only knowledge he had of its contents was derived from some corrupt extracts contained in the collection of materials for the history of ancient Greenland, left by the Icelandic yeoman Bjorn Jonson, of Skardso.

SAGA OF THORFINN KARLSEFNI.

GENEALOGY OF THORFINN KARLSEFNI, HIS VOYAGE TO
GREENLAND, AND MARRIAGE WITH GUDRID, THE
WIDOW OF THORSTEIN ERIKSON.

(Translation from the Manuscript.)

THORD hight* a man who lived at Hofda in Hofda
strand; he married Fridgerda, daughter of Thorer Hyma
and Fridgerda daughter of Kjarval, king of the Irish.
Thord was the son of Bjarni Byrdusmjor, son of Thorvald Ryg, son of Asleik, son of Bjarni Jarnsid, son of
Ragnar Lodbrok. They had a son called Snorri; he married Thorhild Rjupa, daughter of Thord Gellar; their
son was Thord Hesthofdi. Thorfinn Karlsefni hight
Thord's son; Thorfinn's mother hight Thorum. Thorfinn
took to trading voyages, and was thought an able seaman
and merchant. One summer Karlsefni fitted out his
ship, and purposed a voyage to Greenland. Snorri Thorbrandson, of Alptefjord, went with him, and there were
forty men in the ship. There was a man hight Bjarne
Grimolfson, of Breidafjord; another hight Thorhall Ga-
malason, an Eastfjordish man; they fitted out their ship
the same summer for Greenland; there were also forty
men in the ship. Karlsefni and the others put to sea with
these two ships, so soon as they were ready. Nothing is
told about how long they were at sea, but it is to be related that both these ships came to Eriksfjord in the autumn. Erik rode to the ship together with several of

---

*The word *"hight"* means *name,* so that the sentence may be read:
"A man named Thord, who lived at Hofda," etc.

the inhabitants, and they began to deal in a friendly manner. Both the ship's captains begged Erik (Leif) to take
as much of the goods as he wished; but Erik (Leif) on
his side, showed them hospitality, and bade the crews
of these two ships home, for the winter, to his own
house at Brattahlid. This the merchants accepted, and
thanked him. Then were their goods removed to Brattahlid; there was no want of large out-houses to keep the
goods in, neither plenty of every thing that was required,
wherefore they were well satisfied in the winter. But towards Yule Erik (Leif) began to be silent, and was less
cheerful than he used to be. One time turned Karlsefni
towards Erik (Leif) and said: "Hast thou any sorrow,
Erik, my friend? people think to see that thou art less
cheerful than thou wert wont to be; thou hast entertained us with the greatest splendour, and we are bound
to return it to thee with such services as we can command; say now, what troubles thee?" Erik (Leif) answered: "Ye are friendly and thankful, and I have no
fear as concerns out intercourse, that ye will feel the
want of attention; but, on the other hand, I fear that
when ye come elsewhere it will be said that ye have
never passed a worse Yule than that which now approaches, when Erik the Red entertained ye at Brattahlid, in Greenland." "It shall not be so, Yeoman!"* said
Karlsefne; "we have in our ship, both malt and corn; take
as much as thou desirest thereof, and make ready a feast
as grand as thou wilt!" This Erik (Leif) accepted, and
now preparation was made for the feast of Yule, and this

---

*Bondi, a householder.

feast was so grand that people thought they had hardly ever seen the like pomp in a poor land. And after Yule Karlsefni disclosed to Erik (Leif) that he wished to marry Gudrid, for it seemed to him, as if he must have the power in this matter. Erik answered favourably, and said that she must follow her fate, and that he had heard nothing but good of him; and it ended so that Thorfinn married Thurid† (Gudrid), and then was the feast extended; and their marriage was celebrated; and this happened at Brattahlid, in the winter.

EXPEDITION TO AND SETTLEMENT IN VIN LAND BY THORFINN KARLSEFNI.

A. D. 1007.

BEGINNING OF THE VINLAND VOYAGE.

In Brattahlid began people to talk much about that Vinland the Good should be explored, and it was said that a voyage thither would be particularly profitable by reason of the fertility of the land; and it went so far that Karlsefni and Snorri made ready their ship to explore the land in the spring. With them went also the before-named men hight Bjarni and Thorhall, with their ship. There was a man hight Thorvard; he married Freydis, a natural daughter of Erik the Red; he went

---

†The daughter of Thorbjorn is sometimes called Thurid and sometimes Gudrid, in this narrative; and the Editor thinks it probable that she was called by the former name during childhood, but that, afterwards, for religious reasons, the pagan name (derived from the God Thor) was laid aside, and that of Gudrid adopted in its place.

also with them, and Thorvald the son of Erik,* and
Thorhall who was called the hunter; he had long been
with Erik, and served him as huntsman in summer and
steward in winter; he was a large man, and strong,
black and like a giant, silent and foul-mouthed in his
speech, and always egged on Erik to the worst; he was
a bad Christian; he was well acquainted with uninhabited parts, he was in the ship with Thorvard and Thorvald. They had the ship which Thorbjorn had brought
out [from Iceland]. They had in all 160 men,† when
they sailed to the western settlement, and from thence
to Bjanney. Then sailed they two days to the south;
then saw they land, and put off boats, and explored the
land, and found there great flat stones, many of which
were 12 ells broad; foxes were there. They gave the
land a name, and called it Helluland.‡ Then sailed they
two days, and turned from the south to the southeast,
and found a land covered with wood, and many wild
beasts upon it; an island lay there out from the land to
the south-east; there killed they a bear, and called the
place afterwards Bear Island, but the land Markland.
Thence sailed they far to the southward along the land,
and came to a ness; the land lay upon the right; there

---

*Here is again evidently some confusion of names, as Thorvald Erik-
son's death has been previously related in the Saga of Erik the Red, and
Karlsefni was now married to his widow Gudrid; it seems probable that
some other Thorvald accompanied Karlsefne on this voyage.

†Literally "40 men and a hundred" [40 manna oh hundrad] but the
great or long hundred must be understood, consisting of 12 decades, or 120.
Antiq. Amer. p. 137, note b. Thus Tegner, describing the drinking hall of
Frithiof: Not five hundred men (though ten twelves you count to the
hundred), could fill that wide hall, when they gathered to banquet at Yule.

‡The whole of the northern coast of America, west of Greenland, was
called by the ancient Icelandic geographers *Helluland it Mikla*, or Great
Helluland; and the island of Newfoundland simply Helluland, or *Litla
Helluland*.

were long and sandy strands. They rowed to land, and found there upon the ness the keel of a ship, and called the place Kjalarness, and the strands they called Furdu-strands for it was long to sail by them. Then became the land indented with coves; they ran the ship into a cove. King Olaf Tryggvason had given Leif two Scotch people, a man hight Haki, and a woman hight Hekja; they were swifter than beasts. These people were in the ship with Karlsefni; but when they had sailed past Furdustrands, then set they the Scots on shore, and bade them run to the southward of the land, and explore its qualities, and come back again within three days. They had a sort of clothing which they called kjafal, which was so made that a hat was on the top, and it was open at the sides, and no arms to it; fastened together between the legs, with buttons and clasps, but in other places it was open. They staid away the appointed time, but when they came back, the one had in the hand a bunch of grapes, and the other a new sown ear of wheat;* these went on board the ship, and after that sailed they farther. They sailed into a frith; there lay an island before it, round which there were strong currents, there-fore called they it Stream island. There were so many eider ducks on the island that one could scarcely walk in consequence of the eggs. They called the place Stream-frith. They took their cargo from the ship, and prepared to remain there. They had with them all sorts of cattle. The country there was very beautiful. They

---

*Hveitiax nysaid. This was, no doubt, the maize or Indian corn,—the "fruges non seminatas" of Adam of Bremen,—which, as well as beans, pumpkins, and squashes, were found growing in the State of Massachusetts, when first visited by the whites.

undertook nothing but to explore the land. They were there for the winter without having provided food beforehand. In the summer the fishing declined, and they were badly off for provisions; then disappeared Thorhall the huntsman. They had previously made prayers to God for food, but it did not come so quick as they thought their necessities required. They searched after Thorhall for three days, and found him on the top of a rock; there he lay, and looked up in the sky, and gaped both with nose and mouth, and murmured something; they asked him why he had gone there; he said it was no business of theirs; they bade him come home with them, and he did so. Soon after, came there a whale, and they went thither, and cut it up, and no one knew what sort of whale it was; and when the cooked dresesd it then ate they, and all became ill in consequence. Then said Thorhall: "The red bearded was more helpful than your Christ; this have I got now for my verses that I sung of Thor, my protector; seldom has he deserted me." But when they came to know this, they cast the whole whale into the sea, and resigned their case to God. Then the weather improved, and it was possible to row out fishing, and they were not then in want of provisions, for wild beasts were caught on the land, and fish in the sea, and eggs collected on the island.

In the account of these transactions, given in the Saga of Erik the Red, it is stated that a son was born to Gudrid during this autumn (1007); which statement is corroborated in a subsequent part of the present narrative The child was called Snorre, and from this first of European

blood born in America, the celebrated sculptor Thorvald-
son, as well as many other eminent Scandinavians, is
lineally descended.

OF KARLSEFNI AND THORHALL.

So is said, that Thorhall would go to the northward
along Furdustrands, to explore Vinland, but Karlsefni
would go southwards along the coast. Thorhall got
ready, out under the island, and there were no more together than nine men; but all the others went with Karlsefni. Now when Thorhall bore water to his ship, and
drank, then sung he this song:—

> People told me when I came
> Hither, all would be so fine;
> The good Vinland, known to fame,
> Rich in fruits, and choicest wine;
> Now the water pail they send;
> To the fountain I must bend,
> Nor from out this land divine
> Have I quaffed one drop of wine.

And when they were ready, and hoisted sail, then
chaunted Thorhall:—

> Let our trusty band
> Haste to Fatherland;
> Let our vessel brave,
> Plough the angry wave,
> While those few who love
> Vinland, here may rove,
> Or, with idle toil,
> Feted whales may boil,
> Here on Furdustrans
> Far from fatherland.

After that sailed they northwards past Furdustrands, and Kjalarness, and would cruise to the westward; then came against them a strong west wind, and they were driven away to Ireland, and were there beaten, and made slaves, according to what the merchants have said.

Now is to be told about Karlsefni, that he went to the southward along the coast, and Snorri and Bjarne, with their people. They sailed a long time, and until they came to a river which ran out from the land and through a lake, out into the sea. It was very shallow, and one could not enter the river without high water. Karlsefni sailed, with his people, into the mouth, and they called the place Hop. They found there upon the land self-sown fields of wheat, there where the ground was low, but vines there where it rose somewhat. Every stream there was full of fish. They made holes there where the land commenced, and the waters rose highest; and when the tide fell there were secured fish in the holes. There were a great number of all kinds of wild beasts in the woods. They remained there a half month, and amused themselves, and did not perceive anything [new]; they had their cattle with them. And one morning early, when they looked around, saw they a great many canoes, and poles were swung upon them, and it sounded like the wind in a straw stack, and the swinging was with the sun. Then said Karlsefni: "What may this denote?" Snorri Thorbrandson answered him: "It may be that this is a sign of peace, so let us take a white shield and hold it towards them;" and so they did. Upon this the others rowed towards them, and looked with wonder upon those that they met, and went up upon the land. These people were black, and ill favoured, and had coarse hair on the head; they had large eyes and broad cheeks. They remained there for a time, and gazed upon those that they met, and rowed, afterwards, away to the southward, round the ness.

Karlsefni and his people had made their dwellings above the lake, and some of the houses were near the water, others more distant. Now were they there for the winter; there came no snow, and all their cattle fed themselves on the grass. But when spring approached, saw they one morning early that a number of canoes rowed from the south round the ness; so many, as if the sea was sowen with coal; poles were also swung on each boat. Karlsefni and his people then raised up the shield, and when they came together, they began to barter; and these people would rather have red cloth [than anything else]; for this they had to offer skins and real furs. They would also purchase swords and spears, but this Karlsefni and Snorri forbade. For an entire fur skin the Skrellings took a piece of red cloth, a span long, and bound it round their heads. Thus went on their traffic for a time; then the cloth began to fall short among Karlsefni and his people, and they cut it asunder into small pieces, which were not wider than the breadth of a finger, and still the Skrellings gave just as much for that as before, and more.

The Saga of Erik the Red, in giving an account of this transaction, adds that Karlsefni, on the cloth being expended, hit upon the expedient of making the women take out milk porridge to the Skrellings, who, as soon as they saw this new article of commerce would buy the porridge and nothing else. "Thus," says the Saga, "the traffic of the Skrellings was wound up by their bearing away their purchases in their stomachs, but Karlsefni and his companions retained their goods and skins."

It happened that a bull, which Karlsefni had, ran out from the wood and roared aloud; this frightened the Skrellings, and they rushed to their canoes, and rowed away to the southward, round the coast; after that they were not seen for three entire weeks. But at the end of that time a great number of Skrellings boats' were seen coming from the south like a rushing torrent; all the poles were turned from the sun, and they all howled very loud. Then took Karlsefni's people a red shield, and held it towards them. The Skrellings jumped out of their ships, and after this went they against each other and fought. There was a sharp shower of weapons, for the Skrellings had slings. Karlsefni's people saw that they raised up on a pole an enormous large ball, something like a sheep's paunch, and of a blue colour; this swung they from the pole over Karlsefni's men, upon the ground, and it made a frightful crash as it fell down. This caused great alarm to Karlsefni and all his people, so that they thought of nothing but running away, and they fell back along the river, for it appeared to them that the Skrellings pressed upon them from all sides; and they did not stop until they came to some rocks, where they made a stout resistance. Freydis came out and saw that Karlsefni's people fell back, and she cried out: "Why do ye run, stout men as ye are, before these miserable wretches, whom I thought ye would knock down like cattle? and if I had weapons, methinks I could fight better than any of ye." They gave no heed to her words. Freydis would go with them, but she was slower, because she was pregnant; however she followed after them into the wood. The Skrellings pursued her; she found a dead man before her; it was Thorbrand Snorrason, and there stood a flat stone stuck in his head; the sword lay naked by his side; this took she up, and prepared to defend herself. Then came the Skrellings towards her; she drew out her breasts from under her clothes, and dashed them against the naked sword; by this the Skrellings became frightened, and ran off to their ships, and rowed away. Karlsefni and his people then came up, and praised her courage. Two men fell on Karlsefni's side, but a number of the Skrellings. Karlsefni's band was overmatched, and they now drew home to their dwellings, and bound their wounds; and they thought over what crowd that could have been. which had pressed upon them from the land side, and it now appeared to them that it could scarcely have been real people from the ships, but that these must have been optical illusions. The Skrellings found also a dead man, and an axe lay by him; one of them took up the axe, and cut wood with it, and now one after another did the same, and thought it was an excellent thing, and bit well; after that one took it, and cut at a stone, so that the axe broke, and then thought they it was of no use, because it would not cut stone, and they threw it away.

Karlsefni and his people now thought they saw that although the land had many good qualities, still would they be always exposed there to the fear of hostilities from the earlier inhabitants. They proposed, therefore, to depart, and return to their own country. They sailed northwards along the coast, and found five Skrellings clothed in skins, sleeping near the sea. They had with them vessels containing animal marrow mixed with blood. Karlsefni's people thought they understood that these men had been banished from the land; they killed them. After that came they to a ness, and many wild beasts were there, and the ness was covered all over with dung, from the beasts which had lain there during the night. Now came they back to Straumfjord, and there was abundance of everything that they wanted to have. *It is some mens say, that Bjarne and Gudrid remained behind, and 100 men with them, and did not go further; but that Karlsefni and Snorri went southwards, and 40 men with them, and were not longer in Hope than barely two months, and, the same summer, came back.* Karlsefne went then with one ship to seek after Thorhall the hunter, but the rest remained behind, and they sailed northwards past Kjalarness, and thence westwards, and the land was upon their larboard hand; there were wild woods over all, as far as they could see, and scarcely any open places. And when they had long sailed, a river fell out of the land from east to west; they put in to the mouth of the river, and lay by its southern bank.

DEATH OF THORVALD ERIKSON.

It happened one morning that Karlsefni and his people saw, opposite an open place in the wood, a speck which glistened in their sight, and they shouted out towards it, and it was a uniped, which thereupon hurried down to the bank of the river where they lay. Thorvald Erikson stood at the helm, and the uniped shot an arrow into his bowels. Thorvald drew out the arrow, and said: "It has killed me!—to a fruitful land have we come, but hardly shall we enjoy any benefit from it." Thorvald soon after died of this wound. Upon this the uniped ran away to the northward; Karlsefni and his people went after him, and saw him now and then, and the last time they saw him, he ran out into a bay. ˉ

They drew off then, and to the northward, and thought they saw the country of the unipeds, they would not expose their people any longer. They looked upon the mountain range that was at Hope; and that which they now found, as all one, and it also appeared to be equal length from Straumfjord to both places. The third winter were they in Straumfjord. They now became much divided by party feeling, and the women were the cause of it, for those who were unmarried would injure those that were married, and hence arose great disturbance. There was born the first autumn, Snorri, Karlsefni's son, and he was three years old when they went away. When they sailed from Vinland they had a south wind, and came then to Markland, and found there five Skrælings, and one was bearded; two were females, and two boys; they took the boys, but the others escaped, and the Skrellings sank down in the ground. These two boys took they with them; they taught them the language, and they were baptized. They called their mother Vathelldi and their father Uvæge. They said that two kings ruled over the Skrellings, and that one of them was hight Avalldania, but the other Valldidida. They said that no houses were there; people lay in caves or in holes. They said there was a land on the other side, just opposite their country, where people lived who wore white clothes, and carried poles before them, and to these were fastened flags, and they shouted loud; and people think that this was White-man's-Land, or Great Ireland.

Bjarne Grimolfson was driven with his ship into the Irish ocean, and they came into a worm-sea, and straightway began the ship to sink under them. They had a boat which was smeared with seal oil, for the sea-worms do not attack that; they went into the boat, and then saw that it could not hold them all; then said Bjarne: "Since the boat cannot give room to more than the half of our men, it is my counsel that lots should be drawn, for those to go in the boat, for it shall not be according to rank." This thought they all so high-minded an offer that no one would speak against it; they then did so that lots were drawn, and it fell upon Bjarne to go in the boat, and the half of the men with him, for the boat had not room for more. But when they had gotten into the boat, then said an Icelandic man, who was in the ship, and had come with Bjarne from Iceland: "Dost thou intend, Bjarne, to separate from me here?" Bjarne answered:

"So it turns out." Then said the other: "Very different was thy promise to my father, when I went with thee from Iceland, than thus to abandon me, for thou said'st that we should both share the same fate." Bjarne replied: "It shall not be thus; go thou down into the boat, and I will go up into the ship, since I see that thou art so desirous to live." Then went Bjarne up into the ship, but this man down into the boat, and after that continued they their voyage, until they came to Dublin in Ireland, and told there these things; but it is most people's belief that Bjarne and his companions were lost in the worm-sea, for nothing was heard of them since that time.

POSTERITY OF KARLSEFNI AND THURID HIS WIFE.

The next summer went Karlsefni to Iceland, and Gudrid with him, and he went home to Reynisness. His mother thought that he had made a bad match, and therefore was Gudrid not at home the first winter. But when she observed that Gudrid was a distinguished woman, went she home, and they agreed very well together. The daughter of Snorri Karlsefnesson was Hallfrid, mother to Bishop Thorlak Runolfson. They had a son who Thorbjorn hight, his daughter hight Thorunn, mother to Bishop Bjorn. Thorgeir hight the son of Snorri Karlsefnesson, father to Yngvild, mother of Bishop Brand the first. A daughter of Snorri Karlsefnesson was also Steinum, who married Einar, son of Grundarketil, son of Thorvald Krok, the son of Thorer, of Espihol; their son was Thorstein Ranglatr; he was father to Gudrun, who married Jorund of Keldum; their daughter was Halla, mother to Flose, father of Valgerde, mother of Herr Erlend Sterka, father of Herr Hauk the Lagman. Another daughter of Flose was Thordis, mother of Fru Ingigerd the rich; her daughter was Fru Hallbera, Abbess of Stad at Reinisness. Many other great men in Iceland are descended from Karlsefni and Thurid, who are not here mentioned. God be with us! Amen!

VOYAGE OF FREYDIS, HELGI AND FINNBOGI.

A. D. 1011.

FREYDIS CAUSES THE BROTHERS TO BE KILLED.*

Now began people again to talk about expeditions to Vinland, for voyages thereto appeared both profitable and honourable. The same summer that Karlsefni came from Vinland, came also a ship from Norway to Greenland; this ship steered two brothers, Helgi and Finnbogi, and they remained for the winter in Greenland. These brothers were Icelanders by descent, and from Austfjord. It is now to be told that Freydis, Erik's daughter, went from her home at Garde to the brothers Helgi and Finnbogi, and bade them that they should sail to Vinland with their vessels, and go halves with her in all the profits which might be there made. To this

---

*This narrative is contained in the Saga of Erik the Red (Antiq. Amer. p. 65, seq.) but has been transferred to this place, as well to make the chronological order of the various voyages more perspicuous, as on account of the further particulars relating to Karlsefni and Gudrid, with which it concludes.

they agreed. Then went she to Leif her brother, and begged him to give her the houses, which he had caused to be built in Vinland; but he answered the same as before, that he would lend the houses, but not give them. So was it settled between the brothers and Freydis, that each should have thirty fighting men in the ship, besides women. But Freydis broke this agreement, and had five men more, and hid them; so that the brothers knew not of it before they came to Vinland. Now sailed they into the sea, and had before arranged that they should keep together, if it could so be, and there was little difference, but still came the brothers somewhat before, and had taken up their effects to Leif's houses. But when Freydis came to land, then cleared they out their ships, and bore up their goods to the house. Then said Freydis: "Why bring ye in your things here?" "Because we believed," said they, "that the whole agreement should stand good between us." "To me lent Leif the houses," quoth she, "and not to you." Then said Helgi: "In malice are we brothers easily excelled by thee." Now took they out their goods, and made a separate building, and set that building further from the strand, on the edge of a lake, and put all around in good order; but Freydis had trees cut down for her ship's loading. Now began winter, and the brothers proposed to set up sports, and have some amusement. So was done for a time, until evil reports and discord sprung up amongst them, and there was an end of the sports, and nobody came from the one house to the other, and so it went on for a long time during the winter. It happened one morning early that Freydis got up from her bed, and dressed herself, but took no shoes or stockings, and the weather was such that much dew had fallen. She took her husband's cloak, and put it on, and then went to the brothers' house, and to the door; but a man had gone out a little before, and left the door half open. She opened the door, and stood a little time in the opening, and was silent; but Finnbogi lay inside the house, and was awake, and said: "What wilt thou here, Freydis?" She said: "I wish that thou wouldest get up, and go out with me, for I will speak with thee." He did so; they went to a tree that lay near the dwellings, and sat down there. "How art thou satisfied here?" said she; he answered: "Well think I of the land's fruitfulness, but ill do I think of the discord that has sprung up betwixt us, for it appears to me that no cause has been given." "Thou sayest as it is," said she, "and so think I; but my business here with thee, is that I wish to change ships with thy brother, ye have a larger ship than I, and it is my wish to go from hence." "That must I agree to," said he, "if such is thy wish." Now with that they separated; she went home, and Finnbogi to his bed. She got into the bed with cold feet, and thereby woke Thorvard, and he asked why she was so cold and wet. She answered, with much vehemence: "I was gone," said she, "to the brothers, to make a bargain with them about their ship, for I wished to buy the large ship; but they took it so ill that they beat me, and used me shamefully; but thou! miserable man! wilt surely, neither avenge my disgrace nor thine own, and it is easy to see that I am no longer in Greenland, and

233

I will separate from thee if thou avengest not this."
And now could he no longer withstand her reproaches,
and bade his men to get up, with all speed, and take
their arms; and so did they, and went straightway to the
brothers' house, and went in, and fell upon them sleeping, and then took and bound them, and thus led out
one after the other; but Freydis had each of them killed
as he came out. Now were all the men there killed, and
only women remained, and them would no one kill.
Then said Freydis: "Give me an axe!" So was done;
upon which she killed the five women that were there,
and did not stop until they were all dead. Now they
went back to their house after this evil work, and Freydis
did not appear otherwise than as if she had done well,
and spoke thus to her people: "If it be permitted us to
come again to Greenland," said she, "I will take the life
of that man who tells of this business; now should we
say this, that they remained behind when we went
away." Now early in the spring made they ready the
ship that had belonged to the brothers, and loaded it
with all the best things they could get, and the ship
could carry. After that they put to sea, and had a quick
voyage, and came to Eriksfjord with the ship early in the
summer. Now Karlsefni was there, and had his ship
quite ready for sea, and waited for a fair wind; and it is
generally said, that no richer ship has ever gone from
Greenland tha nthat which he steered.

OF FREYDIS.

Freydis repaired now to her dwelling, which, in the meantime, had stood uninjured; she gave great gifts to all her companions, that they should conceal her misdeeds and sat down now in her house. All were not, however, so mindful of their promises to conceal their crimes and wickedness but that it came out at last. Now finally it reached the ears of Leif, her brother, and he thought very ill of the business. Then took Leif three men of Freydis's band and tortured them to confess the whole occurrence, and all their statements agreed. "I like not," said Leif, "to do that to Freydis, my sister, which she has deserved, but this I will predict, that thy posterity will never thrive." Now the consequence was, that no one, from that time thought otherwise than ill of them.

Now must we begin from the time when Karlsefni got ready his ship, and put to sea; he had a prosperous voyage, and came safe and sound to Norway, and remained there for the winter and sold his goods, and both he and his wife were held in great honor by the most respectable men in Norway. But the spring after, fitted he out his ship for Iceland; and when he was all ready, and his ship lay at the bridge, waiting for a fair wind, then came there a southern to him, who was from Bremen in Saxony, and wanted to buy from Karlsefni his house broom. "I will not sell it," said he. "I will give thee a half mark gold for it," said the German. Karlsefni thought this was a good offer, and they closed the bargain. The southern went off with the house broom, but Karlsefni knew not what wood it was; but that was mausur, brought from Vinland. Now Karlsefni put to sea, and came with his ship to Skagafjord, on the northern coast, and there was the ship laid up for the winter. But in spring bought he Glaumbæland, and fixed his dwelling there, and lived there, and was a highly respected man, and from him and Gudrid his wife has sprung a numerous and distinguished race. And when Karlsefni was dead, took Gudrid the management o fthe house with her son Snorri, who was born in Vinland. But when Snorri was married, then went Gudrid abroad, and travelled southwards, and came back again to the house of Snorri her son, and then had he caused a church to be built at Glaumbæ. After this, became Gudrid a nun and recluse, and remained so whilst she lived. Snorri had a son who Thorgeir hight; he was father to Ingveld, mother of Bishop Brand. The daughter of Snorri Karlsefnesson hight Hallfrid; she was mother to Runolf, father to Bishop Thorlak. Bjorn hight a son of Karlsefni and Gudrid; he was father to Thorunn, mother of Bishop Bjarn. A numerous race are descended from Karlsefni, and distinguished men; and Karlsefni has accurately related to all men the occurrences on all these voyages, of which somewhat is now recited here.

GEOGRAPHICAL NOTICES

IN ANCIENT ICELANDIC MSS.

B.—FRAGMENT OF VELLUM CODEX, No. 192.
Supposed to have been written about the end of the 14th Century.

NEXT to Denmark is the lesser Sweden, then is Oeland, then Gottland, then Helsingeland, then Vermeland, and the two Kvendlands, which lie to the north of Bjarmeland. From Bjarmeland stretches uninhabited land towards the north, until Greenland begins. South of Greenland is Helluland; next lies Markland; thence it is not far to Vinland the Good, which some think goes out from Africa; and if it be so, the sea must run in between Vinland and Markland. It is related that Thorfinn Karlsefni cut wood here to ornament his house, and went afterwards to seek out Vinland the Good, and came there, where they thought the land was, but did not effect the knowledge of it, and gained none of the riches of the land. Leif the Lucky first discovered Vinland, and then he met some merchants in distress, at sea, and by God's mercy saved their lives; and he introduced Christianity into Greenland, and it spread itself there, so that a Bishop's seat was established in the place called Gardar. England and Scotland are an island, and yet each is a kingdom for itself. Ireland is a great island. Iceland is also a great island north of Ireland. These countries are all in that part of the world which is called Europe.

237

C. GRIPLA.*

Codex No. 115.

Bavaria is bounded by Saxony; Saxony is bounded by Holstein, then comes Denmark; the sea flows through the eastern countries. Sweden lies to the east of Denmark, Norway to the north; Finmark north of Norway; thence stretches the land out to the north-east and east, until you come to Bjarmeland; this land is tributary to Gardarige. From Bjarmeland lie uninhabited places all northward to that land which is called Greenland, [*which, however, the Greenlanders do not confirm, but believe to have observed that it is otherwise, both from drift timber, which it is known is cut down by men, and also from Reindeer, which have marks upon the ears, or bands upon the horns, likewise from sheep, which stray thither, of which there now are remains in Norway, for one head hangs in Throndhjem, another in Bergen, and many more besides are to be found.*] But there are bays, and the land stretches out toward the southwest; there are Jokels and Fjords; there lie islands out before the Jokels; one of the Jokels cannot be explored; to the other is half a month's sail, to the third a week's sail; this is nearest to the settlement hight Hvidserk; thence stretches the land toward the north; but he who wishes not to miss the settlement, steers to the south-west. Gardar hight the Bishop's seat at the bottom of Eriksfjord; there is a

---

*This remarkable geographical fragment is contained in the celebrated Greenlandic collection of Bjorn Johnson, and was evidently written before the time of Columbus. The name is supposed to be derived from the word *gripa*, to snatch, the collection being of a miscellaneous character. Antiq. Amer. pp. 280-1.

church dedicated to the holy Nicholas; XII churches are upon Greenland in the eastern settlement, IIII in the western.

Now is to be told what lies opposite Greenland, out from the bay, which was before named: Furdustrandir hight a land; there are so strong frosts that it is not habitable, so far as one knows; south from thence is Helluland, which is called Skrellingsland; from thence it is not far to Vinland the Good, which some think goes out from Africa; between Vinland and Greenland is Ginnungagap, which flows from the sea called Mare oceanum, and surrounds the whole earth [*Hæc verbotenus Gripla.*]

MONUMENTS AND INSCRIPTIONS.

THE DIGHTON WRITING ROCK.

SOME remarkable monuments and inscriptions have been found on the eastern shores of North America, which bear testimony to the voyages and settlements recorded in the preceding narratives, and complete the mass of evidence that has been so ably brought forward by Professor Rafn, upon this interesting subject. The Rhode Island Historical Society have applied themselves to the examination of these remains, with a degree of zeal and ability worthy of the occasion, and details of high interest and value have been made known to the corresponding Danish members, through the medium of the distinguished American secretary, Dr. Webb. From these communications it appears that in the western part of the county of Bristol in the State of Massachusetts may still be seen numerous and extensive mounds, similar to the tumuli that are so often met with in Scandinavia, Tartary, and Russia; "also the remains of fortifications that must have required for their construction a degree of industry, labour, and skill, as well as an advancement in the arts, that never characterized any of the Indian tribes. Various articles of pottery are found in them, with the method of manufacturing which they were entirely unacquainted. But above all, many rocks, inscribed with unknown characters, apparently of very ancient origin, have been discovered scattered through different parts of the country: rocks, the constituent parts of which are such as to render it almost impossible to engrave on them such writings without the aid of iron, or other hard metallic instrument. The Indians were ignorant of the existence of these rocks; and the manner of working with iron they learned from the Europeans, after the settlement of the country by the English."

Of such remains, the most important that has yet been discovered is the Assonet rock, or "Dighton writing rock," which is thus described in the Report of a Committee that was appointed by the Rhode Island Historical Society, to examine and report upon this remarkable stone, and who visited it in the month of February, 1830:—

"It is situated six and a half miles south of Taunton, on the east side of Taunton river, a few feet from the shore, and on the west side of Assonet neck, in the town of Berkely, county of Bristol, and Commonwealth of

240

Massachusetts; although, probably from the fact of its being generally visited from the other side of the river, which is in Dighton, it has always been known by the name of the 'Dighton Writing Rock.' It faces northwest, towards the bed of the river, and is covered by the water two or three feet at the highest, and is left ten or twelve feet from it at the lowest tides: it is also completely immersed twice in twenty-four hours. The rock does not occur *in situ,* but shews indubitable evidence of having occupied the spot where it now rests, since the period of that great and extensive disruption, which was followed by the transportation of immense boulders to, and a deposit of them in places at a vast distance from their original beds. It is a mass of well characterized fine grained *greywacke.* Its true colour, as exhibited by a fresh fracture, is a bluish grey. There is no rock in the immediate neighbourhood that would at all answer as a substitute for the purpose for which the one bearing the inscription was selected, as they are aggregates of the large conglomerate variety. Its face, measured at the base, is eleven feet and a half; and in height, it is a little rising five feet. The upper surface forms, with the horizon, an inclined plane of about sixty degrees. The whole of the face is covered, to within a few inches of the ground, with unknown hieroglyphics. There appears little or no method in the arrangement of them. The lines are from half an inch to an inch in width; and in depth sometimes one-third of an inch, though generally very superficial. They were, inferring from the rounded elevations, and intervening depressions, picked in upon the rock, and not chiselled or smoothly cut out. The marks of human power, and manual labour are indelibly stamped upon it. No one who examines attentively the workmanship, will believe it to have been done by the Indians. Moreover, it is a well attested fact, that nowhere, throughout our wide-spread domain, is there a single instance of their recording, or having recorded, their deeds or history on stone."

This remarkable monument had long been an object of interest to American antiquaries, and several drawings and examinations were made of the rock and inscription, at various periods, beginning in the year 1680, but without any satisfactory result; and it remained for Professors Finn Magnusen and Rafn to shew that the whole was a *Runic inscription,* containing various cryptographs, and rude combinations of figures illustrative of the settlements of the Northmen, among which devices may be yet traced the name of THORFINN, and the figures CXXXI. being the number of Karlsefni's associates (151),* which after the departure of Thorhall, accompanied him to Hope.†

---

*Twelve decades being reckoned to the hundred, hence, called by the Icelanders and Scandinavians *stort hundrad* (great hundred). Antiq. Amer. p. 385, ante, p. 88, note*.

†See ante, p. 93. Professor Rafn has gone into an elaborate dissertation upon this inscription, proving by unanswerable arguments its Scandinavian origin. (Antiq. Amer. p. 378, seq.) In this he is fully borne out by the eminent Runologist Finn Magnusen, who shews that the whole of the apparently unmeaning hieroglyphics are illustrative of the Icelandic settlement in Hope :—The well known Runic letter p (Th) on the left hand, at once stamps its Scandinavian or Icelandic origin ; the combined letters which follow the numerals may be decyphered N. M. the initials of norronir menn (Northmen) ; the devices above this, represent the shields (p. 95), under which lies a helmet reversed, indicative of peace. The figure below the name may be intended for a bullock, or some domestic animal, illustrative of their daily pursuits,—the outline of a ship is blended with these ; —the figures of Gudrid and her child Snorri appear on the right ; Karlsefni, protected by a shield from the attacks of the Skrellings, upon the left, while the bows, and missiles of their assailants, more particularly the large ball

A perspective representation of this remarkable rock, together with fac-similes of the several drawings that have been made of the inscription, ending with the most recent and accurate, made by the Committee of the Rhode Island Historical Society in 1830, are appended to the Antiquitates Americanæ; and the analogy between these and inscriptions which have been found both in Sweden and Iceland is shewn by contiguous representations of the Scandinavian remains. The same plate contains also the delineation of a curious fragment of metallic *tessera,* found near Dublin, upon which is inscribed a monogram similar to that seen upon the Assonet Rock, as well as the Runic letter p (th), shewing the Scandinavian origin of the fragment, which may be ascribed to the 9th or 10th century.

The Rhode Island Historical Society have also forwarded to Professor Rafn descriptions and delineations of several other remains which bear a striking analogy to that at Dighton; among these the Portsmouth and Tiverton Rocks form interesting subjects for examination and comparison.*

---

mentioned on page 98, are clearly discernible. Altogether the analogy which this inscription presents to those upon well known Runic monuments —the facility with which the various devices may be made to apply to the incidents and circumstances connected with the Icelandic settlement, and the distinct Roman or Latin letters which form the numerals—leave no reasonable doubt as to its being the work of the Northmen.

*Since the publication of the Antiquitates Americanæ, a still further addition to American monuments has been discovered in the neighborhood of Bahia, as appears from a communication made to the Royal Society of Northern Antiquaries by Dr. Lund, one of its members, residing at Lagoa Santa in Brazil:—It appears, on the authority of a Journal published by a Society lately established at Rio Janeiro, under the name of *Instituto Historico Braziliero,* that the remains of an ancient city, built of hewn stone, have been recently discovered in the neighborhood of Bahia, and that Professor Schuck, one of the members of the Institution, guided by Professor Rafn's work, has deduced from the inscriptions, the Scandinavian origin of these remains. Among the ruins is stated to be a huge column, bearing a remarkable figure, which stretches out the right hand, and points with the fore-finger towards the north pole.

RUNIC STONE AT KINGIKTORSOAK.

BUT traces of the adventurous spirit, and early voyages of the Northmen are to be found in much higher, and far less inviting latitudes, shewing the progress of their course through regions, which even in the present age of high scientific advancement, and maritime enterprise, have tested, and not unfrequently baffled the skill and hardihood of our most distinguished navigators.

In the year 1824, a remarkable Runic stone was found upon the island of Kingiktorsoak, lying in 72° 55′ north latitude and 56° 5′ west longitude.

The following is a representation of this remarkable monument which was transported to Copenhagen, and found on examination, to present a complete inscription in Runic characters:—

which in modern Icelandic orthography would run thus:—

ELLIGR · SIGVATHS : SON : R · OK : BJANNE : TOR-
TARSON : OK : ENRITHI · ODSSON : LAUKARDAK : IN :
FYRIRGAKNDAG HLOTHU ·VARDATE ·OKRYDU :MCXXXV.

or

Erling Sighvatsson and Biarni Thordarsson, and Ein-drid Oddsson, on the seventh day,* before the day of Victory,† erected these stones, and explored. MCXXXV. *1,135*

Some doubts have been expressed by Runic scholars as to the signification of the characters representing the date, but the peculiar formation of the Runes, and other unerring indications shew that the inscription cannot be later than the 12th century.

It appears from various Icelandic documents given in Professor Rafn's work, that the Northmen had two principal stations in the Arctic regions, the one called Greipar, lying immediately south of the island of Disco, in Davis' Straits, and the other called Kroksfjardarheidi, situated on the north-side of Lancaster's sound. Their general name for these regions was Nordrsetur, to which vessels were dispatched from Greenland for the purpose of carrying on the operations of hunting and fishing. But voyages of discovery were also made in this direction; and a clear account of such an expedition, under-taken in the year 1266, follows the narratives which have been given in the preceding pages. It is contained in a letter addressed by a clergyman named Halldor, to a brother ecclesiastic named Arnold, who, after having lived in Greenland, had become chaplain to king Magnus Lagabæter in Norway; and the voyage appears to have been made under the auspices of some clergymen of the

---

*Saturday, Dies Saturni.

†A festival kept by the Northmen previous to the 12th century; it fell on the 25th of April.

Bishopric of Gardar in Greenland. The object of the expedition is stated to have been, to explore regions lying more to the northward than those which they had been hitherto accustomed to frequent, consequently further north than Lancaster's sound. They sailed from Kroksfjardarheidi, but meeting with southerly winds, and thick weather, were obliged to let the vessel run before the wind; on the fogs clearing off they descried several islands, and saw many seals, whales, and bears. They penetrated into the innermost part of the gulf, and saw icebergs lying to the southward, as far as the eye could reach; they observed traces of the Skrælings having inhabited these regions in former times, but were unable to land, in consequence of the bears. They, therefore, went about, and sailed back for three days, when they again found traces of the Esquimaux, upon some islands lying to the southward of a mountain, which they call Snæfell. After this, on St. James's Day (25th July), they proceeded southwards, a long day's rowing (einn mikin dagrodr). It froze during the night, but the sun was above the horizon both night and day; and "it was not higher when on the meridian than that when a man lay across a six oared boat, towards the gunwale, the shade of that side of the boat which was nearest the sun fell on his face; but at midnight was it as high as at home in the settlement, when it is in the northwest." The expedition afterwards returned to Gardar.

These observations are of course very loose and uncertain; the relative depth of the man's position with regard to the gunwale of the boat, would be necessary in order to be able to make anything of the first observation, and the result of the other can only be deduced by presuming the day of the summer solstice to be implied. This, however, is not an unreasonable supposition, more particularly when we find so many other circumstances corroborative of the locality which is thence determined, and Professor Rafn, proceeding upon this assumption, draws out the following result:—

"In the 13th century, on the 25th July, the
    Sun's declination was 17° 54′ North
    Inclination of the Ecliptic, 23° 32′."

If we now assume that the colony, and particularly the episcopal seat of Gardar, was situated on the north side of Igaliko frith, where the ruins of a large church, and of many other buildings, indicate the site of a principal settlement of the ancient colony, consequently in 60° 55′ N. lat. then at the summer solstice, the height of the sun there, when in the N. W. was 3° 40′, which is equivalent to the midnight altitude of the sun on St. James's day (25th July) in the parallel of 75° 46′." Now the parallel of 75° 46′ north latitude, would fall to the northward of Wellington Channel, the highest latitude reached by Parry in his most favourable expedition in search of a North-west passage; and the description of the land seen, and objects met with on the voyage, corresponds well with the characteristics of these regions, as given by the distinguished English navigator. The Northmen sail from Kroksfjardarheidi, a name implying a frith bounded by barren highlands (heidi), and known to be on the north side of Lancaster's sound; this frith must have been of considerable extent, as *three days sailing* are specifically mentioned in that part of the narrative describing their return;—they descry several islands, and meet with many seals, whales, and bears;—they see icebergs lying to the southward, as far as the eye can reach; —they observe traces of the Esquimaux (Skrælings) in various directions; the sun was above the horizon both night and day, and although in the month of July, it froze during the night. There is little doubt, therefore, that these early explorers of the arctic regions, starting from Lancaster's sound, were driven through Barrow's straits, and Wellington Channel, into the Polar sea, from whence they saw the North Georgian Islands, and where they naturally fell in with a multitude of seals, whales, and bears.

It is a startling conclusion, and somewhat mortifying to national pride, to find that these simple navigators of the 13th century, in their humble barks, rivalled the most distinguished arctic explorers of the present day; but however unwilling we may be to admit the evidence of a progress in maritime discovery, which tends to dim the lustre of our own enterprising age, the simple documents in support of these early voyages carry a degree of conviction to the mind which disarms scepticism, and compels us to admit their credibility.

It is a great mistake, however, to suppose that the Northmen of this period were altogether ignorant of astronomical science, and still greater, as some writers have done, to confound them with the Vikings or Pirates of a more barbarous age. The discoverers of America were Merchants, their ships were called trading ships [Kaupskip]; sea-roving had been almost altogether discontinued by the Northmen before the voyages of Bjarne Herjulfson and the descendants of Erik; and all the expeditions which are related in these Sagas were undertaken either for the purposes of discovering new countries, or making settlements in, or trading with, countries that had been already discovered. In the ancient Icelandic work called Rimbegla, which has been before quoted, many rules are given for the measurement of time, the study of astronomy, geometry, etc., and although these are probably translations or compilations from foreign works, they correspond with what the Icelandic clergy taught their people, after the introduction of Christianity. Among these are found scientific rules for finding the course of the sun, moon, and stars, also the division of time thereon depending; information respecting the astronomical quadrant, and its proper use; different methods for ascertaining the spherical figure of the earth; the longitude and latitude of places, and of calculating their distances from each other; the sun's declination; the earth's magnitude and circumference, the times when the ocean could best be navigated, etc.

Early in the eleventh century (1018-1026) the rich chieftain Raudulf, of Oesterdal, in Norway, taught his son Sigurd the science of computing the course of the sun and moon, and other visible celestial bodies, and particularly to know the stars which mark the lapse of time, that he might be able to ascertain the time both by day and by night, when neither the sun nor moon was visible. Even in heathen times we have similar accounts of Icelandic chieftains and their sons, nay even of simple peasants, who paid sedulous attention to the motions of the heavenly bodies, in order from thence to ascertain the true lapse of time; also of their belief in astrology, which was intimately connected with old Scandinavian mythology. Olaus Magnus said that in his time (about 1520) it was generally acknowledged in Sweden that the common people in ancient times had more knowledge of the stars than they possessed in his days.

Some idea may be formed of the character and acquirements of the Scandinavian merchants in the 11th and 12th centuries from the Speculum Regale, a work written in the latter period. Here the merchant is exhorted to make himself acquainted with the laws of all countries, especially those regarding commerce and navigation, as well as with foreign languages, particularly the Italian and Latin, which were then in more general use. He was also enjoined to obtain a complete knowledge of the places and motions of the heavenly bodies, the times of the day, the division of the horizon according to the cardinal and minor points, the movement of the sea, the climates, the seasons best adapted for navigation, the equipping and rigging of vessels, arithmetical calculation, etc. Moreover, to distinguish himself by a becoming and decorous way of living, both as to moral conduct, manners, and attire, etc.: and thus it may be safely inferred that the better educated of the northern merchants in the tenth and eleventh centuries were not so inferior to their southern neighbours, as may be generally supposed.

The extended voyages and commercial intercourse of the Northmen must have also contributed to the amelioration of their habits and character. From the 8th to the 11th centuries they carried on a more active commerce, and a more extensive maritime communication with foreign countries than any other nation in Europe. Such intercourse appears quite incompatible with that extreme degree of ignorance and barbarity in which so many writers would clothe all their actions and enterprises. England, Ireland, Italy, Sicily, France, Spain—were visited by these daring adventurers; true, in the character, and with the spirit, for the most part, of reckless invaders, but that they should have continued to return from such enterprises without exhibiting some modification of that ferocity, which might be expected to yield to the salutary influence of association with more civilized countries, seems scarcely credible. Their long continued intercourse of more than 200 years, with Ireland alone, a country which in the 8th century enjoyed a European reputation for intellectual eminence,* cannot but have had a beneficial influence upon their character and habits, and we should receive with caution all state-

---

*"In the 8th century, indeed, the high reputation of the Irish for scholarship had become established throughout Europe." Moore, Vol. I, p. 289. "As Druidism fell into disrepute, Christian seminaries multiplied . . . Soon after the first foundation, we read of a most noble city and seminary founded at Clonard near the Boyne. In the days of St. Finanus, A. D. 500, we it to contain no less than 3000 scholars, among whom were some of the first eminence for piety and learning. Colgan calls it a repository of all knowledge. . . . About the same time, the academy of Ross, called Ross-Ailithri, in the county of Cork, was formed by St. Fachanus, as Ware notes, and Hanmer, in his Chronicle, tells us that here St. Brandan taught the liberal arts. . . . The schools of Clonfert, Bangor, Rathene, Cashel, etc., were not less remarkable. . . . "

ments upon a subject to which national or religious feeling is likely to have given an exaggerated colouring. Our knowledge of the excesses of the northern invaders is chiefly derived from the evidence of monkish chroniclers, whose Christian faith and feelings were no less outraged by the deeds than the infidelity of the Pagan ravagers, and who writing in many cases long after the events, would naturally aid defective evidence with a fervid zeal and fertile imagination. The particular periods, also, and tribes to which this brutal ferocity of the Northmen is referred, should be more clearly distinguished. The peaceful Norwegian settlers in Iceland, for instance, in the 9th century were very different from those fierce invaders, who, in the same age, shook the kingdoms of Edmund and of Alfred to their centre, and committed barbarities which have called forth the just animadversions of the distinguished historian of the Anglo-Saxons. Flying from the despotic rule of Harald Haarfager, the Norwegian emigrants sought peace and freedom in a remote and sterile island, where the labours of the field, and the trading intercourse necessary to their isolated position were relieved by the relaxation of innocent domestic reunions, and intellectual pursuits; and although some ardent spirit, greedy of fame or plunder, or stimulated by the more honourable ambition of acquiring knowledge and experience by intercourse with foreign lands, might occasionally join the fierce band of the reckless viking, the voyages of the Icelandic Northmen were almost exclusively confined to trade, or discovery, or the formation of peaceful settlements on those

252

shores, which their own enterprise, perseverance, and skill had opened to their connection.

It may, perhaps, be urged in disparagement of the early voyagers in the Polar Seas, that the seasons were then more favourable to arctic discoveries than they have been in later ages, and that therefore the difficulties encountered by modern navigators were unknown to their predecessors; but the popular belief of a milder and more genial climate having formerly prevailed in Europe, is not supported by any satisfactory evidence: indeed the opinions of scientific enquirers would lead to a directly opposite conclusion, and there is, at least, every reason to believe that the periodical changes, which so often call forth complaints, and retrospective comparisons from the aged and infirm, respecting the altered condition of the seasons in the present day, were not less frequent or severe in those favoured periods on which their praises are bestowed.

The supposed settlement on the eastern coast of Greenland (Eystribygd), now nearly inaccessible, has tended to give currency to the popular notion of a less rigorous climate prevailing in those regions, at the period of the Icelandic emigration to that coast, but the able and arduous investigation of Captain Graah has dispelled that illusion, and there is now little doubt that the so called *eastern settlement* extended little further than the south-eastern point of the Greenland coast, the chief and almost only habitations being seated upon the western shore. Of their remains Captain Graah has given highly interesting and minute descriptions, enabling us from these and more recent examinations of several localities on the west coast of Greenland, to trace the vestiges of the old colonies from the most southern fjord at Cape Farewell, up to the neighbourhood of Holsteinborg.

MINOR NARRATIVES.

A.   FROM THE HISTORY OF KING OLAF TRYGGVASON.

ACCORDING TO THE SECOND VELLUM CODEX, No. 61, Fol.

Supposed to have been copied at the end of the 14th or beginning of the 15th Century.

THUS says the holy priest Bede, in the chronicles which he wrote concerning the regions of the earth : that the island which is called Thule in the books, lies so far in the north part of the world, that there came no day in the winter, when the night is longest, and no night in summer, when the day is longest.   Therefore think learned men that it is Iceland which is called Thule, for there are many places in that land, where the sun sets not at night, when the day is longest, and in the same manner, where the sun cannot be seen by day, when the night is longest.   But the holy priest Bede died DCCXXXV years after the birth of our Lord Jesus Christ, more than a hundred and twenty years before Iceland was inhabited by the Northmen.   But before Iceland was colonized from Norway, men had been there whom the Northmen called Papas.   They were Christians; for after them were found Irish books, bells, and croziers, and many other things from whence it could be

254

seen that they were Christian men, and had come from the west over the sea:* English books also shew that, in that time, there was intercourse between the two countries.

B. FROM THE SCHEDÆ OF ARI FRODE.

No. 54, Fol.

At that time was Iceland covered with woods, between the mountains and the shore. Then were here Christian people, whom the Northmen called Papas, but they went afterwards away, because they would not be here amongst heathens; and left after them Irish books, and bells, and croziers, from which could be seen that they were Irishmen. But then began people to travel much here out from Norway, until King Harold forbade it, because it appeared to him that the land had begun to be thinned of inhabitants.

C. FROM THE PROLOGUE TO THE LANDNAMABOK.

No. 53, Fol.

But before Iceland was colonized by the Northmen, the men were there whom the Northmen called Papas; they were Christians, and people think that they came from the west over the sea, for there was found after

---

*Til vestan um haf.   Ireland lying to the west of Norway, from whence the Icelanders had emigrated, was generally spoken of by them with reference to their fatherland, and for the same reason they called the Irish "westmen."   According to a learned enquirer into the origin of the Irish, the literal meaning of the word Ireland is *Westland*, the celtic syllable *iar* or *er* meaning the *west*.   This, however, is disputed by O'Brien, who maintains that the original interpretation of *iar* is "after," or "behind," and considers Eirin to be compounded of *i* and *erin*, the genitive of *ere*, iron, signifying the island of iron or mines, for which Ireland had formerly been famed, and hence ranked by ancient writers among the Cassiterides.   See Wood's Inquiry, concerning the primitive inhabitants of Ireland, p. 1.; O'Brien's Irish Dict. in voce Eirin.

them Irish books, and bells, and croziers, and many more things from which it could be seen that they were West-men; such were found eastwards in Papey, and Papyli, it is also mentioned in English books that in that time, was intercourse between the countries.

The particulars given of Thule by the Irish monk Dicuil, who wrote in the year 825, offer a remarkable confirmation of the Icelandic manuscripts respecting the residence of the Irish ecclesiastics in that region, which, in his work, is evidently identified with Iceland. He speaks of Thule as an uninhabited island, which, however, in his lifetime, about the year 795, had been visited by some monks, *with whom he himself had spoken,* and who had once dwelt upon the island from the first of February to the first of August. They denied the exaggerated statements that had been made by ancient writers respecting the perpetual ice, continued day from the vernal to the autumnal equinox, and corresponding interval of night, but stated that a day's journey further northward, the sea was really frozen, and that with respect to the length of the days and nights, at, and a few days before and after the summer solstice, the sun sank so little below the horizon during the night that one could pursue their ordinary occupations as well as by day-light. The author further describes several islands lying in the north part of the British ocean, and which, with a fair wind, might be reached from the north of Britain in two days and a night; and states that here *nearly a hundred years before,* namely A. D. 725, hermits from Ireland had taken up their abode, but, disturbed by the roving Northmen, had since departed, leaving the place uninhabited. These islands are further described as having upon them a great number of sheep, which circumstance leads to the conclusion that they were the Farœ islands, the name of which is known to be derived from the original Icelandic term *Fareyjar* or sheep islands.

ARI MARSON'S SOJOURN IN GREAT IRELAND,

A. D. 982.

From the Landnamabok, collated with accounts of the same transactions in Hauksbok.

ULF the squinter, son of Hogna the white, took all Reykjanes, between Thorkafjord and Hafrafell; he married Bjorg, daughter to Eyvind the Eastman, sister to Helge the lean; their son was Atli the red, who married Thorbjorg, sister to Steinolf the humble; their son was Mar of Holum, who married Thorkatla, daughter of Hergil Neprass; their son was Ari; he was driven by a tempest to White Man's Land, which some call Great Ireland; it lies to the west in the sea, near to Vinland the Good, and VI days' sailing west from Ireland. From thence could Ari not get away, and was there baptized. This story first told Rafn the Limerick merchant, who had long lived at Limerick in Ireland. Thus said [also] Thorkell Gellerson, that Icelanders had stated, who had heard Thorfinn Jarl of the Orkneys relate, that Ari was recognised in White Man's Land, and could not get away from thence, but was there much respected. Ari married Thorgerd daughter to Alf of Dolum, whose sons were Thorgils, Gudleif and Illugi: this is the family of Reykjaness. Jorund hight a son of Ulf the squinter; he married Thorbjorg Knarrarbringa; their daughter was Thjodhild, who married Erik the Red; their son

257

[was] Leif the Lucky of Greenland. Jorund hight the son of Atli the Red; he married Thordis, daughter of Thorgeir Suda; their daughter was Otkatla, who married Thorgill Kollson. Jorund was also father to Snorri.

VOYAGE OF BJORN ASBRANDSON

TO THE WESTERN HEMISPHERE AND SETTLEMENT IN GREAT IRELAND.

A.D. 999.

BORK the fat and Thordis Surs daughter had a daughter that Thurid hight, and she was married to Thorbjorn the fat, who lived at Froda; he was son of Orm the lean, who had taken and cultivated the farm of Froda. Thurid, daughter of Asbrand of Kamb in Breidavik had he formerly married; she was sister to Bjorn Breidvikinga-happa, who is hereafter mentioned in the Saga, and to Arnbjorn the strong: her sons by Thorbjorn were Ketill the Champion, Gunnlaug and Hallstein. . . .

Now shall something be told about Snorri Godi, that he took up the process about the murder of Thorbjorn his brother-in-law. He also took his sister home to Helgafell, because there was a report, that Bjorn, son of Asbrand from Kamb, began to come there to inveigle her. . . .

Thorodd, hight a man from Medallfellstrand: an honourable man; he was a great merchant, and owned a trading ship. Thorodd had made a trading voyage westwards to Ireland, to Dublin. At that time had Jarl

Sigurd Lodversson, of the Orkneys, sway to the Hebrides, and all the way westward to Man: he imposed a
tribute on the inhabitants of Man, and when they had
made peace the Jarl left men behind him to collect the
tribute; it was mostly paid in smelted silver; but the Jarl
sailed away northwards to the Orkneys. But when they
who had waited for the tribute were ready for sailing,
they put to sea with a south-west wind; but when they
had sailed for a time the wind changed to the south-east
and east, and there arose a great storm, and drove them
northwards under Ireland, and the ship broke there
asunder upon an uninhabited island. And when they had
gotten on shore there came, by chance, the Icelander Thorodd, on a voyage from Dublin. The Jarl's men called out
to the merchantmen to help them. Thorodd put out a boat,
and went into it himself, and when it came up, the Jarl's
men begged Thorodd to help them, and offered him
money to take them home to Sigurd Jarl in the Orkneys;
but Thorodd thought he could not do that, because he
was bound for Iceland; but they pressed him hard, for
they thought it concerned their goods and freedom, that
they should not be left in Ireland or the Hebrides, where
they before had waged war, and it ended so that he sold
them the ship's boat, and took therefore a great part of
the tribute; they steered then with the boat to the Orkneys; but Thorodd sailed without the boat to Iceland,
and came to the south of the land; then steered he westwards, and sailed into Breidafjord, and landed, with all
on board, at Dogurdarness, and went in autumn to winter with Snorri Godi at Helgafell; he was since then

called Thorodd the tribute-buyer. This happened a little after the murder of Thorbjorn the fat. The same winter was at Helgafell Turid the sister to Snorri Godi, whom Thorbjorn the fat had married. Thorodd asked Snorri Godi to give him Thurid his sister in marriage; and because he was rich, and Snorri knew him from a good side, and saw that she required some one to manage her affairs,—with all this together resolved Snorri Godi to give him the woman, and their marriage was held there in the winter at Helgafell. But in the following spring Thorodd betook himself to Froda, and became a good and upright yeoman. But so soon as Thurid came to Froda, began Bjorn Asbrandson to visit there, and there was spread a general report that he and Thurid had unlawful intercourse; then began Thorodd to complain about his visits, but did not object to them seriously. At that time dwelled Thorer Vidlegg at Arnarhvol, and his sons Orn and Val were grown up, and very promising men; they reproached Thorodd for submitting to such disgrace as Bjorn put upon him, and offered Thorodd their assistance, if he would forbid the visits of Bjorn. It happened one time that Bjorn came to Froda, and he sat talking with Thurid. Thorodd used always to sit within when Bjorn was there, but now was he nowhere to be seen. Then said Thurid: "Take care of thy walks, Bjorn, for I suspect that Thorodd thinks to put an end to thy visits here, and it looks to me as if they had gone out to fall upon thee by the way, and he thinks they will not be met by equal force." "That can well be," said Bjorn, and chaunted this stave:—

> O! Goddess of the arm-ring gold*
> Let this bright day the longest hold
> On earth, for now I linger here
> In my love's arms, but soon must fear
> These joys will vanish, and her breath
> Be raised to mourn my early death.

Thereafter took Bjorn his arms, and went away, intending to go home; but when he had gotten up the Digramula, sprang five men upon him; this was Thorodd and two of his servants, and the sons of Thorer Vidlegg. They seized Bjorn, but he defended himself well and manfully; Thorer's sons pressed in hardest upon him, and wounded him, but he was the death of both of them. After that Thorodd went away with his men, and was a little wounded, but they not. Bjorn went his way until he came home, and went into the room; the woman of the house told a maid servant to attend him; and when she came into the room with a light, then saw she that Bjorn was very bloody; she went then in, and told his father Asbrand that Bjorn was come home bloody; Asbrand went into the room, and asked why Bjorn was bloody; "or have you, perhaps, fallen in with Thorodd?" Bjorn answered that so it was. Asbrand then asked how the business had ended. Bjorn chaunted:—

> Easier far it is to fondle,
> In the arms of female fair,
> (Vidlegg's sons I both have slain)
> Than with valiant men to wrestle,
> Or tamely purchased tribute. bear.

---

*Jord, the earth, one of the many wives of Odin and mother of Thor.

Then bound Asbrand his wounds, and he became quite restored. Thorodd begged Snorri Godi to manage the matter about Thorer's sons' murder, and Snorri had it brought before the court of Thorsness; but the sons of Thorlak of Eyra assisted Breidvikinga in this affair, and the upshot was, that Asbrand went security for his son Bjorn, and undertook to pay a fine for the murder. But Bjorn was banished for three years, and went away the same summer. During the same summer Thurid of Froda was delivered of a male child, which received the name of Kjartan; he grew up at Froda, and was soon large and promising.

Now when Bjorn had crossed the sea [to Norway], he bent his way southwards to Denmark, and therefrom south to Jomsborg. Then was Palnatoki chief of the Jomsvikings. Bjorn joined their band, and was named Champion. He was in Jomsborg when Styrbjorn the strong took the castle. Bjorn was also with them in Sweden, when the Jomsvikings aided Styrbjorn; he was also in the battle of Fyrisvall, where Styrbjorn fell, and escaped in the wood with other Jomsvikings. And so long as Palnatoki lived, was Bjorn with him, and was looked upon as a distinguished man, and very brave in all times of trial.

. . . The same summer came the brothers Bjorn and Arnbjorn out to Iceland, to Raunhafnarsos. Bjorn was afterwards called the Champion of Breidavik. Arnbjorn had brought much money out with him, and immediately, the same summer that he came, bought land at Bakke in Raunhofn. Arnbjorn made no display, and

spoke little on most occasions, but was, however, in all
respects, a very able man. Bjorn, his brother, was, on
the other hand, very pompous, when he came to the country, and lived in great style, for he had accustomed himself to the court usages of foreign chiefs; he was much
handsomer than Arnbjorn, and in no particular less able,
but was much more skilled in martial exercises, of which
he had given proofs in foreign lands. In the summer,
just after they had arrived, a great meeting of the people
was held north of the heath, under Haugabret, near the
mouth of the Froda; and thither rode all the merchants,
in coloured garments; and when they had come to the
meeting, was there many people assembled. There was
Thurid, the lady of Froda, and Bjorn went up, and
spoke to her, and no one objected to this, for it was
thought likely that their discourse would last long, since
they, for such a length of time, had not seen each other.
There arose that day a fight, and one of the men from
the northern mountains received a deadly wound, and
was carried down under a bush on the bank of the river;
much blood flowed from the wound, so that there was a
pool of blood in the bush. There was the boy Kjartan,
son of Thurid of Froda; he had a small axe in his hand;
he ran to the bush, and dipped the axe in the blood.
When the men from the southern mountains rode southwards from the meeting, Thord Blig asked Bjorn how
the discourse had turned out betwixt him and Thurid of
Froda. Bjorn said that he was well contented therewith.
Then asked Thord, whether he had that day seen the
lad Kjartan, her and Thorodd's united son. "Him saw

I," said Bjorn. "What do you think of him?" quoth
Thord, again. Then chaunted Bjorn this stave:

> "A stripling lo!
> With fearful eyes
> A woman's image,
> Downwards ran
> To the wolf's lair;—
> The people say
> The youth knows not
> His Viking father."

Thord said: "What will Thorodd say when he hears
of your boy?" Then sung Bjorn:

> "Then will the noble lady,
> When pressing to her breast
> The image of his father
> In her fair arms to rest,
> Admit Thorodd's conjecture,
> For me she ever loved,
> And ever shall I bear her
> Affection deep and proved."

Thord said: "It will be better for ye, not to have
much to do with each other, and that thou turn thy
thoughts from Thurid." "That is surely a good counsel," replied Bjorn, "but far is that from my intention,
although it makes some difference when I have to do
with such a man as Snorri her brother." "Thou wilt
be sorry for thy doings," said Thord, and therewith
ended the talk between them. Bjorn went home now
to Kamb, and took upon himself the management of the
place, for his father was then dead. In the winter he
began his trips over the heath, to visit Thurid; and al-

though Thorodd did not like it, he yet saw that it was not easy to find a remedy, and he thought over with himself, how dearly it had cost him, when he sought to stop their intercourse; but he saw that Bjorn was now much stronger than before. Thorodd bribed, in the winter, Thorgrim Galdrakin to raise a tempest against Bjorn, when he was crossing the heath. Now it came to pass one day that Bjorn came to Froda, and in the evening, when he was going home, was there thick weather, and some rain; and he set off very late; but when he had gotten up on the heath, the weather became cold, and it snowed; and so dark that he saw not the way before him. After that arose a drift of snow, with so much sleet that he could scarcely keep his legs; his clothes were now frozen, for he was before wet through, and he strayed about so that he knew not where to turn; at night he arrived at the edge of a cave, went in, and was there for the night, and had a cold lodging; then sung Bjorn:—

> "Fair one! who dost bring
> Vestments to the weary,*
> Little know'st thou where
> Hid in cavern dreary,
> I now shelter seek;
> He that once on ocean
> Boldly steered a bark,
> Now lies without motion
> In a cavern dark."

And again he chaunted:

---

*To the women of the Northern family was more particularly entrusted the duties of hospitality, among which was included that of bringing dry garments to the traveller who had suffered from the tempestuousness of the weather.

"The swan's cold region I have crossed
All eastwards with a goodly freight,
For woman's love, by tempest tost
And seeking danger in the fight:
But now no woman's couch I tread,
A rocky cavern is my bed."

Bjorn remained three days in the cave, before the
weather moderated; but on the fourth day came he home
from the heath to Kamb. He was much exhausted.
The servants asked him where he had been during the
tempest—Bjorn sang:

"Well my deeds are known
Under Styrbjörn's banner,
Steel-clad Erik slew
Gallant men in battle;
Now on mountain wild,
Met by magic shower,
Outlet could not find
From the Witches power."*

Bjorn was now at home for the winter. In spring
his brother Arnbjorn fixed his residence at Bakka in
Raunhofn, but Bjorn lived at Kamb, and kept a splendid
house. . . .

The same summer bade Thorodd the tribute-buyer his
brother-in-law Snorri Godi to a feast at home at Froda,
and Snorri betook himself thither with twenty men.
And while Snorri was at the feast, disclosed Thorodd to
him, how he felt himself both disgraced and injured by
the visits which Bjorn Asbrandson made to Thurid his

---

*These poetical effusions of Bjorn may, perhaps, appear somewhat
improbable to modern readers, but, the Northmen of this period exhibited
great readiness in a species of rude versification, the melody of which was
chiefly formed on alliteration. "As late as the time of Chaucer," says
Sir Walter Scott, "it was considered as the mark of a Northern man to
'affect the letter.'"

wife, but sister to Snorri Godi: Thorodd said that Snorri
should remedy this bad business.   Snorri was there a few
days, and Thorodd gave him costly presents when he went
away.   Snorri Godi rode from thence over the heath,
and gave out that he was going to the ship in the bay of
Raunhafn.   This was in summer, at the time of hay-
making.   But when they came south on Kamb's heath,
then said Snorri: "Now will we ride from the heath
down to Kamb, and I will tell you," said he, "that I will
visit Bjorn, and take his life, if opportunity offers, but
not attack him in the house, for the buildings are strong
here, and Bjorn is strong and hardy, and we have but little force; and it is well known that men who have come
even so, with great force, have with little success attacked such valiant men inside in the house, as was the
case with Geir Godi, and Gissur the white, when they
attacked Gunnar of Lidarend, in his house, with eighty
men, but he was there alone, and nevertheless were some
wounded, and others killed; and they had staid the attack had not Geir Godi, with his heedfulness, observed
that he was short of arms.   But forasmuch as," continued he, "Bjorn is now out, which may be expected, as it
is good drying weather, so appoint I thee, my kinsman
Mar, to fetch Bjorn the first wound; but consider well,
that he is no man to trifle with, and that wherever he
is you may expect a hard blow from a savage wolf, if
he, at the onset, receives not such a wound as will cause
his death."   And now when they rode down from the
moor to the farm, saw they that Bjorn was out in the
homestead, working at a sledge, and there was nobody

with him, and no weapons had he except a little axe, and a large knife, of a span's length from the haft, which he used for boring the holes in the sledge. Bjorn saw that Snorri Godi with his followers rode down from the moor, into the field, and knew them immediately. Snorri Godi was in a blue cloak, and rode in front. Bjorn made an immediate resolve, and took the knife, and went straight towards them; when they came together, he seized with the one hand the arm of Snorri's cloak, and with the other held he the knife in such a manner as was most easy for him to stab Snorri through the breast, if he should think fit to do so. Bjorn greeted them, as they met, and Snorri greeted him again; but Mar dropped his hands, for it struck him that Bjorn could soon hurt Snorri, if any injury was done to him. Upon this Bjorn went with them on their way, and asked what news they had, but held himself in the same position which he had taken at the first. Then took up Bjorn the discourse in this manner: "It stands truly so, friend Snorri, that I conceal not I have acted towards you in such wise that you may well accuse me, and I have been told that you have a hostile intention towards me. Now it seems to me best," continued he, "that if you have any business with me, other than passing by here to the high road, you should let me know it; but be that not the case, then would I that you grant me peace, and I will then turn back, for I go not in leading strings." Snorri answered: "Such a lucky grip took thou of me at our meeting that thou must have peace this time, however it may have been determined before; but this I beg of thee, that from henceforth, thou cease to inveigle Thurid, for it will not end well between us, if thou, in this respect, continue as thou hast begun." Bjorn replied: "That only will I promise thee, which I can perform, but I see not how I can hold to this so long as Thurid and I are in the same district." "Thou art not so much bound to this place," answered Snorri, "but that thou couldest easily give up thy residence here." Bjorn replied: "True is that which thou sayest, and thus shall it be, since you have yourself come to me, and as our meeting has thus turned out will I promise thee, that Thorodd and thou shalt have no more trouble about my visits to Thuridd for the next year." After this, they separated; Snorri Godi rode to the ship, and then home to Helgafell. The day following rode Bjorn southwards to Raunhofn to go to sea, and he got immediately, in the summer, a place in a ship, and they were very soon ready. They put to sea with a north-east wind, which wind lasted long during the summer; but of this ship was nothing heard since this long time.

The following narrative will shew that Bjorn was driven to that part of the eastern coast of North America, where White Man's Land, or Great Ireland was supposed by the Northmen to be situated, and where, thirty years afterwards (1029), Gudleif Gudlaugson, driven in the same direction by easterly winds, recognised his countryman in a Chief, to whose position and influence both he and his companions were indebted for a safe return to their native land. This narrative is contained in the same Saga from whence the preceding has been derived; but before introducing the sec-

ond period in the history of Bjorn Asbrandson to the notice
of the reader, a short sketch from the able pen of Bishop
Muller, of the general characteristics of the *Eyrbyggja
Saga,* its high position among Icelandic MSS. its well authenticated details, and its consequent claims to credibility
as regards all the leading incidents which it records, will
serve to place the two narratives in their proper light, and
render the whole more worthy of consideration in a historical point of view:

"This Saga contains a number of occurrences and names
of persons that are also mentioned in other places. Thorolf
Mostrarskeg's death is fixed by the annals in 918; of him
and his son Thorstein much is to be found in the Landnamabok; Thorgrim Thorsteinson's death is related at
length in Gisle Surson's Saga; the Landnama mentions
the most of Snorri's actions; the Annals record 'his birth
in 964, and his death in 1031. . . . Besides, many of the
persons named here are also mentioned in the Kristnisaga,
and many are to be found in the Niala and Laxdæla Sagas."

"The author cites the testimony of Ari Frode; he remarks
himself that Snorri appears in many other Sagas, and expressly mentions Laxdæla Saga, and Heidarviga Saga.
Certain circumstances are stated to 'have thus happened
"according to what most people said;" and, we read, "one
sees still the mark of the new barrow, which Arnkel raised
over his father, and where he made a fence across, so that
no animal should come there." It is also stated: "at that
time it was the merchants' custom that they had no cook
on board ship, but that all the ship's company should take
it in turn to cook the victuals: there should also stand a
covered can with drink by the sail." These expressions
prove that the writer of this Saga lived some time after the
events which he here relates; that already a part of the

Saga was current, and that from these statements, and other individual oral relations, he put his work together."

"Again: verses are often introduced, as well by the acting persons as other Skalds who sung of the events. These must, therefore, on the whole, be considered credible, and contain many not unimportant characteristics of the times. Traces of later decoration appear in the description of the hardihood of those who were wounded at the battle of Alptefjord, and of Thorgunna's witchcraft, but it is only natural that somewhat more of superstition should appear in this than in many other Sagas, and the circumstance proves nothing against its antiquity The greater number of these embellishments are no more than what we commonly find, where such superstitious faith is entertained, and the additions are accordant with the credulity of the times. The Eyrbyggja Saga is expressly quoted in the Landnamabok. Besides, we can determine the date of this with greater accuracy than that of most other Sagas: it must have been written before 1264, when Iceland became subject to Norway, because as it is stated: "All should pay tribute to the temple, and be liable for the journeys of the Chief, just as in the present time the Thingmen for their Chief:" hence it follows, that the aristocratic form of society, which ceased when the island became subject to Norway, must have existed at the period in question. The Saga must also have been written whilst Thord Sturleson and his mother yet lived, for it says: "when the church which Snorri Godi had built was removed, his bones were taken up, and brought down to the place where the church now stands; there were present Gudny Bodvar's daughter, Thord and Sighvat Sturleson's mother; and Thord Struleson says, that they were the bones of a middle sized man, and not large. There were also taken up the bones of Bork

the fat, Snorri Godi's uncle: they were very large; also
was taken up the wife of Thordis, Thorbjorn Surs' daughter, Snorri Godi's mother. Gudny says that they were small
women's bones, and as black as if they were singed." This
proves that the writer of the Saga was present with Thord
Sturleson, and his mother. Gudny died in the year 1220
odd, and the Saga must therefore have been written in the
beginning of the 13th century."

VOYAGE OF GUDLEIF GUDLAUGSON TO GREAT IRELAND.

A. D. 1029.

EYRBYGGJA SAGA, CAP. 64. VELLUM FRAGMENT, No. 4456, in 4to.
Collated with the before mentioned MSS.

Gudleif hight a man; he was son of Gudlaug the rich,
of Straumfjord, and brother of Thorfinn, from whom the
Sturlungers are descended. Gudleif was a great merchant, he had a merchant ship, but Thorolf Eyrar Lopt-
son had another, that time they fought against Gyrd, son
of Sigvald Jarl; then lost Gyrd his eye. It happened in
the last years of the reign of King Olaf the Saint, that
Gudleif undertook a trading voyage to Dublin;* but
when he sailed from the west, intended he to sail to Iceland; he sailed then from the west of Ireland,† and met
with north-east winds, and was driven far to the west,
and south-west, in the sea, where no land was to be seen.
But it was already far gone in the summer, and they

---

*Some of the MSS. add *"vestr,"* shewing that Ireland was spoken of
as lying westwards from Iceland.
†Probably Limerick, which was much frequented by the Northmen.

made many prayers that they might escape from the sea; and it came to pass that they saw land. It was a great land, but they knew not what land it was. Then took they the resolve to sail to the land, for they were weary of contending longer with the violence of the sea. They found there a good harbour; and when they had been a short time on shore, came people to them: they knew none of the people, *but it rather appeared to them that they spoke Irish.** Soon came to them so great a number that it made up many hundreds. These men fell upon them and seized them all, and bound them, and drove them up the country. There were they brought before an assembly, to be judged. *They understood so much* that some were for killing them, but others would have them distributed amongst the inhabitants, and made slaves. And while this was going on saw they where rode a great body of men, and a large banner was borne in the midst. Then thought they that there must be a chief in the troop; but when it came near, saw they that under the banner rode a large and dignified man, who was much in years, and whose hair was white. All present bowed down before the man, and received him as well as they could. Now observed they that all opinions and resolutions concerning their business, were submitted to his decision. Then ordered this man Gudleif and his companions to be brought before him, and when they had come before this man, spoke he to them in the North-

---

*This is a very remarkable passage, and affords the strongest grounds for believing that the country to which they were driven had been previously colonized from Ireland. The Northmen, from their intercourse with the Irish ports, might be supposed to have had just sufficient knowledge of the language to detect its sounds (here probably corrupted), and understand the general meaning of the words.

THE NORSE DISCOVERY OF AMERICA

came. They answered him, that the most of them were
Icelanders. The man asked which of them were Icelanders? Gudleif said that he was an Icelander. He
then saluted the old man, and he received it well, and
asked from what part of Iceland he came. Gudleif said
that he was from that district which hight Borgafjord.
Then enquired he from what part of Borgafjord he came,
and Gudleif answered just as it was. Then asked this
man about almost every one of the principal men in
Borgafjord and Breidafjord; and when they talked thereon, enquired he minutely about every thing, first of
Snorri Godi, and his sister Thurid of Froda, and most
about Kjartan her son. The people of the country now
called out, on the other side, that some decision should
be made about the seamen. After this went the great
man away from them, and named twelve of his men
with himself, and they sat a long time talking. Then
went they to the meeting of the people, and the old man
said to Gudleif: "I and the people of the country have
talked together about your business, and the people have
left the matter to me; but I will now give ye leave to
depart whence ye will; but although ye may think that
the summer is almost gone, yet will I counsel ye to remove from hence, for here are the people not to be trusted,
and bad to deal with, and they think besides that the
laws have been broken to their injury." Gudleif answered: "What shall we say, if fate permits us to return to our own country, who has given us this freedom?" He answered: "That can I not tell you, for I

274

like not that my relations and foster-brothers should make such a journey hereto, as ye would have made, if ye had not had the benefit of my help; but now is my age so advanced, that I may expect every hour old age to overpower me; and even if I could live yet for a time, there are here more powerful men than me, who little peace would give to foreigners that might come here, although they be not just here in the neighbourhood where ye landed." Then caused he their ship to be made ready for sea, and was there with them, until a fair wind sprung up, which was favourable to take them from the land. But before they separated took this man a gold ring from his hand, and gave it into the hands of Gudleif, and therewith a good sword; then said he to Gudleif: "If the fates permit you to come to your own country, then shall you take this sword to the yeoman, Kjartan of Froda, but the ring to Thurid his mother." Gudleif replied: "What shall I say, about it, as to who sends them these valuables?" He answered: "Say that he sends them who was a better friend of the lady of Froda, than of her brother, Godi of Helgafell; but if any man therefore thinks that he knows who has owned these articles, then say these my words, that I forbid any one to come to me, for it is the most dangerous expedition, unless it happens as fortunately with others at the landing place, as with you; but here is the land great, and bad as to harbours, and in all parts may strangers expect hostility, when it does not turn out as has been with you." After this, Gudleif and his people put to sea, and they landed in Ireland late in harvest, and were in Dublin for the winter. But in the summer after, sailed they to Iceland, and Gudleif delivered over there these valuables; and people held it for certain, that this man was Bjorn, the Champion of Breidavik, and no other account to be relied on is there in confirmation of this, except that which is now given here.

The reader will no doubt come to the same conclusion drawn by the Icelanders respecting the identity of the aged chief, to whose generosity and friendly feeling Gudleif and his companions were so much indebted, and unhesitatingly pronounce him to have been none other than Bjorn Asbrandson, the Champion of Breidavik, who, it will be remembered, had set sail about thirty years before, with a northeast wind, and had not since been heard of. The remarkable accordance of all the personal details, to which the writer evidently attaches the principal importance, with the historical events, which are only incidentally alluded to, enable us to determine dates and intervals of time with a degree of accuracy that places the truth of the narrative beyond all question, and gives a high degree of interest to these two voyages. The mention of Sigurd Jarl of the Orkneys, Palnatoki, Styrbjorn the nephew of Erik of Sweden, the battle of Fyrisvold, Snorri Godi, "the latter part of the reign of king Olaf the saint," gives a chronological character to the narratives, and enables us to fix with confidence, nearly the exact period of the principal events. Hence it appears that Gudleif Gudlaugson, sailing from the west of Ireland in the year 1029, with a N. E. wind, is driven far to the south and south-west, where no land was to be seen, and that after being exposed for many

days to the violence of the winds and waves, he at length
finds shelter upon a coast, where Bjorn Asbrandson, who
had left Iceland with N. E. winds thirty years before, had
become established as chief of the inhabitants of the country. He finds him, as might naturally have been expected,
"stricken in years," and "his hair was white," for Bjorn
had left Iceland for Jomsborg in the prime of life, had,
after taking part in the achievements of the Jomsvikings
up to the death of Palnatoki in 993, returned to and resided in Iceland until 999, and now thirty winters had
passed over his head since his ultimate departure from his
native land. The locality of the newly discovered country
is next to be determined: Now if a line be drawn running
N. E. to S. W. the course of Bjorn Asbrandson, from the
western coast of Iceland, and another in the same direction
(the course of Gudleif Gudlaugson) from the west coast of
Ireland, they would intersect each other on the southern
shores of the United States, somewhere about Carolina or
Georgia. This position accords well with the description
of the locality of their country, given by the Skrælings to
Thorfinn Karlsefne, and which the Northmen believed to
be White Man's land or Great Ireland, as also with the
geographical notices of the same land which have been
already adduced; and when to these evidences be added
the statements of Gudleif and his companions respecting
the language of the natives, *"which appeared to them to be
Irish,"* there is every reason to conclude that this was
the Hvitramannaland, Albania, or Ireland ed mikla of the
Northmen.

The notices of the country contained in these two narratives are, doubtless, scanty, and merely incidental, the
object of the narrators being evidently to trace the romantic

and adventurous career of the Champion of Breidavik, and the perilous voyage of his countrymen, but this very circumstance is an argument in favour of the honesty of the statement as regards the supposed Irish settlement; and the simple and unpretending character of both narratives, supported, as they are, by historical references, confirmatory of the principal events, gives to these incidental allusions a degree of importance to which they would not otherwise be entitled.

Professor Rafn is of opinion that the White Man's Land, or Great Ireland of the Northmen was the country situated to the south of Chesapeake Bay, including North and South Carolina, Georgia, and East Florida. It is well known that the Esquimaux Indians formerly inhabited countries much further south than they do at present, and a very remarkable tradition is stated to be still preserved amongst the Shawnese Indians, who emigrated 87 years ago, from West Florida to Ohio, that Florida was once *inhabited by white men, who used iron instruments.* A German writer also mentions an old tradition of the ancestors of the Shawnese having come *from beyond the sea.*

Various circumstances shew that Great Ireland was a country, of the existence of which the Icelandic historians had no doubt; it is spoken of in the Saga of Thorfinn Karlsefne as a country well known by name to the Northmen; in the account of Ari Marson's voyage, and the geographical fragment, its position is pointed out:—"west from Ireland, near Vinland the good"—"next and somewhat behind Vinland," and the following extract, taken from the collection of Bjorn Johnson, will shew that a Chart had actually been made of this distant land:—

"Sir Erlend Thordson had obtained from abroad the

geographical chart of that Albania, or land of the White men, which is situated opposite Vinland the good, of which mention has been before made in this little book, and which the merchants formerly called Hibernia Major or Great Ireland, and lies, as has been said, to the west of Ireland proper. This chart had held accurately all those tracts of land, and the boundaries of Markland, Einfœtingjaland, and little Helluland, together with Greenland, to the west of it, where apparently begins the good Terra Florida." This Sir Erlend was priest of the parish of Staden in Steingrimsfjord, on the west coast of Iceland, in the year 1568, but no further information has been obtained respecting the chart, which probably contained the outlines of all the countries known to the Northmen soon after their discovery of the American continent.

From what cause could the name of Great Ireland have arisen, but from the fact of the country having been colonized by the Irish? Coming from their own green island to a vast continent possessing many of the fertile qualities of their native soil, the appellation would have been natural and appropriate; and costume, colour, or peculiar habits, might have readily given rise to the country being denominated White Man's Land by the neighbouring Esquimaux. Nor does this conclusion involve any improbability: we have seen that the Irish visited and inhabited Iceland towards the close of the 8th century, to have accomplished which they must have traversed a stormy ocean to the extent of about 800 miles; that a hundred years before the time of Dicuil, namely in the year 725, they had been found upon the Farœ islands; that in the 10th century, voyages between Iceland and Ireland were of ordinary occurrence; and that in the beginning of the

11th century, White Man's Land or Great Ireland is mentioned,—not as a newly discovered country,—but as a land *long known by name* to the Northmen. Neither the Icelandic historians nor navigators were, in the least degree, interested in originating or giving currency to any fable respecting an Irish settlement on the southern shores of North America, for they set up no claim to the discovery of that part of the Western continent. their intercourse being limited to the coasts north of Chesapeake Bay. The discovery of Vinland and Great Ireland appear to have been totally independent of each other: the latter is only incidentally alluded to by the Northern navigators; with the name they were familiar, but of the peculiar locality of the country they were ignorant, nor was it until after the return of Karlsefni from Vinland in 1011, and the information which he obtained from the Skrellings or Esquimaux who were captured during the voyage, that the Northmen became convinced that White Man's Land or Great Ireland was a part of the same vast continent, of which Helluland, Markland, and Vinland formed portions.

The traces of Irish origin which have been observed among some of the Indian tribes of North and Central America tend also to strengthen the presumption that these countries had been colonized from Ireland at some remote period of time. Rask, the eminent Danish philologist, leans to this opinion which he founds upon the early voyages of the Irish to Iceland and the similitude between the Hiberno-Celtic, and American Indian dialects. "It is well known," he says, "that Iceland was discovered and partially inhabited by the Irish before its discovery and occupation by the Scandinavians; and when we find that the Icelanders, descended from the Scandinavians, discovered North

America, it will appear less improbable that the Irish, who, at that period, were more advanced in learning and civilization, should have undertaken similar expeditions with success :" the name of *Irland it Mikla* he also considers to be a sufficient indication of the Irish having emigrated thither from their own country.

It seems to be generally admitted by historians and antiquaries that the main stream of colonization has flowed from east to west, the Celts preceding the Teutonic and Sarmatian races, by a long interval of time. Herodotus, four centuries before the Christian era, places the Celts beyond the pillars of Hercules, and upon the borders of the most westerly region in Europe, and Cæsar in the first century finds them in Gaul and Britain; that their successors, the Goths, should have driven them to seek for regions still further westward is therefore in full accordance with the course of their former migrations, and the same nomadic principle which brought them from Asia to the British isles, might have wafted them in later ages to the western world.

The illustrious Leibnitz seems to have contemplated the possibility of such a remote Celtic settlement when he wrote:—"And if there be *any island beyond Ireland,* where *the Celtic language* is in use, by the help thereof we should be guided, as by a thread, to the knowledge of still more ancient things."

The remarkable narrative of Lionel Wafer who resided for several months amongst the inhabitants of the Isthmus of America, contains some remarkable passages bearing upon this subject, and which, as the author had no preconceived opinions on the affinity of languages, or favourite theory to uphold, are deserving of notice: speaking of their language, he says:—

"My knowledge of the Highland language made me the more capable of learning the Darien Indians' language, when I was among them, for there is some affinity; not in the signification of the words of each language, but in the pronunciation, which I could easily imitate, both being spoken pretty much in the throat, with frequent aspirates, and much the same sharp or circumflex tang or cant." This writer, however, had evidently not paid much attention to the affinities of the two languages which he compares and finds only to resemble in pronunciation, for many of the words which he afterwards adduces as examples of the Indian language, bear a marked similitude to those of the Celtic, as may readily be seen by the following comparison:

AMERICAN-INDIAN.	CELTIC.
Tautah—Father	Taduys (Welsh), Tad (Corn.) Tat (Armoric) Dad or Daddy (vulg. Irish).
Namah—Mother	Naing (Irish).
Poonah—Woman	Bean (Ir.), Bun (Armor.).
Neenah—Girl	Neean (ancient Scotch).
Nee—the Moon	Neul, a star—light—neultaib njme, the stars of heaven(Ir.).
Eechah (pron. Eetsha)—Ugly	Etseact—Death (Ir.)—the ugliest of all things.
Paeechah—Foh! Ugly	Pah, prefixed to a word in Welsh augments its signification.
Eechah Malooquah, an expression of great dislike	Malluighe or malluigte, cursed, accursed (Irish).
Cotchah, sleep	Codalta and Codaltac, sleepy (Ir.).
Caupah(pron. Capa), hammock	Cába, a cloak, Caban, tent, cottage (Ir.), Caban, ib.(Welsh).

Eetah, got	Ed, to take, handle (Irish).
Doolah, water	Tuile, a flood (Ir.).
Copah, drink	Ceóbac, drunkenness (Ir.).
Mamaumah, fine	Ma, ma, ba, would be nearly the sound of the repetition of the word ba, which signifies good in Irish: the m and b are also often used indiscriminately. See O'Brien—Remarks on letter M.
Eenah, to call	Enwi, to name (Welsh), Henu, a name (Armor.).

Wafer further says: "Their way of reckoning from score to score is no more than what our old English way was, but their saying, instead of thirty-one, thirty-two, etc., one score and eleven, one score and twelve, etc., is much like the Highlanders of Scotland and Ireland, reckoning eleven and twenty, twelve and twenty, etc.; so for fifty-three, the Highlanders say thirteen and two score, as the Darien Indians would two score and thirteen, only changing the place. In my youth I was well acquainted with the Highland or primitive Irish language, both as it is spoken in the north of Ireland, particularly at the Navan upon the Boyne, and about the town of Virgini upon Lough Rammer in the Barony of Castle Raghen, in the County of Cavan; and also in the Highlands of Scotland, where I have been up and down in several places. . . . I learned a great deal of the Darien language in a month's conversation with them."

Wafer's description of the dress of this tribe of American Indians, presents also a remarkable coincidence with the short notices of the inhabitants of White Man's Land, as given to Karlsefni by the Esquimaux:—

"They have a sort of long cotton garment of their own, some *white,* others of a rusty black, shaped like our carters' frocks, hanging down to their heels, with a fringe of the same of cotton, about a span lang, and short, wide, open sleeves, reaching but to the middle of the arms. These garments they put on over their heads. . . . When they are thus assembled, they will sometimes walk about the place or plantation where they are, with their robes on; and I once saw Lacenta (a chief) thus walking about with two or three hundred of these attending him, as if he was mustering them: and I took notice that those in the black gowns walked before him, *and the white after him, each having their lances of the same colour with their robes.* . . . They were all in their finest robes, which are *long white gowns,* reaching to their ancles, with fringes at the bottom, and in their hands they had half pikes."

The affinity between the American-Indian and Celtic languages, and consequent probability of an European settlement having been formed upon the shores of New Spain before the arrival of the Spaniards, appears to have been entertained by many writers of eminence in the 17th century. In the remarkable work entitled the "Turkish Spy," we find the author positively affirming the similarity of the two languages, and stating the tradition of an early European settlement:

"This prince (Charles II.) has several nations under his dominions, and 'tis thought he scarce knows the just extent of his territories in America. There is a region in that continent inhabited by a people whom they call Tuscorards and Doegs. *Their language is the same as is spoken by the British or Welsh.* . . . Those Tuscorards and Doegs of America are thought to descend from them. . . . It is certain that when the Spaniards first conquered Mexico they were surprised to hear the inhabitants discourse of a strange people, that formerly *came thither in corraughs,* who taught them the knowledge of God, and of immortality, instructed them also in virtue and morality, and prescribed holy rites and ceremonies of religion. 'Tis remarkable also what an Indian King said to a Spaniard, viz.: That in foregoing ages a strange people arrived there by sea, to whom his ancestors gave hospitable entertainment; in regard they found them men of wit and courage, endued also with many other excellencies: but he could give no account of their origin or name. . . . The British language is so prevalent here, that the very towns, bridges, beasts, birds, rivers, hills, etc., are called by British or Welsh names." "Who can tell," truly adds the author, "the various transmigrations of mortals on earth, or trace out the true originals of any people?"

The improbability of the Irish having, at any very remote period of time, been in possession of vessels of sufficient power and capacity to enable them to accomplish a voyage across the Atlantic may, perhaps, be urged as an objection to this supposed early migration to the American coast; but, without resting upon their ancient Spanish or Carthaginian connexion, a very little enquiry will show, that at least in the first centuries of the Christian era they were amply provided with the means of accomplishing a voyage to the New World, which, from the western coast of Ireland, little exceeds 1600 miles.

O'Halloran states, on the authority of the Psalter of Cashel, said to be the oldest Irish MS., that Moghcorb, King of Leath Mogha, or Munster, prepared *a large fleet* in the year 296, and invaded Denmark; and that in the following century (A. D. 367), Criomthan, who in the Psalter of Cashel is styled Monarch of Ireland and Albany, and leader of the Franks and Saxons, prepared a formidable fleet, and raised a large body of troops, which were transported to Scotland, for the purpose of acting in conjunction with the Picts and Saxons against the Roman wall, and devastating the provinces of Britain. In 396, an expedition, upon a most extensive and formidable scale, was undertaken by the celebrated Niall of the Nine Hostages, one of the most distinguished princes of the Milesian race: "Observing," says Moore, "that the Romans, after breaking up the line of encampment along the coast opposite to Ireland, had retired to the eastern shore and the northern wall; Niall perceived that an apt opportunity was thus offered for a descent upon the now unprotected territory. Instantly summoning, therefore, all the forces of the island, and embarking them on board such *ships* as he could collect, he ranged, with his *numerous navy*, along the whole coast of Lancashire," etc. It was to this expedition that the poet Claudian, lauding the achievement of his patron Stilicho, alluded, in the memorable lines:—

> By him defended, when the neighbouring hosts
> Of warlike nations spread along our coasts;
> When Scots† came thundering from the Irish shores,
> And the wide ocean foamed from hostile oars.
>
> De Laudab, Stil. Lib. 2.

---

†The Irish are supposed to have obtained the name of Scots or Scoti from the Scotic or Scythic origin of the Spanish settlers under the sons of Milesius, whose invasion Moore places "about a century or two" before the Christian era; other more enthusiastic national historians take us back to 800 years before that period; and O'Halloran fixes the landing on the 17th of May, A. M. 2736, or 1264 years before the birth of Christ. The name Scoti, he derives from Scota, the wife of Niulus, High Priest of Phœnius, the inventor of letters, and ancestor of Milesius, in proof of which is given a quotation from an Irish poem of the 9th century, entitled, Canam bunadhas na Nagaoidheal, or "Let us rehearse the origin of the Irish."

This same Niall extended this enterprise to the coast of Brittany, and ravaged the maritime districts of the northwest of Gaul, during which expedition was captured the great Christian apostle, St. Patrick.

That such expeditions could have been carried on by means of the little fragile currachs, to which mode of transport some writers would limit the sea expeditions of the Irish at this period, seems scarcely credible, and while allowing full force to the fearless and enterprising spirit of the gallant Scoti, and the "contempto pelagi," alluded to by Eric of Auxerre, we must allow them some more rational means for conveying a body of troops across the British and Gallic channels than these frail barks.

Not that the currachs were insufficient for individual enterprise of a more peaceful character, and it seems probable that the monks of the 8th century launched themselves on the northern ocean in these simple hide-covered skiffs, and thus effected a passage to their island retreats; for we find St. Cormac committing himself to the sea in a similar bark, and on one occasion he is said to have been out of sight of land for fourteen days and nights.

But the remarkable passage in Tacitus, which has been so often cited by Irish historians in proof of the early maritime importance of their country, would lead to the conclusion that at a period anterior to that now under consideration, the Irish were possessed of ships, or vessels of no mean size or description. "Ireland," the Roman historian says, "situated midway between Britain and Spain, and convenient also to the Gallic sea, connected a most powerful portion of the empire by considerable mutual advantages; the soil and climate, and the dispositions and habits of the people do not differ much from those of

Britain: *the approaches and harbours are better known, by reason of commerce and the merchants."* "From this it appears," says Moore, "that though scarce heard of till within a short period by the Romans, and almost as strange to the Greeks, this sequestered island was yet in possession of channels of intercourse distinct from either; and that whilst the Britons, shut out from the continent by their Roman masters, saw themselves deprived of all that profitable intercourse which they had long maintained with the Veneti and other people of Gaul, Ireland still continued to cultivate her old relations with Spain, and saw her barks venturing on their accustomed course, between the Celtic Cape, and the Sacred Promontory, as they had done for centuries before."

That Ireland must have been included amongst the Cassiterides which are known to have been visited by the Phœnicians, before the Gallic invasion of Britain, seems to be admitted by all unprejudiced writers upon this subject,* and that the mystery, in which these wily traders sought to conceal their commercial monopoly, has led to the obscurity in which the records of their voyages is involved. That the nautical knowledge and equipments of the Celtic population of Spain and Ireland must have received considerable advancement from this connection, is a natural consequence. Inhabiting the maritime regions of the Spanish peninsula, they were necessarily brought into immediate contact with the Carthaginian merchants, who had formed settlements on the same coast, and from whom they probably obtained not only their knowledge of naviga-

---

*"We may therefore admit, without much chance of error, that the Cassiterides visited by the Phœnicians, were the British *islands*, though the Romans understood by the name the islands of Scilly, with perhaps, part of the coast of Cornwall."

tion, but of those religious rites and ceremonies which were afterwards developed in the form of Druidism.

That the latter was not of British origin seems obvious. Cæsar's description of its observances is only reconcilable with his account of Britain, on the assumption that the chief seat of the Druids was in Ireland, for while he describes the Gauls as deriving their knowledge of Druidism from the British, he represents the latter as inferior in civilization to the Gauls. Even in the time of Tacitus the Britons are represented as *ferocæ,* a state of barbarism obviously incompatible with the creation of a highly wrought mysterious superstition, implying considerable intellectual advancement and scientific knowledge: a superstition, be it remembered, which is known to have existed amongst the Phœnicians and Carthaginians.

The Roman knowledge of the British isles was extremely limited and imperfect; before the time of Tacitus they were ignorant of the insular position of Britain, and the acquaintance of Agricola with Ireland was principally derived from the doubtful information of a faithless Irish chief, who sought the Roman camp to betray his country. Ireland also, according to Ptolemy, was formerly called *Little Britain,* therefore when Cæsar speaks of the Gauls repairing to Britain in order to become instructed in the mysteries of Druidism, the term may have been intended as a general expression for the British isles.*

---

*It should be recollected that Cæsar merely mentions the origin of the Druids as traditionary: "Disciplinam *existimatur* reperta esse in Britannia," &c. Ibid. Sharon Turner would appear to lean to the opinion of Druidism having originated with the Phœnicians or Carthaginians: "If this system," he observes, "was the creature of a more civilized people, none of the colonizers of Britain are so likely to have been its parents as the Phœnicians or Carthaginians; the fact so explicitly asserted by Cæsar, that the Druidical system began in Britain, and was thence introduced into Gaul, increases our tendency to refer it to those nations. The state of Britain was inferior in civilization to that of Gaul, and therefore it seems more reasonable to refer the intellectual parts of Druidism to the foreign visitors *who are known* to have cultivated such subjects, than to suppose them to have originated from the rude unassisted natives."

The Druids, Cæsar tells us, are concerned in divine matters, superintend public and private sacrifices, interpret religious rites, determine controversies, inheritance, boundaries of land, rewards and punishments. . . . "They are said to learn by heart a great number of verses, for which reason some continue in the discipline twenty years."— *"They use written characters."*—"Much besides they discourse, and deliver to youth, upon the stars, and their motion, on the magnitude of the world and the earth, on the nature of things, on the influence and power of the immortal Gods."

This particular class, combining the double office of judge and priest, although common in the time of Cæsar to the British isles, would naturally be found most enlightened in that part of the three kingdoms, whose direct communication with Spain, from a remote period, brought it into more immediate contact with the Phœnician navigators; and the appellations of "Sacred Isle," and "Sacred Promontory," in the works of Ptolemy and Avienus, lead us involuntarily to the conclusion that, hundreds of years before the Roman invasion of Britain, Ireland was the depository of those Phœnician superstitions which afterwards became adopted throughout the British Isles under the form of Druidism.

The root of the word Druid is to be found with little variation in the Hiberno-Celtic language of the present day, *Draoj* signifying a Druid, magician or wise man, and *Draoideacht* or Draoide-achta, magic or the Druidical form of worship; the golden ornaments in the shape of a half moon, which have been frequently found in the Irish bogs, are supposed to have been connected with these superstitions, of which lunar worship formed a part, and add to the numerous testimonies in proof of its great antiquity.

But the high state of perfection, if it may be so called, in which the Druidical form of worship existed in Ireland, and the superior acquirements of her Pagan priesthood to those of the British, is best evinced by the vestige of the Ogham or occult character in which their mysteries were recorded, and which presents a marked resemblance to the secret mode of writing, known to have been used for similar purposes by the hierarchies of the East.

It may therefore be presumed without much stretch of credulity that the same communication with the Phœnician settlers on the coast of Spain which transmitted these eastern superstitions to the Irish shore, may have also brought with it some knowledge of navigation, and the construction of ships; and therefore, that we are not driven to the hide-covered currach for a means of transporting the Celtic settlers to the American coast.

Or if the theory of those be adopted, who would bring the first colonists of Ireland from Belgic, or Celtic Gaul, the description of that people by Cæsar will furnish equal evidence of maritime knowledge at a period sufficiently early to transport an expedition to America in the first centuries of the Christian era. The Veneti, inhabiting that district of Armoric Gaul, now known by the name of Vannes, are stated to have had vessels of considerable bulk and power, and admirably adapted as well for coasting voyages, as a stormy sea. The hull was of oak, the beams a foot in breadth, and fastened with iron, the bottom flat, the sails of leather, and what to nautical men may, perhaps, appear somewhat wonderful in those early days, the anchors were secured by means of *chain cables.*

Looking therefore, either to the Phœnician, Carthaginian, Iberian, Belgic, Gallic, or Scythic intercourse of an early period,—to the more continuous Scandinavian occupation of later years,—or to the primitive mode of transport of the simple skiff, it is evident that ample nautical means were not wanting in Ireland to transfer any part of her population to the western shores of America long before the period when Great Ireland became known to the Northmen.

The absence of any notice of such a migration in Irish Annals,—if such be the case,—is no argument against the probability of its existence. The most brilliant period of Irish History remains unsupported by Irish manuscripts. Of that enlightened age when pupils from all parts of Europe sought learning from Irish seminaries and Irish ecclesiastics,—when Columbkill dispensed the light of Christianity to the Picts, Columbanus to the French, Gallus to the Swiss, and the brothers Ultan and Foilan to the Belgians, —when Virgilius, the Apostle of Carinthia, astounded the German bishops with his superior knowledge of cosmography and science—not one authentic *written* record now remains.*

Invasion from without, and internal dissension from within, have swept away all written testimonies of a time, when the intellectual and religious eminence of Ireland attracted the attention and admiration of neighbouring nations, and obtained for her the just distinction of "Sacred Island" and "School of the West:" it cannot therefore be a matter of surprise that the records of earlier history should

---

*This point is ably handled by Mr. Moore, who shews that the arguments against ancient Irish history, founded upon the non-existence of any authentic MSS. prior to the 9th century (Psalter of Cashel), applies with much greater force to the comparatively modern periods above mentioned, the records of which are never questioned. Hist. Ir. Vol. I., p. 308.

have been lost amid the ravages of such general devastation.*

But further examination of Icelandic Annals may possibly throw more light upon this interesting question, and tend to unravel the mystery in which the original inhabitants of America are involved. Lord Kingsborough's splendid publication† in 1829 first brought to the notice of the British public the striking similitude between Mexican and Egyptian monuments; the ruins of Palenque, Guatemala and Yucatan, the former rivalling the pyramids of Egypt or the ruins of Palmyra, were only known to a few hunters until the end of the 18th century, and modern travellers are still engaged in bringing the hidden wonders of this and other regions of the vast American continent to the knowledge of the literary world

The argument founded upon the absence of Irish records might as reasonably be applied to these later publications of the north; and why, may it as well be asked, was the discovery of American by the Northmen in the 10th century not satisfactorily established until the nineteenth?—The

---

*O'Halloran charges the English Government with a wholesale destruction of Irish MSS. previous to the reign of James I.:—
"What the false piety and mistaken zeal of the early Christians left unfinished, the Danes continued, and the Saxon and Norman invaders completed.....In Ireland, until the accession of James I, it was a part of state policy to destroy or carry off all the manuscripts that could be discovered. "What the president Carew," says the author of the Analect (p. 555) "did in one province (Munster), Henry Sidney and his predecessors did all over the kingdom, being charged to collect all the manuscripts they could, that they might effectually destroy every vestige of antiquity and letters throughout the kingdom! The learned Archdeacon Lynch, with many others, give too many melancholy instances of the kind." Hist. Ireland, V. I. p. 94. "Many of these precious remains," says Moore, "were, as the author of Cambrensis Eversus tells us, actually torn up by boys for covers of books, and by tailors for measures. It was till the time of James I., says Mr. Webb, an object of government to discover and destroy every literary remain of the Irish, in order the more fully to eradicate from their minds every trace of their ancient independence." Moore's Hist. of Ireland, V. I. p. 309, note.

†"Mexican Antiquities," a work upon which this lamented nobleman expended (at least) £30,000 and the best years of his life, but the circulation of which, from the small number of copies printed, and the inaccessible price (£150) to the majority of the reading public, was necessarily very limited.

name of Vinland was, doubtless, known to Torfæus; and Wormskiold, Malte Brun and others, following the erroneous calculation which he had made of its locality, fixed it in a latitude with which the physical features of the country did not correspond:* hence the whole statement in the Sagas was long looked upon as fictitious; but the more accurate recent investigations of Danish archæologists have set the question at rest, and the discovery of America by the Northmen has assumed its proper position in the history of the tenth century.

The existence of a Celtic or Irish settlement upon the south-eastern shores of North America, does not preclude the co-existence of other races upon the western and northern shores. A colony from western Ireland may have been planted on the east, while tribes from eastern Asia had settled on the west; and both have driven before them the less civilized, or more feeble Scythic wanderers, who may have entered at the north: all emanating,—but by distinct and separate channels,—from the one great center, which peopled the wide spread sphere, and thus multiplying, in every region and every clime, the living evidences of those sacred records which offer peace and immortality to man.

---

*Torfæus, in consequence of an erroneous interpretation of the passage, pp. 64, 65, in the Saga of Erik the Red, relating to the length of the day, which he took to be eight hours instead of nine, fixed the latitude of Vinland at 49 degrees, being that of Newfoundland.

THE NORSEMEN IN AMERICA.

BY RASMUS B. ANDERSON, LL. D.

CHAPTER I.

NORUMBEGA.

THE early discovery of this country by the Norsemen is of interest to every American. It is the first coming of Europeans to this continent. It is the first chapter of civilization in the Western world. It is also the first chapter of the history of the Christian Church in America; for Leif Erikson and his followers had been converted to Christianity and Leif was himself a missionary sent out by the king of Norway to preach the gospel of the Gallilean to the Norse colonists in Greenland.

Before the landing of the Pilgrims at Plymouth Rock in 1620, the shores of North America had been visited by the so-called French voyageurs. Some of these explorers wrote accounts of their voyages, and in their narratives and on maps which they published there is frequent mention of the name Norumbega. The name is found with a variety of spellings, Norumbegue, Norumbergue, sometimes with the initial "n" omitted, Anorabegra, Anorumbega, etc. It is applied to a country, river and city located somewhere in the eastern part of the United States or Canada. It is said to have been discovered by Verrazzano in 1524. The site of the city was given on a map published at Antwerp in 1570. In 1604 Champlain ascended the Penobscot River in Maine, supposing that stream to be the Norumbega. But after going twenty-two leagues he discovered no indications of a city or of civilization except an old moss-grown cross in the woods. American historians have found much difficulty in identifying Norumbega. The fact is the statements of the various French authorities are conflicting. As stated, the first mention is by Verrazzano on his map published in Antwerp in 1524, and later, that is, in 1539, Parmentier found the name Norumbega applied to a country lying southwest from Cape Breton. Allefonsce, under Roberval, in 1543, determined the fact of there being two Cape Bretons, of which the more southern, referred to by Parmentier, was in the forty-third degree and identical with Cape Anne. Within the limit of this forty-third degree was a river, at the mouth of which, according to Allefonsce, were many rocks and islands; up which river, as Allefonsce estimated, fifteen leagues from the mouth was a city called Norumbegue. "There was," Allefonsce said, "a fine people at the city and they had furs of many animals and wore mantles of martin skins." Allefonsce was a pilot by profession and on him particularly rests the identity of one of the Cape Bretons which Cape Anne and the fact of there being a river with a city on its banks, both bearing the name Norumbega between Cape Anne and Cape Cod. Wytfiiet, in 1597, in an augment to Ptolemy, says, "Norombega, a beautiful city and a grand river, are well-known." He gives on his map a picture of the settlement, or villa, at the junction of two streams, one of which is called the Rio Grande. Thevet in his texts places Fort Norumbegue at the point where Wytfliet placed the city, that is, at the junction of two streams, and Thevet says "To the north of Virginia is Norumbega, which is well-known as a beautiful city and a great river. Still one can not find whence this name is derived, for the natives call it Agguncia. At the entrance of the river there is an island very convenient for the fishery." Thevet describes the fort as surrounded by fresh water and at the junction of two streams. The city of Norumbega on his map is lower down the river. The French, who occupied the fort, called the fort Norumbega. As stated, the identification of Norumbega has greatly puzzled American historians, and the country, river and city have from time to time been located at various points from Virginia to the St. Lawrence. Most authorities have referred Norumbega to New England, while Lok, in 1582, seems to have believed that the Penobscot in Maine formed its southern boundary. Before 1880 this view seems to have been very generally adopted by American scholars. Our poet, J. G. Whittier, made Norumbega the subject of one of his most beautiful poems.

In connection with the poem, the poet gives the following explanatory note, which well represents the concensus of opinion of American scholars before 1880: "Norembega, or Norimbegue, is the name given by early French fishermen and explorers to a fabulous country south of Cape Breton, first discovered by Verazzano in 1524. It was supposed to have a magnificent city of the same name on a great river, probably the Penobscot. The site of this barbaric city is laid down on a map published at Antwerp in 1570. In 1604, Champlain sailed in search of the Northern Eldorado, twenty-two leagues up the Penobscot from the Isle Haute. He supposed the river to be that of Norembega, but wisely came to the conclusion that those travelers who told of the great city had never seen it. He saw no evidence of anything like civilization, but mentions the finding of a cross, very old and mossy, in the woods."

In 1881 Arthur James Weise, of Troy, N. Y., published a work called "The Discovery of America to the Year 1525." In the closing pages of this work he takes up the subject of Norumbega, and arrives at the conclusion that the name is a contraction of the old French L'Anormeeberge (the grand scarp), and claims that the adjective "anormee" and the noun "berge" definitely describe the wall of rocks known as the Palisades, on the Hudson river, above New York city. Weise has no doubt that by the term Norumbega river the Hudson is meant, and that the country around the Palisades was called by the French explorers La Terre d'Anormeeberge, afterwards contracted and corrupted into Norumbega and its other variations heretofore named. In identifying the river called by one of the French writers Norombega with the present Hudson, Weise lays great stress upon the statement by the same writer that the water of the river was salty to the height of forty leagues, and shows that the Hudson is brackish beyond the city of Poughkeepsie. According to Weise, the city of Norumbega must have occupied the site of the present Albany, the capital of New York. Weise's arguments seemed so conclusive, particularly his interpretation of the name, that his view was very generally accepted by students of American history everywhere.

Passing on to the year 1890, we come to an entirely new theory. Before presenting this in detail it may interest my readers to learn a few facts leading up to it. In 1873 I suggested to the famous Norwegian violinist, Ole Bull, that Leif Erikson, the first white man who planted his feet on American soil, ought to be honored with a monument. Ole Bull accepted the suggestion with the greatest enthusiasm, and he and I together immediately prepared plans for its realization. During the spring of 1873 we arranged a number of entertainments in Wisconsin and Iowa, the proceeds of which made the nucleus of the Leif Erikson monument fund. At these entertainments Ole Bull played the violin and the writer sandwiched in short addresses to the audiences while the artist rested. Later, that same year, I accompanied Ole Bull to Norway, and there a series of entertainments were arranged for the same purpose. At one of these entertainments the distinguished Norwegian poet, Bjornstjerne Bjornson, delivered an address. A sum of money was realized from the entertainments in Norway for the monument fund. A few years later Ole Bull made his American home in Cambridge, Mass.; there he was successful in organizing a committee for the purpose of carrying out our plans in regard to the Leif Erikson monument. The committee was a most brilliant one.

In it were found James Russell Lowell, Henry Wadsworth Longfellow, Oliver Wendell Holmes, Thomas S. Appleton, Prof. E. N. Horsford, the Governor of Massachusetts, the Mayor of Boston and many other distinguished people. Funds were rapidly raised, and America's most distinguished sculptress, Miss Anne Whitney,* was engaged to produce in bronze a statue of Leif Erikson in heroic size. In due time the statue was completed and placed at the end of Commonwealth Avenue in Boston. The statue represents Leif Erickson as he discovers the first faint outlines of land far away on the horizon, and with his right hand he shades his eyes from the dazzling rays of the sun. The statue does not represent my idea of a long bearded and shaggy haired Norseman of the tenth century. Miss Whitney has made Leif smooth faced, with the general outlines of the Roman. She seems to have taken the splendid physique and features of Ole Bull for her model. But it is certainly a great work of art. No less authority than James Russell Lowell declared it to be the finest work of sculpture hitherto produced in America. A perfect replica, cast in the same mold as the original, was presented by a Milwaukee lady to the city of Milwaukee, where it can be seen by my readers. It stands on the lake front, a little north of the Chicago & Northwestern railway station, near the well-known Juneau monument.

It will be observed that Prof. Horsford was mentioned as one of the committee in Cambridge. Prof. Eben Nor-

---

*Miss Anne Whitney was born in Watertown, Mass. She opened a studio as sculptress in Boston in 1873, and has made among other notable works, a statue of Samuel Adams and one of Harriet Martineau.

ton Horsford, born July 27th, 1818, was the son of a distinguished missionary among the Indians. The son, Eben, acquired from his father, who was thoroughly familiar with many Indian dialects, an extensive knowledge of Indian words. He studied science both in America and in Europe under Prof. Liebig, and became Professor of Science in Harvard University in 1847, a position which he filled with distinction for sixteen years. Fortune smiled on him. He became wealthy and was able to devote his time exclusively to scientific and literary pursuits. He was a large hearted man and gave generously of his wealth to educational institutions. Wellesley College is under great obligations to him.

The organization of the Leif Erickson committee in Cambridge attracted his attention to the subject of the Norse discovery of America. The result was that he practically abandoned his other studies and concentrated all his energies on investigations bearing on the Norse voyages to this country. He was particularly interested in locating the landfall of Leif Erikson and in identifying the country explored by him and his countrymen from the tenth to the fourteenth century. Some idea can be formed of Prof. Horsford's enthusiasm in this cause when we learn that he spent more than $50,000 in making explorations, in publishing books and maps, and in building monuments and memorials in honor of the Norse discoverer. He was the orator at the unveiling of the Leif Erikson monument in Boston.

In 1890, Prof. Horsford presented an entirely new theory in regard to the perplexing question of Norumbega.

In this year appeared his "Discovery of the Ancient City of Norumbega." In it he claims to have found the precise site of the ancient city, and locates it with absolute confidence on the Charles river, in Massachusetts, at its junction with Stony Brook, near Walton. He makes Norumbega identical with the Vinland of the Norseman, claiming that Norumbega is not derived from the old French *D'Anormee Berge,* but is a corruption of the old name *Norvegr* and that it has borne that name among the aborigines ever since the Norse explorers in the tenth and following centuries made their headquarters there. He takes Norumbega to be the name the French voyageurs did not bestow but found. So thoroughly convinced was Prof. Horsford of the correctness of his theory that he built on the site which he identified as Norumbega a costly tower in commemoration of the Norse discoverers and colonists. Prof. Horsford found at and around the junction of Stony Brook with Charles river evidences of a great industry involving, among other things, a graded area some four acres in extent, paved with field boulders. At the base of the bluffs along Stony Brook there are ditches or canals extending far into the country and above the ditches are walls made of boulders from three to five feet high. The existence of these works has long been known, but their origin has never been satisfactorily interpreted. It is certain that they existed before the landing of the Pilgrim Fathers in 1620. It is equally certain that they are the handiwork of man. They are too extensive to have been produced by the French or English explorers previous to 1620. They can scarcely be ascribed to the aborigines, for they differ widely from any works known to have been constructed by the natives of this country. The old Norse sagas tell us that the Norseman carried timber from Vinland to Greenland and Prof. Horsford suggests that the canals were filled with water at high tide and that logs were floated down to where their ships lay in the Charles river. He supposes that the walls above the canals were constructed to protect the canals from being filled with debris from the bluffs. When the immediate shores of the river had been cleared of wood the shores of the tributaries flowing into the river became the field of activity and maple blocks were sent floating down the stream; and where the streams were remote from the bases of the slopes on either side the sources of water were at hand. Canals, or nearly level troughs, were dug to transport the logs to the streams and ultimately to the Charles. Dams and ponds were necessary at the mouths of the streams to prevent the blocks from going down the Charles without a convoy and out to sea to be lost. There is an admirable canal, walled on one side, extending for a thousand feet along the western bank of Stony Brook in the woods above the Tiverton railroad crossing, between Walton and Weston. The Cheesecake Brook is another and Cold Spring Brook another, and there is an interesting dry canal near Murray Street, not far from Newtonville. It may be seen from the railroad cars on the right, a little to the east of Eddy Street, approaching Boston. Prof. Horsford found throughout the basin of the Charles numerous canals, ditches, deltas, boom-dams, ponds, fish-ways, forts, dwellings, walls, terraces of theatre and amphitheatre, and he insisted that there was not a square mile drained into the Charles River that lacked an incontestable monument of the presence of the Norsemen. I have myself gone over the most of this ground in company with Prof. Horsford and listened to his enthusiastic interpretations of these strange remains. It may seem as an undeserved dignity to speak of these ditches as canals, but they are so named in the old deeds in Weston, and if you look at them on the left of the highway, between Sibley's and Weston, with the stone wall on either side, you will not wonder that the word canal, as well as ditch, should have suggested itself. They are so called on the published town maps of Millis and Holliston. Prof. Horsford, as indicated, bought a tract of land at the junction of Stony Brook with Charles River, consecrating it to the memory of the Norsemen, and set up in Weston, at the mouth of Stony Brook, a magnificent tower. Over the tablet, set in the wall of the tower, is poised the Icelandic falcon about to alight with a new world in his talons. On the tablet is given the following inscription:

A. D. 1000.   A. D. 1889.

NORUMBEGA.

City—Country—Fort—River.

Norumbega—Nor'mbega.
Indian utterance of Norbega, the Ancient Form of Norvega, Norway, to which the Region of Vinland was Subject.

City.

At and near Watertown,
Where Remain To-day
Docks, Wharfs, Walls, Dams, Basin.

Country:

Extending from Rhode Island to the St. Lawrence.
First Seen by Bjarni Herjulfson, 985 A. D.
Landfall of Leif Erikson on Cape Codd, 1000 A. D.
Norse Canals, Dams, Walls, Pavements.
Forts, Terraced Places of Assembly, Remain To-day.

Fort:

At Base of Tower and Region About
Was Occupied by the Breton French in the 15th, 16th and
17th Centuries.

River:

The Charles,
Discovered by Leif Erikson 1000 A. D.
Explored by Thorwald, Leif's Brother, 1003 A. D.
Colonized by Thorfinn Karlsefni 1007 A. D.
First Bishop Erik Gnupson 1121 A. D.
Industries for 350 Years.
Masur-wood (Burrs), Fish, Furs, Agriculture.
Latest Norse Ship Returned to Iceland in 1347.

Prof. Horsford mentioned as considerations that led
to the erection of the tower:

"1. It will commemorate the discovery of Vinland
and Norumbega in the forty-third degree, and the identification of Norumbega with Norway, the home country
to which this region was once subject by right of discovery and colonization.

"2. It will invite criticism, and so sift out any errors of interpretation into which, sharing the usual fortune of the pioneer, I may have been led.

"3. It will encourage archæological investigation in a fascinating and almost untrodden field, and be certain to contribute in the results of research and exploration, both in the study and the field, to the historical treasure of the commonwealth.

"4. It will help by reason of its mere presence, and by virtue of the veneration with which the tower will in time come to be regarded, to bring acquiescence in the fruit of investigation, and so allay the blind skepticism, amounting practically to inverted ambition, that would deprive Massachusetts of the glory of holding the Landfall of Leif Erikson, and at the same time the seat of the earliest colony of Europeans in America."

In the old Norse sagas (histories) in which the Norse voyages to America are described, it is stated that when Leif Erikson came to Vinland he first sailed up a river, that the river then widened into a lake, that he crossed this lake and then sailed up another river as far as his ship could float. Such a description might doubtless apply to various points on the northeast coast, but it certainly applies well to the Charles river.

In 1887, at a scientific gathering in Cambridge, Prof. Horsford announced that he had studied the saga of Erik the Red and that he interpreted the brief but clear statement therein to refer to Leif's sailing across the mouth of Cape Cod Bay opening out northeast to the sea from the Race to the Gurnet; his coasting westerly along

the Gurnet from Scituate Beach past the Cohasset Rocks
to Nantasket, his entrance into Boston harbor, his running aground on an ebb-tide off the site of Long Wharf,
his floating on the returning flood up into the reach or
strait of Charles river, on to the expansion of the back
bay, and later winding through the salt meadow and
marshes up the Charles, beyond the bay to the south end
of Symond's Hill at the so called Gerry's Landing in
Cambridge, near which he built his large house, as indicated in the details given concerning Leif, Thorwald
and Thorfin Karlsefne in the sagas. At the same time
Prof. Horsford stated that if any remains of Leif's house
in Vinland should ever be found they would be located
between Symond's Hill, the ancient bluff extending eastward some hundred yards from the Cambridge City Hos-
pital, and the angle of the Cambridge City Cemetery,
about a quarter of a mile to the south. The place where
Leif landed would be, Horsford insisted, the first place
going up the Charles, where, landing on an even keel,
permitting a plank to be run out to the shore was possible. It was the spot determined for Gerry's Landing,
the great point in the earlier days of the colony for re-
ceiving goods from the sea and transporting them on
wagons to the interior. Mr. Horsford made careful investigations in this vicinity and discovered in the turf a
ridge, the outlines of which correspond with the outlines
of an Icelandic house in the saga time. The old Norse
house had a fire place in the centre of the floor and the
smoke escaped through an opening in the roof. Prof.
Horsford was so sure that this characteristic of the

house near Gerry's Landing would be found that he announced it to the workmen, who of course showed the greatest incredulity. He told them that if they would dig a trench along the middle of the house they would uncover a fire place. The turf and blown sand were a foot thick. He indicated the spot where the hearth would be found. His prediction was verified. An area of about four feet in diameter, covered by boulders, was exposed. Some were more fine grained and compact, preserving their original shape, but pitted at the surface as if they had been exposed to prolonged heat. Others were cracked into several pieces. Others still, being originally fissile gneiss finely stratified sand and argillaceous material, were resolved into different fragments like slate. One of the blocks that had preserved its general form, but with all its corners rounded, was observed to be of a dull red as if covered with reddish brown rouge. Horsford said: "If this redness is due to peroxide of iron I shall find the interior of a greenish shade due to the presence of mineral combinations with protoxide of iron." A lapidary cut the stone into thin slices. Horsford says: "As I expected, in the interior where, though heated, it had been protected from the air, the color was of a dull bottle green. The outer surface where it had been heated and exposed to the air was reddish brown. Charcoal was found, as might have been expected, at the border of the hearth."

Mr. Horsford found on the south side of the outline a marked depression, as if there had been a door. If there were door posts they should have had something to stand on. On digging down a foot or more on either side of the door-way a boulder of two-thirds of a bushel basket capacity was found. The outline of the house of logs might have been expected to rest on stone as a protection against the decay of the logs. Such stone foundations were found in probing the ground with an iron rod at a depth of about one foot and were at various points uncovered. The whole outline of the house is a regular parallelogram. Prof. Horsford had this interesting place enclosed and suitably marked.

On the last night of the year 1892, Eben Norton Horsford called his daughter Cornelia to talk with her about the traces of the house built on the banks of the Charles River, both by Thorfin Karlsefni and Snorre Thorbrandson, two Icelanders who came from Greenland in three ships with 151 men and seven women and their live stock, intending to establish a colony in Vinland, in the year 1007. Prof. Horsford asked his daughter, "What will you find in Thorfin's house if I find a fire place in Leif's house? And if I found foundations of walls at Leif's house, what will you find to correspond with that at Thorfin's house?" Then he instructed her to buy the land herself, and in the spring, when the frost was out of the ground, to get an iron rod and strike it into the earth to find the fire place, and afterwards to find the foundation walls in the same way; because he wanted her to have the pleasure of making a discovery herself. The next day, January 1st, 1893, our dear old Prof. Horsford died suddenly in his library. Miss Cornelia Horsford afterwards got her mother's permission to fin-

ish and edit her father's unpublished works, and during
the long days and evenings, while the ground was still
covered with snow, she read all the books about the ancient Norsemen and their customs to learn what she
might happen to find when the time came in the spring
for her to look for the remains of Thorfin's long house
on the bank of the river. On the 19th of April, when
the frost was out of the ground, she began her search for
the remains of the long house of Thorfin's party. It is
no easy matter to find the foundations of a house after
they have been buried several hundred years, even when
they can be traced by ridges of earth. For an hour, she
says, she watched the earth thrown up, and probed the
ground in vain. At noon she went for Mr. Scorgie,
who had made the search at Leif's house under her father's direction, and asked him to show her how to find
the foundations and fire place of this house. He soon
found them for her. The ring of the iron rod against
the stone as he struck on the north wall was distinct and
sharp, and in the afternoon he had outlined with the rod
two walls about sixty-four feet long, having first found
the end wall at the south. She was troubled by the fact
that she found two fire places, but in examining the
Yuglinga saga of Snore Sturlason, Chap. 34, she found
that large buildings sometimes had more than one fire
place. The stones which showed the action of heat were
neatly laid together, with a few clam shells and oyster
shells near by. She did not carry the excavations any
further because her father did not wish to have the ridges
destroyed by which he discovered the site of the house.

Near by, and yet undisturbed, there are traces of other houses.

In 1892 I visited Prof. Horsford and he took me first to the junction of Stony Brook with Charles River, and showed me the magnificent monument he there had erected. He pointed out to me the four acres of solid pavement and showed me the long stretches of canals and stone walls. Afterwards he took me down to Gerry's Landing and he made me discover the site of Leif Erikson's house myself. I left him and went to where I could see a ridge in the form of a parallelogram in the sod, and walked slowly over its four sides, Prof. Horsford in the meantime clapping his hands. The stone from the fire place he subsequently had cut into thin slices, and one of these he sent me as a present on Christmas, 1892, only a week before his death. Prof. Horsford had not the slightest doubt that he had identified and explained satisfactorily the Norumbega of the French voyageurs. He had the fullest faith that Norumbega was a corruption of the ancient name Norvegr, that this name had been given to the aborigines by the Norsemen and that the aborigines had handed it down from generation to generation and had spoken it to the French voyageurs. He made the most careful investigations and found that no house had been built near Gerry's Landing since 1620. He therefore became absolutely convinced that the outlines which he described must be referred back to the house built in this country in the tenth and eleventh centuries by Leif Erikson and the other Norse explorers. Prof. Horsford was very anxious to convince me that he was right and my readers are doubtless anxious to know my opinion about the matter. I am sorry that I am not able to express a conviction on the subject. Horsford's discoveries are most startling, but they seem to prove too much. I am hospitably disposed to the basin of the Charles River as the site of Vinland and the operations of the Norse discoverers. All the descriptions in the sagas apply remarkably well to the Charles River with its surrounding country, and it is more than probable that Leif Erikson trod the ground now occupied by Harvard university. The remains pointed out by Horsford, both those near Weston and those near Gerry's Landing, deserve to be carefully studied, and it is possible that a thorough investigation will confirm many of Horsford's conclusions.

CHAPTER II.

NORSE VOYAGES IN THE TENTH AND FOLLOWING CENTURIES.

If we go back to the middle of the ninth century we find what is now Norway divided into thirty odd districts, called fylkes, and governed by kinglets, or jarls. These rulers were elected and obtained their positions by the grace of the people in convention assembled. But about this time there appeared in Norway a man named Harald Fairhair, who with his prime minister, Guthorm, succeeded in subjugating all the kinglets in Norway, and united the various fylkes into one kingdom. The last battle was a naval engagement at Hafursfjord, near Stavanger, in July, 872. In this battle the last of the kinglets was conquered, and Harald became monarch of all Norway. His usurpation of power created great dissatisfaction and resulted in a large emigration to France, to the British Isles, to the Hebrides, Orkneys and Shetland Isles, to the Fareys and particularly to Iceland. Iceland had been discovered in 860, and had been visited several times by Norsemen between that time and 874, in which year the settlement of Iceland began. The flower of the Norwegian people emigrated, and it was not long before Iceland had a population of more than 50,000 souls. In Iceland a republic was organized which flourished for four hundred years; and it was during the time of the republic that the grand old poetic and historic literature of Iceland was produced.

Here it is proper to add that the Norsemen were the discoverers of pelagic navigation. Let me here state with all the emphasis that I am able to compress into so many words, that the navigation of the ocean was discovered by the old Norse Vikings. Before them, the only navigation known was coast navigation. The Norsemen were excellent ship-builders and knew how to calculate time by the sun, moon and stars, and into every history of the world, and into every encyclopedia I would have the fact conspicuously stated that pelagic navigation was discovered by the Norsemen.

Iceland became the hinge upon which the door swings which opened America to Europe. In the voyages between Norway and Iceland—a distance of about 800 miles—the sailors would occasionally be overtaken by cloudy and stormy weather and drift beyond Iceland, and so they could not help finding their way by accident to Greenland and other countries to the west and southwest of Iceland. And so it happened that in the year 876 a Norwegian mariner, by name Gunbjorn, reported that he had seen land far to the west of Iceland.

If the reader will now go with me to the southwestern part of Norway, about the middle of the tenth century, we shall find living there in a district called Jadern a man called Erik (often spelled Eirik) the Red. He was called the "Red" on account of his red hair and red beard and ruddy complexion. It also appears that he had a somewhat fiery and combative disposition. He now and then quarrelled with his neighbours, and on one occasion he had the misfortune of becoming guilty of manslaughter. For this reason he decided to emigrate from Norway, and he removed with his family to the western part of Iceland. But while he left his neighbors and the dust and sky of Jadern behind him, he carried his fiery nature with him and it was not long before he got into trouble with his new neighbors in Iceland. He therefore decided to emigrate from Iceland also and to go in search of the land seen nearly a hundred years before by Gunbjorn far to the west of Iceland. He left Iceland with a few companions in 982 and found an extensive country far to the west of Iceland. He remained there making explorations for three years and decided to found a colony there. He was anxious to give the country a name that might be attractive to settlers, and in discussing this question with his companions, they agreed on naming the country Greenland, reasoning that no name would be better suited to attract immigrants.

Greenland belongs entirely to the Western Hemisphere and is accordingly a part of America. The discovery of Greenland was in fact the discovery of America, and Erik the Red was the first European who ever boomed real estate on the Western Continent, and he boomed it successfully. He succeeded in founding in Greenland a colony which flourished for several hundred years. The Icelandic sagas contain elaborate accounts of this colony and give us the names of a number of the bishops who resided there.

Erik the Red returned to Iceland in 985, and in 986 he, with a considerable number of followers, emigrated to Greenland. Among those who emigrated with Erik the Red was one Herjulf Bardson. Herjulf Bardson had a son, by name Bjarne. Bjarne was a viking merchant. He had a custom of spending one year with his father in Iceland and the next year abroad, acquiring fee and fame, that is, wealth and reputation. In 986 he chanced to be absent on a viking expedition and, on returning to Iceland in the summer, he learned that his father had emigrated with Erik the Red to Greenland. Desiring to spend the next winter with his father, as was his custom, he asked his sailors whether they would go with him. They all said they would. "But we have none of us ever been in the Greenland sea," said Bjarne. "We mind not that," said his men, "we are willing to go wherever you will lead." And so Bjarne and his men at once set sail from Iceland. They were overtaken by foggy and stormy weather and sailed on and on, not knowing whither they were sailing. The fog and storm lasted for several weeks, then the sky cleared, the sun shone again, and lo behold they could see land in the distance! They saw that they were much too far south. The land, which was hilly and well wooded, did not correspond to the descriptions which they had received of Greenland. It was getting late in the season, so they did not go ashore, but proceeded northward. On their journey northward they discovered two other countries, but as neither of them could be Greenland they did not land. They hastened on until they finally reached Greenland in safety and happened to land near the colony founded by Erik the Red. We have no time to go into details, but it is evident that the first land seen by Bjarne, Herjulf's son, must have been some part of New England; the second land was probably Nova Scotia, and the third Newfoundland. And thus Bjarne, in the year 986, was the first pale-faced man whose eyes looked upon the American continent.

Erik the Red was the chief of the colony in Greenland. His family consisted of three sons, Leif, Thorvald and Thorstein, all bright, stalwart and enterprising young men.

In the year 1000, the same year as that in which Christianity was adopted as the religion of Iceland, Leif Erikson chanced to be in Norway. Norway had just been converted to Christianity and the ruler at this time was the famous King Olaf Trygvason. Leif Erikson met the king, and the king became very fond of him. He persuaded Leif to accept the Christian religion and be baptised. Then King Olaf sent for Leif and told him that he had a double mission for him. "In the first place," said King Olaf, "I want you to go and look up those lands which were seen by Bjarne and secure more definite information about them, and in the second place, I want you to go as a missionary to Greenland and preach the gospel of the White Christ to the colonists there."

Leif agreed to carry out the king's wishes. In the summer of the year 1000 he set sail for the far West. He decided to investigate the lands seen by Bjarne before going to Greenland. On his way west, he first reached the land which Bjarne reported he had seen, that is, Newfoundland. He anchored his ship off the coast, went ashore, and, exploring the land somewhat, found that it was hilly and extensively covered with large, flat stones. He decided to name the country after its most conspicuous peculiarities, and called it Helluland (land of flat stones). Then he proceeded towards the southwest and reached the second land seen by Bjarne (that is, Nova Scotia), which he also explored somewhat, and found that it was a heavily wooded country. On account of the large forests he called it Markland (timberland). Then he sailed on to the first country seen by Bjarne, that is, some part of New England, and here, the saga tells us, he first entered a bay and then a river, then the river widened into a lake, which he crossed, then he entered a river on the other side of the lake and sailed up this river as far as it was deep enough for his viking ship. As the reader will see, this can be applied to the Boston Harbor, to the Charles River between Boston and Cambridgeport, to the Back Bay between Boston and Cambridge and to the Charles River up as far as Gerry's Landing, near which our Professor Horsford claimed to have found the site of Leif Erikson's house and fireplace.

After having landed, Leif Erikson and his party, thirty-one in number, pulled the vessel ashore and at once went to work to build a house for the winter. The party was divided into two groups to explore the country in different directions on alternate days. On one evening, when the exploring party returned to the camp, one man was missing. This was a German, by name Tyrker, who, though a prisoner of war, was Leif Erikson's special favorite. Leif Erikson became very much alarmed and anxious. He feared that Tyrker might have been slain by natives or devoured by wild beasts. Therefore with his men Leif immediately set out in search of Tyrker. But they had not gone far from the camp when they met their missing fellow mate in a very excited state of mind. The cause of his excitement was the fact that he had found ripe wild-grapes. He had his arms full of grapes, and was devouring the fruit with all his might, and when spoken to by Leif Erikson, he only answered in his native tongue, "Weintrauben! Weintrauben!! Weintrauben!!!" He was born in a country where the grape grew, and, having been absent from Germany for many years, the finding of grapes in this western world overwhelmed him with delight. The sagas tell us that grapes were found in great abundance on every hand, and from this circumstance Leif gave the country the name of Vinland, and history at the same time obtained the interesting fact that a German accompanied these daring Argonauts of the Christian era.

The sagas give very full and interesting accounts of the various products of Vinland and of the natives or aborigines with whom our Norse explorers came in contact. This part of the subject is fully treated in preceding chapters of this volume. What I desire particularly to emphasize at this point is the fact that Leif Erikson was the first European and the first Christian who planted his feet on American soil and, as such, he deserves a conspicuous place in the history of our country. He represents the first chapter of civilized and Christian history of America.

In the spring Leif Erikson loaded his vessel with as much timber as it would carry and, in obedience to the instructions of King Olaf, proceeded to Greenland to preach the gospel of the Gallilean to Erik the Red's colony there. He was successful, and had the good fortune to convert the whole colony to the Christian religion, except the aged Erik the Red. The latter stubbornly refused to be persuaded. He declared that his faith in Odin and Thor, and particularly in his own might and main, had been sufficient for him through his long life, and he would not forsake the Gods of his childhood in his old age. And so Erik the Red died as he had lived, a heathen.

In the Greenland colony there was much talk about

Vinland the Good, and it was the general opinion that the country had been far too little explored. It was therefore agreed in the year 1002 that Leif's brother, Thorwald, should make an expedition to Vinland. He set out with a good crew of men and reached Vinland in safety, where he occupied the house built by Leif two years before. He came into conflicts with the natives, and in one of these he lost his life, an arrow from one of the aborigines piercing his heart. His comrades buried him in Vinland, and Thorwald's was the first Christian grave made in this Western World. His grave was marked by two crosses, one at the head and one at the foot. Then the little band of Norsemen, having lost their leader, returned to Greenland.

Two years later, 1005, it was decided that the youngest brother, Thorstein, should proceed to Vinland, partly for the purpose of bringing back the body of his brother Thorwald. Thorstein's wife was Gudrid, a noble, refined, intelligent and enterprising woman, and an ornament to her sex. Gudrid went with her husband on this expedition, but the party did not reach Vinland. The weather was unfavorable and the vessel drifted far to the north. Thorstein was taken sick and died, and the widow, Gudrid, took the vessel back to Erik's fjord in Greenland.

Leif Erikson and his sister-in-law, Gudrid, lived at the farm Brattahlid in Greenland, and if the reader now will go with me to that northern country in the year 1006 we will find that there had just arrived in the colony a distinguished and wealthy man from Norway. His

name was Thorfin Karlsefni. He visited frequently at
Brattahlid, and with each visit his admiration of Gudrid
increased. The spark of love soon grew into an un-
controllable flame and he asked the young widow to become his wife. The matter was referred to Leif Erikson, who had the disposal of his sister-in-law, and he
at once consented, and accordingly the nuptials of Gudrid and Thorfin were celebrated in grand style during
the Christian holidays of the year 1006. The honey-
moon was spent in Greenland, and I fancy that when the
sun's rays began to warm the atmosphere the following
spring that the young couple took many a walk on the
sea shore, and I take it also that much of their conversation turned on Vinland, the Good, and the prospects
offered for founding a settlement in that beautiful and
fertile country. Gudrid was a bright and enterprising
young woman and, while there is no record of the fact, I
can imagine that she looked smiling into Thorfin's face
and talked to him somewhat in this fashion: "I wonder that you, Thorfin, with all your wealth and with all
your splendid men should choose to live in this God-
forsaken country instead of seeking out the famous Vinland and planting a colony there. Just think what an
agreeable change it would be for all of us! Thick and
leafy woods instead of these willow bushes that are good
for nothing except to save our cattle from starvation
when the hay crop gives out. Longer summers and
shorter and less cold winters instead of the barren wastes
of this country. Surely, I think this land was woefully
misnamed when Erik the Red called it Greenland."

Of course Gudrid pleaded as only a woman can plead, and Thorfin was persuaded. He resolved to plant a colony in Vinland, and in the summer of 1007 he organized a party of one hundred and fifty-one men and seven women, who sailed in three ships from Greenland to Vinland. That Thorfin and Gudrid intended to make a permanent settlement in Vinland is also evident from the fact that they took cattle and sheep with them. The party reached Vinland in safety, and remained there three years, but the frequent conflicts with the aborigines made their life a very precarious one, and they finally decided to abandon the colony, and return to Greenland. Powder and firearms had not yet been invented, and the superior intelligence of the Norsemen was not sufficient to protect them against the swarms of natives that surrounded them and were as well armed as the Norsemen. It is, however, to be recorded that during their stay in Vinland, Thorfin and Gudrid got a son. They named him Snorre. He was born in the summer of 1008, and was the first white and the first Christian child who saw the light of day in America.

The sagas—that is to say, the histories—written in Iceland, describing these voyages of the Norsemen, give very full accounts of the daily life in the Vinland colony, of the explorations, of the natives of America, of the various kinds of products of the soil, of the climate, etc., and it is interesting to read these first recorded descriptions of a land that has since become so prominent in the history of the world, and which is now so dear to all of us who call it our home.

The sagas tell of various other voyages to Vinland, particularly of one in the year 1011. In 1121 it is stated, in various places in the sagas, that a bishop named Erik Upse went to find Vinland. It is nowhere stated whether he actually reached Vinland or returned and we are simply left to conjecture as to the purpose and result of his journey. All we know with certainty is that he "started for Vinland." However, it is by no means likely that the church would send a bishop to Vinland before a colony was planted there. We know now by the manuscript reports shown among the Vatican Exhibits at the World's Fair, 1904, that the Catholic See of Greenland extended its jurisdiction over all the new discoveries of Lief and Thorvald, and Karlsefni. It was common for priests to accompany voyages, but bishops took charge of the Church interests of colonies and, therefore, by the sending of bishop Erik Upse to Vinland it is reasonably certain that a colony had been planted there and was maintained for several years. This inevitable conclusion is fortified, if not confirmed, by references contained in official reports made by the bishops of Greenland to the Church at Rome.

The last expedition mentioned in the sagas was in 1347, 145 years before the rediscovery by Columbus. In that year it is stated that a vessel came from Markland (Nova Scotia) to Iceland with a cargo of wood. But this, as the reader will see, carries us down to a memorable period in European history. It brings us to the breaking out of the terrible black plague, or black death. The ravages of the black plague were so enormous, they

so much decimated the population of all European countries that much time was required for recuperation. It
took more than one hundred years for Europe to recover
sufficiently to be able to engage in new enterprises either
at home or abroad. We can form some conception of
the character of the black death when we learn that it
reduced the population of Norway alone from 2,000,000
to 300.000. The black death has been handed down in
tradition from generation to generation, even to the
present time. The Norwegian peasants speak of it as
an old hag marching through the country with a rake in
one hand and a broom in the other. If she came to a valley in Norway where there were a few good people she
used the rake, and the virtuous would escape between the
fingers of the rake. But when she found a valley where
all the people were wicked she used the broom and did
not leave a soul to tell the tale of what had happened.
Some of the remote valleys thus swept clean have been
rediscovered within the last century. The black death
also visited Iceland and Greenland and committed similar depredations there. It is evident that this scourge
left no surplus population for exploring and colonizing
lands beyond the sea.

If the communication between the north of Europe
and Greenland and Vinland could have been continued a
hundred years longer, that is, until the middle of the
fifteenth century, or until the countries had recuperated
from the ravages of the black plague and until after the
discovery of the compass and of powder and fire arms,
then there is no doubt but that the Norse colonies would

have become permanent, and America would have become the scene of Norse settlements and Norse enterprises. The Norse language would have taken possession of this country from sea to sea and there is little doubt that his article of mine would have been written in the Norse tongue instead of in English. Meanwhile it is certain that Bjarne Herjulfson was the first European whose eyes beheld the American continent, that Leif Erikson was the first pale-faced man whose feet trod on American soil, that his brother Thorvald was the first Christian buried beneath our sod, that Thorfin Karlsefni was the first to attempt the planting of a colony on our shores, that the noble and intelligent Gudrid was the first white woman to honor America with her presence, and that Thorfin's and Gudrid's son Snorre was the first white child born in America.

In this connection it is interesting to note the fact that the first white man to visit the extreme western part of America was the Dane, Vitus Bering, after whom Bering Strait bears its name. Bering discovered the extreme western coast of this country in 1728. The Norwegian, Leif Erikson, stands at the rising, and the Dane, Vitus Bering, at the setting sun, and clasp the great American continent in their strong Scandinavian arms. The Swedes, too, should be remembered, for when this country was in the throes of the great civil war, did not Sweden give us her great son, John Ericsson, who invented for us the Monitor?

"Truth crushed to earth will rise again." The facts of these Norse voyages have long lain darkened and hid

in old neglected libraries, and so truth may long lie unknown under the dust and rubbish of the ages; but it is
like a ray of light from a star in some far-off region of
the universe. After thousands of years that ray reaches
some other heavenly body and gives it light.

CHAPTER III.

COLUMBUS AND THE NORSEMEN.

THERE is no direct evidence on this subject, that is to
say, there is no statement either by Columbus or by any
one of his contemporaries that he possessed any knowledge of Norse voyages to the Western continent. But
there is a considerable amount of indirect or circumstantial evidence, and it is believed that circumstantial evidence, when a sufficient number of strong links are
found, is even more to be relied on than direct evidence.
In weighing the circumstantial proofs to be presented I
would request my reader not to judge these proofs singly,
but rather united. One of the wires in the Brooklyn
bridge would not carry a horse, but the thousands of
wires twisted together form the strong cables that sus-
tain the great bridge and all that immense traffic between New York and Brooklyn. Thus either one of the
arguments which I propose to present, though the steel
in it is of excellent quality, may not, when considered
alone, be of sufficient strength; but when the various
arguments are twisted together by the reader I trust they

will constitute for him a cable of evidence strong enough to unite the voyages of Columbus with those of the Norsemen.

1. It will be remembered that in the year 1007 Thorfin Karlsefni and his gifted wife, Gudrid, undertook to colonize Vinland; that the emigrants from Greenland, more than 150 in number, remained in Vinland for three years, but that on account of frequent conflicts with the aborigines, making life a very precarious one, the colonists decided to return to Greenland. Some years after their return to Greenland Thorfin Karlsefni died, and then it is related in the sagas that his widow, Gudrid, in accordance with a well established custom in the North, made a pilgrimage to Rome. The sagas emphasize the fact that she was well received in that ancient city and greatly admired for her intelligence, courtesy and dignified manners. Now, does any one of my readers regard it as probable, or even possible, that Gudrid could spend a day, or a week, or a month in Rome and not tell how she had crossed the unexplored Western ocean, called the Sea of Darkness, and that she had spent no less than three years in a land washed by the western waves? Reports of Greenland, Helluland, Markland and Vinland may have come to Rome through other channels, but Gudrid brought personal evidence.

2. I stated in the preceding chapter that Bishop Erik Upse went to find Vinland in the year 1121. At this time the Church in the north of Europe, including Iceland, Greenland and the countries beyond Greenland, was under the jurisdiction of the Archbishop of Lund, in

327

Southern Sweden. Rome had been visited by Gudrid and had received information concerning Vinland from another important source, which I shall mention later on, and the Vatican paid much attention to geographical discoveries, and took pains to collect all possible information. Every new discovery meant an enlargement of Christendom—a new field for the preaching of the gospel. I therefore think it highly probable that Bishop Erik set out for Vinland in obedience to instructions from the Vatican through the Archbishop of Lund.

3. If you will take your 'cyclopedia and look up the name Adam Bremensis, or Adam of Bremen, you will find that this Adam ranks away up as one of the most distinguished writers in Europe in the eleventh century. Adam was superintendent or master of schools in Bremen and a devoted student of history. Space does not permit me to give an extensive account of Adam's life and works. What I desire especially to call attention to here is the fact that he was deeply interested in the ecclesiastical history of the north of Europe, where the Christian religion had recently been introduced in Denmark by St. Ansgar, in Norway by Olaf Trygvason, in Greenland by Leif Erikson, and he decided to write a book on the propagation of Christianity in the North. In order to equip himself properly for this work he visited Denmark. There he met the Danish king, Svend Estridson, a nephew of Canute the Great. King Svend was himself a very intelligent and scholarly man. "He knew the events of the barbarians by heart, as if they were written." That is to say, he was thoroughly familiar with the his-

tory of the Norsemen. Adam not only received from the king a gracious and hospitable reception, but also an abundance of valuable information, and the king took pains to introduce him to the best-informed men near his court. On his return to Bremen, Adam wrote his book on the propagation of Christianity in the North of Europe, one of the best works on that subject extant. The volume consists of four books, the first three being devoted to a description of the introduction of Christianity in Denmark, Sweden, Norway, etc. But Adam, fearing that his readers might not be well up in the geography of the countries discussed, devotes the fourth book to a geographical description of the various lands in the North of Europe. In this book he first describes Denmark, then Sweden, then Norway, then Iceland, and then Greenland, and he gives a very satisfactory account of the climate, products and population of these countries. When he has described Iceland, he says that beyond Iceland is Greenland, and when he has completed his description of Greenland, he says, listen! "The same king (Svend Estridson) also informed me about the discovery of one more region in that ocean—a region named Vinland, because the grapes grow there spontaneously, producing the best of wine; and corn, too, without being sown, grows there in abundance. This is no fabulous conjecture, but is based on positive statements of the Danes (hæc compermus non fabulosa opinione, sed certa relatione Danorum)." This book, written in Latin by Adam of Bremen, was published between the years 1072 and 1076. I say published. Of course, printing was not yet invented, but the book was published in the same manner as other books before the invention of the art of printing. The book was read by intelligent people throughout Europe, it being scattered in numerous manuscripts, and we find evidence of its being discussed in the twelfth century by Helmold, in the thirteenth and fourteenth centuries by Albert of Stade and others, and in the beginning of the sixteenth century by Albert Krantz. Several manuscripts are now in existence, and since 1876 a new one has been found in Leyden and another in Vienna. The fact is that Adam's book was never forgotten between the time of its first publication and the introduction of printing. The biographers of Columbus inform us that he was deeply interested in geographical studies, that he searched with diligence every work within his reach, that in his study he was surrounded by the best historical and geographical works. Can the reader, therefore, for a moment doubt that one of the books read and studied by the distinguished Genoese navigator was this very book above described, and written by the great scholar, Adam of Bremen?

4.   In my mind there is not a shadow of doubt that a copy of Adam of Bremen's work must have fallen into the hands of Christopher Columbus, and the reason for this conviction will appear in the next link in this remarkable chain of evidence. The life of Christopher Columbus was written by his own son, Ferdinand, in a volume published in 1521, a book easily found in every well-stocked library. From this book we know positively that while the design of attempting the discovery

in the West was maturing in his mind, Columbus made a voyage to the North of Europe and visited Iceland. This was in February, 1477, and in his conversation in Iceland with the Bishop, and other learned men there, he must have been informed of the extraordinary fact that their countrymen had discovered Greenland, Hellu- land, Markland, and Vinland, beyond the western ocean, and that Vinland seemed to extend southward indef- initely. This was a circumstance not likely to rest quietly in the active and speculative mind of the great navigator. My readers will observe that when Colum- bus was in Iceland, in the year 1477, fifteen years before he rediscovered America, only 130 years had elapsed since the last Norse expedition to Vinland. There were undoubtedly people still living whose grandfathers had crossed the Atlantic, and it would be altogether unrea- sonable to suppose that he who was constantly talking about geography and navigation could possibly visit Ice- land and hear nothing about the land in the West. In the volume by Ferdinand Columbus is quoted a letter received by Ferdinand, the son, from Christopher, the father, narrating that in February, 1477, he had sailed from Bristol, in England, to Iceland. In it he gives his son considerable information in regard to the extent, cli- mate, tides, etc., of Iceland. But Ferdinand does not quote the whole letter. He ends the quotation by "etc." The "etc." may have related to private matters between father and son, and hence of no interest to the public, but the reader will admit the possibility of its containing information in regard to Norse voyages that the son did not think best to publish.

5. If you will study the life of Columbus, you will find that he persistently maintained a firm conviction that there was land in the West. When, at the Rabida convent, he was forced to give the reasons for his conviction, he stated that he based this conviction, first, on the nature of things; second, on the reports of navigators; and third, on the authority of learned writers. The nature of things doubtless has reference to the rotundity of the earth. The reports of navigators may refer to information scattered throughout Europe concerning the Norse voyages, but more particularly to what Columbus gathered in conversation with people in Iceland. The authority of learned writers would seem to point directly to the work of Adam and Bremen, above described.

Columbus stated before he left Spain that he expected to find land soon after sailing about 700 leagues, hence he knew the breadth of the ocean, and must have had a pretty definite knowledge of the situation of Vinland. His biographers say that he underestimated the size of the earth, and hence guessed accurately the breadth of the ocean. May I ask, is it not equally logical when I say he knew the breadth of the ocean, and hence he underestimated the circumference of the earth? This reasoning will be plain when we consider that the Norsemen furnished no knowledge of the existence of the great Pacific ocean, and hence it was reasonable for Columbus to assume that the Vinland visited by the Norsemen was some part of Eastern Asia. The whole history of the rediscovery by Columbus proves that he must have possessed previous knowledge of America, and it makes Columbus a greater man, in my estimation, that he formed his opinion in regard to land in the West by a chain of logical deductions based upon thorough study and research. It is to the credit of Columbus, I say, that he investigated the nature of things; that he paid the closest attention to all reports of navigators, and that he diligently searched the learned writers, including Adam of Bremen. The fact that he was a great genius enabled him to gather up all those scattered gleams of knowledge that fell without effect upon ordinary minds. With all the above means of knowledge at his command, we can understand how the theory in regard to land in the West was fixed in the mind of Columbus with singular firmness. We can understand how he never spoke in doubt or hesitation, but with as much certainty as if his eyes had already beheld the promised land. It would be absurd for him to hold such firm conviction on merely presumptive evidence, and such a view of Columbus can not be maintained without great damage to him. I hold that I am vindicating the great name of the Genoese navigator by insisting that he based his certainty upon equally certain facts, which he possessed the ability and patience to study out, and the keenness of intellect to put together, and this view gives historical importance to the discovery of America by the Norsemen. Care should always be taken to vindicate great names from accident. The life of Columbus furnishes us an example of what human genius and laudable enterprise can accomplish.

A farmer on the prairies of South Dakota needs water for his cattle. He proceeds to dig a well. When he has penetrated seventy-five or a hundred feet into the earth, his pick and shovel come in contact with brick and mortar. He calls the attention of a physician, a clergyman and a lawyer in his neighborhood to this fact. Extensive excavations are undertaken, and lo and behold! an ancient city of the size of Chicago is exhumed. The farmer stumbled on this discovery. It was a mere accident. There was a man in America who was anxious to find the location of ancient Troy. He visited every library in Christendom, examined every volume and manuscript that contained any reference to Troy. Having gathered all the light furnished by the libraries, he said to himself, not unlike our dear Horsford, "If I now search in that particular locality in Asia Minor, I shall find the remains of ancient Troy." This was Henry Schlieman. Guided by all the light supplied to his intelligence, by all the libraries in Christendom, he proceeded to a certain locality in Asia Minor, and lo and behold! he found in his excavations the remains of the famous Troy. The Columbus in whom you have been believing is like my South Dakota farmer. He stumbles upon America by mere chance and accident, but the Columbus whom I preach unto you with all the ardor and sincerity of my nature is like our Henry Schlieman. He rediscovered America after a systematic study of every avenue of information; and the visit of Gudrid to Rome, the sending of Erik Upse as a bishop to Vinland, the perusal of Adam of Bremen's book, and his own remarkable journey to Iceland in 1477 gave him a torch that lighted his pathway across the Sea of Darkness.

Further investigations, particularly in the great Vatican library in Rome, has brought forth more evidence. Indeed, there are a number of other points bearing on Columbus' sources of knowledge which I have not discussed. I have contented myself with giving the five strongest links in the chain of circumstantial evidence, and by these I hope to have made some converts among my readers. And while the knowledge of the discovery by the Norsemen, and of Columbus' relation thereto, lay for a long time hidden or neglected beneath the dust of unstudied libraries, let us take this lesson, that truth will conquer and that honor will at length be given to whom honor is due.

On my suggestion the Norsemen in America have adopted a Leif Erikson or Grape Festival, to be celebrated on the first Wednesday of October in each year. It is a festival to commemorate the first landing of white men upon our shores. It is a festival to commemorate the first chapter of Christian and civilized history in America. As Leif Erikson and his followers found grapes in abundance and called the country Vinland, so grapes are to be the chief emblem at these festivals. The tables are to be decorated with grape leaves and the guests are to feast on grapes. Many of these festivals have already been celebrated during the past seven years.

Let us remember Erik the Red, who founded a settlement in Greenland. Let us remember Bjarne Herjulfson, the first white man whose eyes beheld any part of the American continent. Let us remember Leif Erikson, the first white man and the first Christian who planted

335

his feet on American soil. Let us remember Thorwald Erikson, the first Christian buried beneath American sod. Let us remember Thorfin Karlsefni, the first white man who attempted to colonize America. Let us remember his wife Gudrid, the first white and Christian woman to visit our shores. And let us not forget her little son Snorre, the first white child to see the light of day on this continent. Let us recognize the Norsemen in their true capacity as navigators and discoverers, and as the first people to venture out upon the boundless ocean in ships. The Norsemen were the discoverers of pelagic navigation. It is my firm conviction that the more you study the history of the Norse voyages, the history of Columbus, and of the centuries between Leif Erikson and Columbus, the more you will become convinced that Columbus possessed knowledge of the Norse voyages. It certainly was the Norsemen who taught him pelagic navigation. When you rear a monument to Columbus, make the pedestal large enough to supply room for a description of his Norse forerunners. This will give the monument of Columbus a higher and more conspicuous position.

In the next chapter I shall attempt to show that America was visited by the Irish in the tenth and the eleventh centuries. I there propose to show that the subject of discovering in America can not be treated exhaustively without bringing back to the mind fond recollections of the Emerald Isle, which was at one time the school of Western Europe.

CHAPTER IV.

DISCOVERY OF AMERICA BY THE IRISH.

In the preceding chapter I intimated that the Irish have some claim to the honor of having discovered America before Columbus. It is a large subject, and all I am able to do at this time is to give the particular facts and traditions, and some hints in regard to their proper interpretation. The name of St. Brendan (or Brandan, as it is sometimes written) is well known, at least it may be found in the larger cyclopedias. He was an Irish monk, famous for his voyages upon the sea to strange lands. The traditions handed down to us from the Middle Ages contain many legends in regard to him. He belongs to the sixth century after Christ, and hence to an age where fact and fiction are strangely mingled. His death is said to have occurred A. D. 577. Report has it that he went on a nine years' voyage, and visited unknown lands. These lands are described in the work "De Fortunatis Insulis," published in the eleventh century, in the Latin language, and translated into French about the year 1120. Versions of his voyages appeared also in German, English and Dutch. Popular tradition has identified the Fortunate Islands of St. Brendan with America, and given this Irish saint the credit of discovering the western continent.

According to one legend, St. Brendan, conducted by

an angel, descended to the lower world, where he wit-
nessed the torments of the Devil and of the damned, and
subsequently he came to the Fortunate Islands, and
finally he visited Paradise. At the end of the nine years
he returned to Ireland, and gave an account of his adventures. The less superstitious interpreted St. Brendan's voyages as referring to existing countries, and I
now hasten to declare it here as a fact that the reports
concerning St. Brendan constituted one of the causes
which led the Spanish and Portuguese to undertake voyages of discovery in the western ocean. Thus St. Brendan is one of the links in that chain of influences operat-
ing on the mind of the great Genoese navigator.

There is evolution in history, as well as in other things.
The voyages of the Phœnicians and of the Greek Pytheas
were germs that budded in the explorations of the Irish
and of the Welsh, blossomed in the expeditions of the
Norsemen, and culminated and bore fruit in the discovery of America by Columbus. The Phœnicians and Columbus are the two ends of the long chain of events in
the opening of the new world to civilization. Columbus
was a scholar, who studied industriously all books and
manuscripts that contained any information about voyages and discoveries. His searching mind sought out
the writings of Adam of Bremen and the works relating
to St. Brendan. It is in this wise that we are able to
explain the firm conviction that Columbus invariably expressed in his reference to land in the west. In that
way we are able to account for the absolute certainty and
singular firmness with which he talked of land across the

ocean, and thus, too, we can account for his accurate knowledge of the breadth of the ocean.

It is now my privilege to call the attention of my readers once more to the Icelandic sagas, and show from them corroborations of the above theory concerning the discovery of America by the Irish. There was a powerful chieftan in Iceland, by name Are Marson, and the sagas tell us that in the year 983, that is, three years before Vinland was seen by Bjarne Herjulfson, he was driven to Great Ireland by storms, and was there baptized. The first author of this account was his contemporary, Rafn, surnamed the Limerick Trader, he having long resided in Limerick, Ireland. The illustrious Icelandic sagaman, Are the Wise, descendant in the fourth degree from Are Marson, states on this subject that his uncle, Thorkel Gellerson (whose testimony he on another occasion declares to be worthy of all credit), had been informed by Icelanders, who had their information from Thorfin Sigurdson, Earl of Orkney, that Are Marson had been recognized in Great Ireland, and could not get away from there, but was held there in great respect. This statement, therefore, shows that in those times (about the year 983) there was an occasional intercourse between the western part of Europe, that is to say, the Orkneys and Ireland, and the Great Ireland or Whitemen's Land of America. The sagas from which we get our information about Leif Erikson expressly state that Great Ireland lies to the west in the sea, near Vinland the Good, six days' sail west from Ireland. Doubtless the "VI" has arisen through some mistake or carelessness of the transcriber of the original manuscript, which is now lost, and was erroneously written for XX, or XI, or perhaps XVI, which would correspond with the distance. Such a mistake might easily have been caused by a blot or defect in the manuscript.

It must have been in this same Great Ireland that Bjorn Asbrandson, surnamed the Champion of Breidavik, spent the latter part of his life. He had been adopted into the celebrated band of Jormsborg warriors, under Palnatoke. His relations with Thurid of Froda, in Iceland, a sister of the powerful official Snorre, drew upon him the enmity and persecution of the latter, in consequence of which he found himself obliged to quit Iceland forever, and in 999 he set sail with a northeast wind.

And now comes the most interesting part of this story. Gudleif Gudlaugson, the ancestor of the celebrated historian, Snorre Sturlason, had made a trading voyage to Dublin, in Ireland, but when he left that place again, with the intention of sailing around Ireland and returning to Iceland, he met with long-continued northeasterly winds, which drove him far to the southwest in the ocean, and late in the summer he and his company came at last to an extensive country, but they knew not what land it was. They went on shore, whereupon a crowd of the natives, several hundred in number, came against them and laid hands on them and bound them. They did not know to what race these people belonged, but it seemed to them that their language resembled Irish. The natives now took counsel whether they should kill the strangers or make slaves of them. While they were deliberating, a large company approached, displaying a banner, close to which rode a man of distinguished appearance, who was far advanced in years and had gray hair. The matter under deliberation was referred to his decision, when to their astonishment it was discovered that he was none other than the above named Bjorn Asbrandson. He caused Gudleif to be brought before him, and addressing him in Icelandic, asked him whence he came. On Gudleif's reply that he was an Icelander, Bjorn made many inquiries about his acquaintances in Iceland, and particularly about his beloved Thurid of Froda and her son, Kjartan, supposed to be his own son, and who at that time was the proprietor of the estate of Froda. In the meantime, the natives becoming impatient and demanding a decision, Bjorn selected twelve of his company as counselors, and took them aside with him, and some time afterward he went toward Gudleif and his companions, and told them that the natives had left the matter to his decision. He thereupon gave them their liberty, and advised them, although the summer was then far advanced, to depart immediately, because the natives were not to be depended upon and were difficult to deal with, and, moreover, conceived that an infringement on their laws had been committed to their disadvantage. He gave them a gold ring for Thurid and a sword for Kjartan, and told them to charge his friends and relations not to come over to him, as he had now become old and might daily expect that old age would get the better of him; that the country was large, having but few harbors, and that strangers must everywhere expect a hostile reception. Gudleif and his company accordingly set sail again, and found their way back to Dublin, where they spent the winter; but the next summer they repaired to Iceland and delivered the presents, and everybody was convinced that it was really Bjorn Asbrandson, the Champion of Breidavik, that they had met with in this far-off country.

The date of Gudleif's voyage is the year 1029, and my readers may easily find the account in chapter 64 of the Eyrbyggja Saga. The portion of America here referred to is supposed to be situated south of the Chesapeake Bay, and includes North and South Carolina, Georgia and East Florida. In the saga of Thorfin Karlsefni, chapter 13, it is distinctly called "Irland-it-Milka," that is, Great Ireland. The presumption is that the name Great Ireland arose from the fact that the inhabitants seemed to Gudlaugson's party to speak Irish; that the country presumably had been colonized by the Irish long before Gudlaugson's visit, and that they, coming from their own green island to a vast continent possessing many of the fertile qualities of their own native soil, found such an appellation natural and appropriate. I see nothing improbable in this conclusion; for the Irish, who visited and inhabited Iceland toward the close of the eighth century, to accomplish which they had to traverse a stormy ocean to the extent of eight hundred miles; who as early as 725 were found upon the Fareys (voyages between Ireland and Iceland in the tenth century were of ordinary occurrence)—a people so familiar with the sea were certainly capable of making a voyage across the Atlantic Ocean.

The geography of the western world, according to the old Norsemen, consisted of (1) Helluland (Newfoundland), (2) Markland (Nova Scotia), (3) Vinland (Massachuesetts or some part of New England), and then (4) stretching far to the south of Vinland lay Whitemen's Land or Great Ireland.